The Tanner Lectures on Human Values

THE TANNER LECTURES
ON HUMAN VALUES

X

1989

Wm. Theodore de Bary, Anthony Quinton, Barry Stroud
Albert O. Hirschman, Robert A. Dahl, Javier Muguerza
Grethe B. Peterson, *Editor*

UNIVERSITY OF UTAH PRESS — Salt Lake City
CAMBRIDGE UNIVERSITY PRESS — Cambridge, London, Melbourne, Sidney

CAMBRIDGE UNIVERSITY PRESS
Cambridge, New York, Melbourne, Madrid, Cape Town,
Singapore, São Paulo, Delhi, Tokyo, Mexico City

Cambridge University Press
The Edinburgh Building, Cambridge CB2 8RU, UK

Published in the United States of America by Cambridge University Press, New York

www.cambridge.org
Information on this title: www.cambridge.org/9780521176385

First published by the Tanner Lectures on Human Values 1989
First paperback edition by Cambridge University Press 2011

A catalogue record for this publication is available from the British Library

ISBN 978-0-521-37341-8 Hardback
ISBN 978-0-521-17638-5 Paperback

THE TANNER LECTURES ON HUMAN VALUES

The purpose of the Tanner Lectures is to advance and reflect upon scholarly and scientific learning that relates to the entire range of human values.

To receive an appointment as a Tanner lecturer is a recognition of uncommon capabilities and outstanding scholarly or leadership achievement in the field of human values. The lecturers may be drawn from philosophy, religion, and humanities and sciences, the creative arts and learned professions, or from leadership in public or private affairs. The lectureships are international and intercultural and transcend ethnic, national, religious, or ideological distinctions.

The Tanner Lectures were formally founded on July 1, 1978, at Clare Hall, Cambridge University. They were established by the American scholar, industrialist, and philanthropist, Obert Clark Tanner. In creating the lectureships, Professor Tanner said, "I hope these lectures will contribute to the intellectual and moral life of mankind. I see them simply as a search for a better understanding of human behavior and human values. This understanding may be pursued for its own intrinsic worth, but it may also eventually have practical consequences for the quality of personal and social life."

Permanent Tanner lectureships, with lectures given annually, are established at nine institutions: Clare Hall, Cambridge University; Harvard University; Brasenose College, Oxford University; Princeton University; Stanford University; the University of California; the University of Michigan; the University of Utah; and Yale University. Each year lectureships may be granted to not more than four additional colleges or universities for one year only. The institutions are selected by the Trustees.

The sponsoring institutions have full autonomy in the appointment of their lecturers. A major purpose of the lecture program is the publication and wide distribution of the Lectures in an annual volume.

The Tanner Lectures on Human Values is a nonprofit corporation administered at the University of Utah under the direction of a self-perpetuating, international Board of Trustees. The Trustees meet annually to enact policies that will ensure the quality of the lectureships.

The entire lecture program, including the costs of administration, is fully and generously funded in perpetuity by an endowment to the University of Utah by Professor Tanner and Mrs. Grace Adams Tanner.

Obert C. Tanner was born in Farmington, Utah, in 1904. He was educated at the University of Utah, Harvard University, and Stanford University. He has served on the faculty of Stanford University and is presently Emeritus Professor of Philosophy at the University of Utah. He is the founder and chairman of the O. C. Tanner Company, manufacturing jewelers.

GRETHE B. PETERSON
University of Utah

CONTENTS

PREFACE TO VOLUME X

The Tanner Lectures on Human Values were established at Clare Hall, Cambridge University, in 1978. Annual lectures have been delivered at the six institutions which were named the original permanent sponsors of the lectureship: Clare Hall, Cambridge University; Harvard University; Brasenose College, Oxford University; Stanford University; the University of Michigan; and the University of Utah.

The University of California and Yale University were added to the institutions which are designated as permanent sponsors in 1987, and Princeton University was added in 1988. .

In addition, lectures have been delivered at Utah State University, the Hebrew University of Jerusalem, Australian National University, Jawaharlal Nehru University, the University of Helsinki, the University of Warsaw, the University of Buenos Aires, the Universidad Complutense de Madrid, and the Chinese University of Hong Kong.

The Tanner Lectures on Human Values are published in an annual volume. A general index to Volumes I through V is included in Volume V.

Volume X of the Lectures is comprised of lectures delivered during the academic year 1987–88, except for lectures by F. Van Zyl Slabbert and Louis Blom-Cooper, which were delivered early in the academic year and appeared in Volume IX.

In addition to the Lectures on Human Values, Professor Tanner and the Trustees of the Tanner Lectures have funded special lectureships at selected colleges and universities which are administered and published independently of the series of lectures published in the annual volumes.

Two Hundred Years of Reactionary Rhetoric:
The Case of the Perverse Effect

ALBERT O. HIRSCHMAN

THE TANNER LECTURES ON HUMAN VALUES

Delivered at
The University of Michigan

April 8, 1988

ALBERT O. HIRSCHMAN was born in Berlin in 1915. He studied economics in Paris, London, and Trieste before coming to the United States. He joined the Federal Reserve Board in 1946 and worked on the financial problems of postwar reconstruction in western Europe. He lived in Bogotá, Colombia, from 1952–56 where he was a financial advisor for the National Planning Board and a private consultant.

Since 1956 Dr. Hirschman has taught at Yale, Columbia, Harvard, and the Institute for Advanced Study in Princeton, where he is now professor of social science, emeritus.

Among his many books are *National Power and the Structure of Foreign Trade* (1945), *Essays in Trespassing* (1981), and *Rival Views of Market Society* (1986). Among other honors, he is a Distinguished Fellow of the American Economic Association.

My lecture will be a progress report on a book I am trying to write. Principally I shall present here the shortened text of its first chapter, but to begin with I would like to tell you about the conception of the work as a whole — as I see it at present.

GENERAL OUTLINE

My starting point is a famous 1949 lecture by the English sociologist T. H. Marshall on the "development of citizenship" in the West.[1] Marshall distinguished between the civil, political, and social dimensions of citizenship and then proceeded to explain, very much in the spirit of the Whig interpretation of history, how the more enlightened human societies had tackled one of these dimensions after the other, conveniently allocating about one century to each of the three tasks. According to this scheme, the eighteenth century witnessed the major battles for the institution of *civil* citizenship — from freedom of speech, thought, and religion to the right to even-handed justice and other aspects of individual freedom or, roughly, the "Rights of Men" of the natural law doctrine and of the American and French revolutions. In the course of the nineteenth century, it was the *political* aspect of citizenship, that is, the right of citizens to participate in the exercise of political power, that made major strides as the right to vote was extended to ever larger groups. Finally, the rise of the welfare state in the twentieth century extended the concept of citizenship to the *social and economic* sphere, by recognizing that minimal conditions of education, health, economic well-being, and security are basic to the life of a civilized being as well as

[1] "Citizenship and Social Class," Alfred Marshall Lectures given in Cambridge, England, in 1949, reprinted in T. H. Marshall, *Class, Citizenship, and Social Development* (New York: Doubleday, 1965), chap. 4.

to the meaningful exercise of the civil and political attributes of citizenship.

When Marshall painted this magnificent canvas of staged progress, the third battle for the assertion of citizenship rights, the one being waged on the social and economic terrain, seemed to be well on its way to being won, particularly in the Labor-party-ruled, social-security-conscious England of the immediate postwar period. A generation or so later, it appears that Marshall had been overly optimistic on that score and that the notion of the socioeconomic dimension of citizenship as a natural complement of the civil and political dimensions had run into considerable difficulties and stands in need of substantial rethinking. This point was recently made by Ralf Dahrendorf and it is surely well taken.[2]

But does it go far enough? Is it not true that not just the last but each and every one of Marshall's three progressive thrusts have been followed by ideological counterthrusts of extraordinary force? And have not these counterthrusts been at the origin of convulsive social and political struggles often leading to setbacks for the intended progressive programs as well as to much human suffering and misery? The backlash so far experienced by the welfare state may in fact be rather mild in comparison with the earlier onslaughts and conflicts that followed upon the assertion of individual freedoms in the eighteenth century or upon the broadening of political participation in the nineteenth. Once we contemplate this protracted and perilous seesawing of action and reaction we come to appreciate more than ever the profound wisdom of Whitehead's well-known observation: "[T]he major advances in civilization are processes which all but wreck the societies in which they occur."[3] It is surely this statement rather than any

---

[2] Dahrendorf was addressing the initial meeting, held in 1985, of a group assembled by the Ford Foundation to consider and make recommendations on social welfare policy. His brief but pointed remarks on that occasion set me off on the present study.

[3] Alfred N. Whitehead, *Symbolism: Its Meaning and Effect* (1927; repr. New York: Capricorn Books, 1959), p. 88.

account of smooth, unrelenting progress that catches the deeply ambivalent essence of the story so blandly entitled the "development of citizenship."

THREE REACTIONS

There are good reasons, then, for focusing on the *reactions* to the successive forward thrusts. To start with, I shall briefly state what I understand by the "three reactions," or reactionary waves, particularly since they may well be more diverse and diffuse than Marshall's fairly straightforward trio.

The first reaction is the movement of ideas following (and opposing) the assertion of equality before the law and of civil rights in general — Marshall's civil component of citizenship. There is a major difficulty in isolating this movement: the most emphatic assertion of these rights occurred in the early stages and as a result of the French Revolution so that the contemporary reaction against them was intertwined with opposition to the Revolution and all its works. To be sure, any opposition to the Declaration of the Rights of Man and the Citizen was motivated more by the events that led to the Declaration's being issued than by the text itself. But the radical counterrevolutionary discourse that soon emerged refused to distinguish between positive and negative aspects of the French Revolution or to concede that there were any positive ones. Anticipating what was later to become a slogan of the Left (*La révolution est un bloc*), the early adversaries of the Revolution considered it as a cohesive whole. Significantly, the first general indictment of the Revolution, Edmund Burke's *Reflections on the Revolution in France* (1790), started with a sustained polemic against the Declaration of the Rights of Man. Taking the ideology of the Revolution seriously, the counterrevolutionary discourse encompassed rejection of the text the revolutionaries were most proud of. In this manner it became a fundamental intellectual current, laying the groundwork for much of the modern conservative position.

The second reactionary wave was much less self-consciously counterrevolutionary or counterreformist than the first. Few writers specifically proclaimed the objective of rolling back the advances of popular participation in politics that were achieved through extensions of the franchise in the nineteenth century. One can nevertheless *construct* an ideological countermovement out of several influential currents that arose at about the time when the major breakthroughs in the struggle for the extension of the franchise occurred. From the last third of the nineteenth century to the First World War and beyond, a vast and diffuse literature — embracing philosophy, psychology, politics, and belles-lettres — amassed every conceivable argument for disparaging the "masses," the majority, parliamentary rule, and democratic government. Even though it made few proposals for alternative institutions, much of this literature implicitly or explicitly warned of the dire dangers threatening society as a result of the trend to democratization. With the benefit of hindsight, it is easy to argue that such writings shared in the responsibility for the self-destruction of democracy in Italy and Germany during the interwar period. To the extent the claim is justified, the second reaction must be given credit, if that is the correct term, for having produced history's most striking instance of the self-fulfilling prophecy. Curiously, the reaction that was least consciously intent on rolling back the ongoing trends or reforms became the one to have — or to be later accused of having had — the most destructive impact.

We are now coming to the third reactionary wave: the contemporary critique of the welfare state and the attempts to roll back or "reform" some of its provisions. But these topics need not, perhaps, be gone over at this point. As direct, day-to-day observers of this movement we have a certain commonsense understanding of what is involved. At the same time, while a very large literature has by now criticized every aspect of the welfare state from the economic and political points of view, and in spite of determined assaults upon social welfare programs and institutions by a variety of powerful political forces, it is too early to appraise the outcome of this new reactionary wave.

THREE "REACTIONARY" THESES

As will be apparent from this brief account, the size of my topic is truly enormous. In trying to get hold of it I must be severely selective. It is therefore useful to point out right away what I am *not* attempting here. In the first place, I shall not write yet another volume on the nature and deep roots of conservative thought. Rather, my aim is to delineate formal types of argument or rhetoric, and my emphasis will thus be on the major polemical postures and maneuvers likely to be engaged in by those who set out to debunk and roll back "progressive" policies and movements of ideas. Second, I am not going to embark on a broad and leisurely historical retelling of the successive reforms and counter-reforms, theses and countertheses since the French Revolution. Rather, I shall focus on common or typical arguments unfailingly made by the three reactive movements just noted. These arguments will constitute the basic subdivision of my text. It is in conjunction with each argument that the "three reactions" will be drawn upon to ascertain the specific shape the argument has taken in various historical contexts.

Which are the arguments and how many are there? I must have an inbred urge toward symmetry. In canvassing for the principal ways of criticizing, assaulting, and ridiculing the three successive "progressive" thrusts of Marshall's story I have come up with another trio: that is, with three reactive-reactionary theses which I call the *perversity thesis*, the *futility thesis*, and the *jeopardy thesis*. Let me explain briefly what I mean by each.

The *perversity thesis*, or *thesis of the perverse effect* — perhaps the most basic and certainly the most elementary, least sophisticated of the three — is closely connected with the semantic origin of the term "reaction." As Starobinski has shown, the couple "action" and "reaction" came into current usage as a result of Newton's third law of motion, which asserted that "to every Action there is always opposed an equal Reaction." Having thus been singled out for distinction in the prestigious science of mechanics, the two concepts spilled over to other realms and were widely used in the analysis of society and history in the eighteenth century.[4]

No derogatory meaning whatsoever attached at first to the term "reaction." The remarkably durable infusion of this meaning took place during the French Revolution and, specifically, after its great watershed, the events of Thermidor.[5] It is already noticeable in Benjamin Constant's youthful tract *Des réactions politiques*, written in 1797 expressly to denounce what he perceived as a new chapter of the Revolution in which the reactions against the excesses of the Jacobins might themselves engender far worse excesses.[6] This very thought may have contributed to the pejorative meaning that was soon attached to the term "reaction." A more fundamental reason is that the spirit of the Enlightenment, with its belief in the forward march of history, survived the Revolution, even among its critics, notwithstanding the Terror and other mishaps. One could deplore the "excesses" of the Revolution, as Constant certainly did, and yet continue to believe both in history's fundamentally progressive design and in the Revolution's being part of it. Such must have been the dominant contemporary attitude. Otherwise it would be hard to explain why those who "reacted" to the Revolution in a predominantly negative manner came to be perceived and denounced as "reactionaries."

The semantic exploration of "reaction" points straight to an important characteristic of "reactionary" thinking. Because of the stubbornly progressive temper of the modern era, "reactionaries"

---

[4] Jean Starobinski, "La vie et les aventures du mot 'réaction,'" *Modern Language Review* 70 (1975), pp. xxi–xxxi.

[5] F. Brunot, *Histoire de la langue française, des origines à 1900* (Paris: Colin, 1905–53), vol. 9, pt. 2, pp. 843–44.

[6] Benjamin Constant, *Ecrits et discours politiques*, ed. O. Pozzo di Borgo (Paris: Jean-Jacque Pauvert, 1964), vol. 1, pp. 21–91.

live in a hostile world. They are up against an intellectual climate that attaches a positive value to the lofty objective proclaimed and actively pursued by their adversaries. Given this state of public opinion, reactionaries are not likely to launch an all-out attack on that objective. Rather, they will endorse it, sincerely or otherwise, but then attempt to demonstrate that the action undertaken in its name is ill-conceived; indeed, they will most typically argue that this action will produce, via a series of unintended consequences, the *exact contrary* of the objective that is being pursued.[7]

This, then, is the thesis of the perverse effect, to which I shall devote the bulk of this lecture. But let me briefly tell you about the remaining two theses.

My second "reactionary" argument is what I call the *futility thesis*. While the thesis of the perverse effect proclaims that the alleged progress will in fact lead to regress, the futility thesis asserts, to the contrary, that the attempt at change is abortive, that in one way or another any change is or was largely surface, façade, cosmetic, hence illusory, as the "deep" structures of society remain wholly untouched.

It is curious that the French, rich in revolutionary experiences as they are, should have given this argument its classic epigrammatic expression with the maxim, coined in 1840 by the journalist Alphonse Karr (1808–90), *plus ça change plus c'est la même chose*. Instead of a law of motion we have here a law of no-motion. Turning it into a strategy for avoiding change yields the well-known paradox of the Baron of Lampedusa in his novel *The Leopard*: "Everything must change here so that everything will remain the same." Both conservatives and, even more, revolutionaries have eagerly adopted this aphorism from Sicilian society as the leitmotif or epigraph for studies that affirm the failure and futility of reform, particularly in Latin America. Finally, there is the inevitable Lewis Carroll, whose equally proverbial saying in

---

[7] For a broad survey of perverse effects by a sociologist, see Raymond Boudon, *Effets pervers et ordre social* (Paris: Presses Universitaires de France, 1977).

Alice in Wonderland, "Here it takes all the running you can do, to keep in the same place," expresses yet a different facet of the futility thesis.

All of these spirited statements deride or deny efforts at, and possibilities of, change while underlining and perhaps celebrating the resilience of the status quo. The conservative bias of the epigrams thus serves to offset the opposite bias of language with its derogatory connotation, as just noted, for "reaction" and "reactionary." It is of course difficult to argue at one and the same time that a certain movement for social change will be sharply counterproductive, in line with the perverse-effect thesis, and will have no effect at all, in line with the futility thesis. For this reason, the two arguments are generally made by different critics.

Nevertheless the two arguments have something in common: both are remarkably bald — therein lies, of course, much of their appeal. In both cases it is shown how actions undertaken to achieve a certain purpose miserably fail to do so: either no change occurs at all or the action yields an outcome that is the opposite of the one intended. Then there is a third, more moderate way of arguing against a change which, because of the prevailing state of public opinion, one does not care to attack head-on (this, I have claimed, is one of the hallmarks of "reactionary" thinking): this one asserts that to move in a certain direction, though feasible and even desirable if viewed in isolation, carries with it unacceptable costs of one sort or another. The trouble with this argument is that it normally involves a difficult and subjective comparison of highly heterogeneous benefits and costs; it will therefore carry less general conviction than a demonstration that an intended change is simply abortive or counterproductive.

The comparison of costs and benefits becomes rather more homogeneous and therefore more compelling when it takes a special, privileged form: that of focusing on a new reform in relation to one that has already been accomplished. If it can be argued that the two reforms are in some sense competitive or mutually exclusive so that the older will be endangered by the new one, then an element of comparability enters into the argument and the evaluation can proceed in vaguely common "coins of progress": does it make sense to sacrifice the old progress for the new one? Moreover, with this argument the reactionary takes on once again the progressive's clothes and argues as though both the new and the old progress were desirable, and then shows typically how a new reform, if carried out, would mortally *endanger* an older, highly prized one that has only recently been put into place. The older, hard-won conquests or accomplishments, so it is argued, are still fragile, still need to be consolidated and would be placed in jeopardy by the new program. I therefore call this argument the *jeopardy thesis*: it involves a more complex, historically grounded argument than the other two.

In line with T. H. Marshall's tripartite division of "progress" into the civil, political, and socioeconomic dimensions of citizenship, the jeopardy thesis should make its *first* fully articulated appearance with the *second* reactionary wave, the one that criticizes the extension of the franchise and of democracy. It will be claimed that this extension imperils the earlier conquest of individual liberty, that undue insistence on participation or "positive liberty" represents a danger for precious "negative liberty." Next, as the jeopardy thesis is used against the welfare state, it can deploy a double-barreled argument. The welfare state, so it will be argued, is likely to endanger earlier advances with regard to individual rights (the first dimension of citizenship) and also with regard to democratic governance (the second, nineteenth-century dimension). All of these arguments have indeed profusely surfaced, as I hope to demonstrate in due course.

So much by way of an overview of the three theses. I think I will be able to show that jointly they account for the bulk of the arguments in the reactionary arsenal.[8] I now return to the first

---

[8] I should add that the arguments, particularly the perversity and futility theses, are not the exclusive property of "reactionaries." Most generally these arguments

thesis, that of the perverse effect, tracing it through the three reactions.

THE THESIS OF THE PERVERSE EFFECT

The argument of the perverse effect asserts not merely that a movement or policy will fall short of its goal or will occasion unexpected costs or negative side effects: rather, so goes the argument, *the attempt to push society in a certain direction will result in its moving all right, but in the opposite direction.* Being simple, intriguing, and devastating (if true), the argument has proven popular with generations of "reactionaries" as well as fairly effective with the public at large. In current debates it is also often referred to as the counterintuitive or counterproductive effect of some allegedly progressive public policy.

THE REACTION TO THE FRENCH REVOLUTION

As with many other key elements of "reactionary" thinking, the argument of the perverse effect was "invented" in the wake of the French Revolution. Actually, there was little need for inventive genius: as *liberté, egalité, fraternité* turned into the dictatorship of the Comité de Salut Public (and later into that of Bonaparte), the thought that certain attempts to reach for liberty are bound to lead to tyranny instead almost forced itself upon one's mind. What was remarkable was that Edmund Burke predicted such an outcome as early as 1790, in his *Reflections on the Revolution in France.* Here he prognosticated that "an ignoble oligarchy, founded on the destruction of the crown, the church, the nobility, and the

---

will be made by groups that are out of power and oppose or criticize actions, any kind of actions, that are proposed or have already been taken. Whenever "reactionaries" find themselves in power and are able to carry out their own programs and policies, they may in turn be attacked by "liberals" or "progressives" along the lines of the perversity or futility theses, whenever one or the other can be plausibly invoked. Toward the end of the larger work I have in progress, I plan to comment briefly on "liberal" rhetoric, and particularly on its resemblances to, and differences from, the "reactionary" variety I will have surveyed.

people [would] end all the deceitful dreams and visions of the equality and the rights of men." [9] Also, he conjured up the spectacle of military interventions during various civil disorders and exclaimed, "Massacre, torture, hanging! These are your rights of men!" [10]

The argument took root and was to be repeated in many forms, particularly by foreign observers who were trying to draw "lessons" for their countries from what was happening in France. Thus, Friedrich Schiller wrote in 1793: "The attempt of the French people to install the holy Rights of Man and to conquer political liberty has only brought to light its impotence and unworthiness in this regard; the result has been that not just this unhappy people, but alongside it a considerable part of Europe and a whole century have been thrown back into barbarism and servitude." [11] Perhaps the most general, if heavy-footed, formulation is that of the German romantic political economist Adam Müller, who proclaimed when the Revolution and its Napoleonic aftermath had run their course: "The history of the French Revolution constitutes a proof, administered continuously over thirty years, that man, acting by himself and without religion, is unable to break any chains that oppress him without sinking in the process into still deeper slavery." [12] Here Burke's conjectures have been turned into a rigid historical law that could serve as an ideological prop for the Europe of the Holy Alliance.

Burke's uncanny ability to project the course of the French Revolution has been attributed to the very strength of his pas-

[9] Edmund Burke, *Reflections on the Revolution in France* (Chicago: Regnery, 1955), p. 276.

[10] Ibid., 313.

[11] Letter of July 13, 1793, to Herzog Friedrich Christian von Augustenburg, in *Schiller's Briefe*, ed. Fritz Jonas (Stuttgart: Deutsche Verlagsanstalt, 1892–96), vol. 3, p. 333.

[12] Cited in Carl Schmitt, *Politische Romantik*, 2d edition (Munich: Duncker & Humblot, 1925), p. 170.

sionate engagement with it.[13] But it may be suggested that his formulation of the perverse effect has an intellectual origin as well: he was steeped in the thought of the Scottish Enlightenment which had stressed the importance of the unintended effects of human action. The best-known application of this notion was the Invisible Hand doctrine of Adam Smith, with whose economic views Burke had expressed total agreement.

Smith, like Mandeville and others (such as Pascal and Vico) before him, had shown how individual actions motivated by greed or, less insultingly, by self-interest can have a positive social outcome in the shape of a more prosperous commonwealth. Expressing these ideas with poetic pith toward the end of the century, Goethe defined his Mephisto as "a part of that force that ever wills evil, but ever brings forth good."

In this manner the intellectual terrain was well prepared for arguing that on occasion the opposite might happen. This was exactly what Burke did when he was faced with the unprecedented undertaking of the French Revolution to reconstruct society: he made good and evil switch places in Mephisto's statement and asserted that the social outcome of the revolutionaries' striving for the public good would be evil, calamitous, and wholly contrary to the goals and hopes they were professing.

From one point of view, then, Burke's proposition looks (and may have looked to him) like a minor variation on a well-known eighteenth-century theme. From another, it was a radical ideological shift from the Enlightenment to romanticism and from optimism about progress to pessimism. It seems possible to me that large-scale and seemingly abrupt ideological shifts often take place in this fashion. Formally they require only a slight modification of familiar patterns of thought, but the new variant has an affinity to very different beliefs and propositions and becomes *embedded* in them to form a wholly new gestalt so that in the end the

---

[13] By Conor Cruise O'Brien in his introduction to Burke's *Reflections* (Harmondsworth: Penguin Books, 1969), pp. 70–73.

intimate connection between the old and the new is almost unrecognizable.

In the present case the old was the slow emergence of a new kind of hope for world order. From the sixteenth century on it was widely agreed that religious precept and moral admonition could not be relied on to restrain and reshape human nature so as to guarantee social order and economic welfare. But with the rise of commerce and industry in the seventeenth and eighteenth centuries, influential voices proposed that some of the very ineradicable "vices" of men, such as persistent self-seeking, could, properly channeled, produce a minimally workable and perhaps even a progressive society. To Pascal, Vico, and Goethe this paradoxical process suggested the intervention of a Providence that is remarkably benign, forgiving, and helpful as it transmutes evil into good. The optimistic message of this construction was enhanced further when the pursuit of self-interest through trade and industry lost its stigma and was accorded social prestige instead. At that point there was no longer a sharp contrast between the means and the end, or between process and outcome, and the need for the magical intervention of Divine Providence became less compelling — Adam Smith in fact barely allowed it to survive, secularized and a bit anemic, as the Invisible Hand.[14]

The thinking about unintended outcomes of human action received a new impulse with the events of the French Revolution. As the strivings for liberty ended up in terror and tyranny, the critics of the Revolution perceived a new and striking disparity between individual intentions and social outcomes. Consequently Divine Providence was pressed back into active service but in a shape that was anything but benign: her task now was to *foil* the

---

[14] In his 1966 lectures on *The Role of Providence in the Social Order* (Philadelphia: American Philosophical Society, 1972), and particularly in the third lecture, "The Invisible Hand and Economic Man," Jacob Viner demonstrates the continued hold teleological thought had on Adam Smith. It is significant, nevertheless, that Smith introduced the secular term "Invisible Hand" as a substitute for the Divine Providence which had long been routinely invoked in previous writings expressing a teleological view of nature and society.

designs of men, whose pretensions to build an ideal society were
to be exposed as naive and preposterous, if not as criminal and
blasphemous. *Der Mensch in seinem Wahn* (man in his delu-
sion), that "worst of terrors," as Schiller put it in one of his best-
known poems (*Das Lied von der Glocke*), had to be taught a
salutary if severe lesson.

Joseph de Maistre in particular endows the Divine Providence
he sees at work throughout the Revolution with refined cruelty.
In his *Considérations sur la France* (1797) he regards it as a
providential development for the Revolution to have generated
its own lengthy internecine conflicts; for, so he argues, if there
had been an early successful counterrevolution, the revolutionaries
would have had to be tried in official courts and then one of two
things would have happened: either the verdicts would have been
considered excessive by public opinion or, most likely, they would
have fallen far short of full justice in being limited to just a few
great criminals (*quelques grands coupables*). Here Maistre proclaims: "This is precisely what Providence did not want" and this
is why she cleverly arranged matters in such a way that much
larger numbers were made to "fall under the blows of their own
accomplices." [15]

Maistre's construction of Divine Providence is exceptional in
its elaborate and expert vengefulness. But the basic feature of the
reactionary argument that invokes the "perverse effect" has remained unchanged: man is held up to ridicule — by Divine Providence and by those privileged social analysts who have pierced her
designs — for in setting out to improve the world radically he
goes radically astray. What better way to show him up as half-
foolish and half-criminal than to prove that he is achieving the
exact opposite of what he is proclaiming as his objective?

---

[15] Joseph de Maistre, *Considérations sur la France*, ed. Jean-Louis Darcel
(Geneva: Slatkine, 1980), pp. 75, 74.

THE FIN-DE-SIÈCLE REACTION TO THE SPREAD
OF A DEMOCRATIC POLITICAL ORDER

The identical line of reasoning surfaces again during our next episode, the broadening of the franchise in the course of the nineteenth century. New reasons for affirming the inevitability of a perverse outcome of that process were now put forward by the emergent social sciences. To appreciate the climate of opinion in which these arguments arose it is useful to recall first contemporary attitudes toward the masses and toward mass participation in politics.

Europe had long been a highly stratified society with the lower classes being held in the utmost contempt by both upper and middle classes. A not particularly aristocratic person like Burke wrote, in the *Reflections*: "The occupation of a hairdresser, or of a working tallow chandler cannot be a matter of honor to any person . . . to say nothing of a number of other more servile employments . . . . the state suffers oppression if such as they . . . are permitted to rule." Later on, he comments in passing on the "innumerable servile, degrading, unseemly, unmanly, and often most unwholesome and pestiferous occupations to which by the social economy so many wretches are inevitably doomed." [16]

Such remarks, made in an off-hand manner, suggest that Burke's primary emotion toward the "lower orders" was not so much class antagonism and fear of revolt as utter contempt, a feeling of total separateness, even outright physical revulsion, much as in caste societies. This mood carried over into the nineteenth century and could only have been enhanced by the cityward migration of impoverished rural folk that came with industrialization. Shortly it was indeed compounded with fear as Burke's "wretches" took to staging violent political outbreaks, particularly in the 1840s. After one such episode in 1845 in nearby Lucerne, the young Jacob Burckhardt wrote from Basel: "Con-

---

[16] *Reflections*, pp. 75, 228.

ditions in Switzerland — so disgusting and barbarous — have
spoilt everything for me and I shall expatriate myself as soon as
I can. . . . The word freedom sounds rich and beautiful, but no
one should talk about it who has not seen and experienced slavery
under the loud-mouthed masses, called the 'people'. . . . I know
too much history to expect anything from the despotism of the
masses but a future tyranny, which will mean the end of history.''[17]

It would be easy to collect additional evidence on the extent
to which the idea of mass participation in politics, be it in the
watered-down form of universal suffrage, seemed aberrant and
potentially disastrous to a good part of Europe's elites. Universal
suffrage was one of Flaubert's favorite *bêtes noires*, a frequent
butt for his passionate hatred of human stupidity. With heavy
irony, universal suffrage (*suffrage universel*) figures in his *Dic-
tionnaire des idées reçues* as the "last word of political science";
in his letters he pronounced it "the shame of the human spirit"
and the equal of (or worse than) other absurd notions, such as
the divine right of kings or the infallibility of the pope.[18]

Elsewhere in Europe similar feelings prevailed. The more
universal suffrage extended its sweep across Europe, the more
strident became the elite voices that stood or arose in unrecon-
ciled opposition to it. For Nietzsche popular elections were the
ultimate expression of the "herd instinct," a telling term he coined
to denigrate all trends toward democratic politics. Even Ibsen,
acclaimed in his time as a progressive critic of society, harshly
attacked the majority and majority rule. In *An Enemy of the
People* (1882), the play's hero (Dr. Stockmann) thunders: "Who
forms the majority in any country? I think we'd all have to agree
that the fools are in a terrifying, overwhelming majority all over
the world! But in the name of God it can't be right that the fools
should rule the wise! . . . The majority has the power, unfortu-

[17] *The Letters of Jacob Burckhardt*, ed. A. Dru (London: Routledge & Kegan
Paul, 1955), p. 93.
[18] Gustave Flaubert, *Correspondance* (Paris: Conard, 1930), pp. 282, 33.

nately . . . but the majority is not right! The ones who are right are a few isolated individuals like me! The minority is always right!" [19]

In this manner, the undoubted advance of democratic political forms in the second half of the century took place in the midst of a diffuse mood of skepticism and hostility. Then, toward the century's end, this mood found a more sophisticated expression as medical and psychological discoveries showed human behavior to be motivated by irrational forces to a much greater extent than had been acknowledged before. The idea of basing political governance on universal suffrage could henceforth be exposed as a belated product and, indeed, obsolete relic of the Enlightenment with its abiding belief in the rationality of the individual. This belief would now be denounced not just as "shallow," the standard romantic critique, but as plain wrong.

Among the several political ideas that can be considered to be, in this manner, "reactions" to the advances of the franchise and of democracy in general, one of the more prominent and influential was articulated by Gustave Le Bon in this best-selling *Psychologie des foules*, first published in 1895. It also exemplifies once again the attraction of "reactionary" thinkers to the perverse effect.

Le Bon's principal argument challenges commonsense understandings in the manner of what is known to economists as the *fallacy of composition*: what applies to the individual, so he argues, does not necessarily hold for the group, much less for the crowd. Impressed by recent medical research findings on infection and hypnosis and unaware of the simultaneously proceeding work of Freud that would shortly show individuals themselves to be subject to all manner of unconscious drives, Le Bon based his theory on a sharp dichotomy between the individual and the crowd: the individual was rational, perhaps sophisticated and

---

[19] Henrik Ibsen, *An Enemy of the People*, act IV.

calculating; the crowd was irrational, easily swayed, unable to
weigh pros and cons, given to unreasoning enthusiasms, and so on.
Even though occasionally the crowd is accorded some good points
because of its ability to engage in acts of selfless abnegation (sol-
diers in battle), there is no doubt that Le Bon looks at the crowd
as a lower, though dangerously vigorous, form of life: "None too
good at reasoning, the crowd is on the contrary much given to
action." [20] This action takes typically the form either of anomic
outbreaks by "criminal crowds" or of enthusiastic, hypnotic mass
movements organized by demagogic leaders who know how to
enslave the crowd according to a few simple rules obligingly supplied by Le Bon.

In fin-de-siècle Europe, Le Bon's theory had obvious political
implications. It saw the prospects for national and international
order as quite gloomy: with the franchise spreading, Le Bon's
irrational crowds were installed as important actors in an ever-
larger number of countries. Moreover, the book's last two chapters, "Electoral Crowds" and "Parliamentary Assemblies," supplied various specific arguments against modern mass-based democracy. Here Le Bon does not argue directly against universal suffrage; rather, like Flaubert, he speaks of it as an absurd dogma
which is unfortunately bound to cause a great deal of harm just as
did earlier superstitious beliefs. "Only time can act on them,"
he wrote, assuming the stance of a resigned chronicler of human
folly.[21] This nonreformist position then permits Le Bon to outline
coldly the disastrous consequences of universal suffrage: anticipating our contemporary "public choice" theorists, he first demonstrates how parliamentary democracy fosters a tendency toward
ever more public spending, in response to the pressure of sectional
interests. The perverse effect is appealed to in the final, crowning
argument of the book: vaunted democracy will increasingly turn

---

[20] Gustave Le Bon, *Psychologie des foules* (Paris: Félix Alcan, 1895), p. 4.
[21] Ibid., 169.

into the rule of bureaucracy through the many laws and regulations that are being passed in "the illusion that equality and liberty will be better safeguarded thereby." [22] In support of these views he cites Herbert Spencer's book *The Man versus the State* (1884), a collection of late essays. Here was indeed a contemporary scientific authority figure who had taken a strongly conservative turn. Spencer too had chosen the perverse effect as his leitmotif, particularly in the essay entitled "The Sins of Legislators," where he puts forward an extravagantly general formulation: "uninstructed legislators have in past times continually increased human suffering in their endeavours to mitigate it." [23]

Once again, then, a group of social analysts found itself irresistibly attracted to deriding those who aspire to change the world for the better. And it is not enough to show that these naive *Weltverbesserer* (world improvers) fall flat on their face: it must be proven that they are actually, if I may coin the corresponding German term, *Weltverschlechterer* (world worseners), that they leave the world in a worse shape than prevailed before any "reform" had been instituted.[24] Moreover, the worsening must be shown to occur along the very dimension where there was supposed to be improvement.

THE REACTION TO THE RISE OF THE WELFARE STATE

This sort of argument was to achieve special prominence during the third reactionary phase to which I now turn: the present-day assault on the economic and social policies that make up the modern welfare state.

In economics, more so than in the other social and political sciences, the perverse-effect doctrine is closely tied into a central

[22] Ibid., 187.

[23] Herbert Spencer, *The Man versus the State* (Caldwell, Idaho: Caxton Printers, 1940), p. 86.

[24] The term *Weltverbesserer* has a derisive meaning in German, probably as a result of the reaction against the Enlightenment.

tenet of the discipline: the idea of a self-regulating market. To the extent that this idea is dominant, any public policy aiming to change market outcomes, such as prices or wages, automatically becomes noxious interference with beneficent equilibrating processes. Even economists who are favorable to some measures of income and wealth redistribution tend to regard the most obvious "populist" measures of that sort as counterproductive.

The perverse effect of specific interferences — a minimum-wage law or the decreeing of a maximum price for bread — has often been argued for by tracing through demand and supply reactions to such measures. As a result of, say, a price stop for bread, it is shown how flour will be diverted to other final uses and how some bread will be sold at black-market prices, so that the average price of bread may go up rather than down as was intended. Similarly, after a minimum wage is imposed less labor will be hired, so that the income of the workers may fall rather than rise.

There is actually nothing certain about such perverse effects. In the case of minimum-wage legislation, in particular, it is conceivable that the underlying demand and supply curves for labor could shift as a result and that the officially imposed rise in wages could have a positive effect on labor productivity and consequently on employment. But the mere possibility of demonstrating an outright perverse outcome as the first-order effect of interferences with market outcomes — under the famous *ceteris paribus* clause of partial equilibrium reasoning — makes for a powerful debating point which is bound to be brought up in any polemic.

The long discussion about problems of social assistance to the poor provides ample illustration. Such assistance is admittedly and often self-consciously rank interference with "market outcomes" that assign some members of society to the low end of the income scale. The economic argument on the ensuing perverse effects was first put forward during the debates about the Poor Laws in England. The critics of these laws, from Defoe to Burke, and from Malthus to Tocqueville, scoffed at the notion that the

Poor Laws were merely a "safety net," to use a current term, for those who had fallen behind, through no fault of their own, in the race for a livelihood. Given the human "proclivity to idleness," to use Mandeville's phrase, this "naive" view neglected the supply reactions, the incentives built into the arrangement: the availability of the assistance, so it was argued, acts as a positive encouragement to "sloth" and "depravity," and thus *produces* poverty instead of relieving it. Here is a typical formulation of this point by an early nineteenth-century English essayist:

> The Poor-laws were intended to prevent mendicants; they have made mendicancy a legal profession; they were established in the spirit of a noble and sublime provision, which contained all the theory of Virtue; they have produced all the consequences of Vice. . . . The Poor-laws, formed to relieve the distressed, have been the arch-creator of distress.[25]

A century and a half later, one reads in the most highly publicized attack on the welfare state in the United States, Charles Murray's *Losing Ground* (1984):

> We tried to provide more for the poor and produced more poor instead. We tried to remove the barriers to escape from poverty and inadvertently built a trap.[26]

Except for a slight toning down of nineteenth-century coloratura, the melody is exactly the same. The perverse effect would seem to work unremittingly under both early and late capitalism.

Not that the ideological scene has remained unchanged throughout these 150 years. The success of Murray's book owes in fact much to the rather fresh look of its principal point, epitomized in its title — almost any idea that hasn't been around for a

---

[25] Edward Bulwer-Lytton, *England and the English* (New York: Harper, 1833), vol. 1, p. 129. Part of this passage is cited in Gertrude Himmelfarb, *The Idea of Poverty: England in the Early Industrial Age* (New York: Knopf, 1984), p. 172.

[26] Charles Murray, *Losing Ground: America's Social Policy, 1950–1980* (New York: Basic Books, 1984), p. 9.

long time has a good chance of being mistaken for an original insight. What actually happened is that the idea went into hiding, for reasons that are of some interest to our story.

As Karl Polanyi showed memorably in *The Great Transformation* (1944), the English Poor Laws, especially as supplemented and reinforced by the Speenhamland Act of 1795, represented a last-ditch attempt to rein in, through public assistance, the free market for labor and its effects on the poorest strata of society. By supplementing low wages, particularly in agriculture, the new scheme helped to ensure social peace and to sustain domestic food production during the age of the Napoleonic Wars.

But once the emergency was over, the accumulating drawbacks of the system of combining relief and wages came under strong attack. Supported by belief in the new political economy "laws" of Bentham, Malthus, and Ricardo, the reaction against the Speenhamland Act became so strong that in 1834 the Poor Law Amendment Act (or "New Poor Law") fashioned the workhouse into the exclusive instrument of social assistance. In response to the critics of the more generous earlier system, workhouse assistance was now organized so as to do away once and for all with any conceivable perverse effect. To this end, the new arrangements were meant to deter the poor from resorting to public assistance and to stigmatize those who did by "imprisoning [them] in workhouses, compelling them to wear special garb, separating them from their families, cutting them off from communication with the poor outside and, when they died, permitting their bodies to be disposed of for dissection." [27]

It was not long before this new regime aroused in turn the most violent criticism. As early as 1837 Disraeli inveighed against it in his election campaign: "I consider that this Act has disgraced the country more than any other upon record. Both a moral crime

[27] This is a paraphrase of a passage in William Cobbett's tract *A Legacy to Labourers* (1834), quoted in Himmelfarb, *The Idea of Poverty*, p. 211.

and a political blunder, it announces to the world that in England poverty is a crime." [28]

Critics of the law came from a wide spectrum of opinion and social groups. A particularly powerful and influential indictment was Charles Dickens's novel *Oliver Twist*, published in 1837–38. A strong anti–Poor Law movement arose, complete with demonstrations and riots, during the decade following enactment and, as a result, the provisions of the law were not fully applied, especially in the north, the center of both the opposition and the textile industry.[29] It became uncomfortably clear that there were many evils — loss of community, forgoing of common decency, and internal strife — that could be worse than the alleged "promotion of idleness" whose elimination had been so singlemindedly pursued by the 1834 statute.

The experience with the New Poor Law was so searing that the argument which had presided over its adoption — essentially claiming the perverse effect of social welfare assistance — remained discredited for a long time. This may in fact be one reason for the rather smooth, if slow, emergence of welfare-state legislation in England during the late nineteenth and early twentieth centuries.

Eventually, however, the argument reappeared, particularly in the United States. But even in this country it was not put forward at first in its crude form as in the statement already cited from Murray's *Losing Ground*. Rather, it looks as though, to be reintroduced into polite company, the old-fashioned perverse effect needed some special, sophisticated attire. Thus, one of the early general attacks on social welfare policy in this country had the intriguing title "Counterintuitive Behavior of Social Systems." [30] Written by Jay W. Forrester, a pioneer in the simulation of social

[28] Cited in Himmelfarb, *The Idea of Poverty*, p. 182.

[29] See Nicholas C. Edsall, *The Anti–Poor Law Movement, 1834–44* (Manchester, England: Manchester University Press), 1971.

[30] *Technology Review* 73, no. 3 (Jan. 1971).

processes by computer models and an influential adviser to the Club of Rome, the article is a good example of what the French call "intellectual terrorism." At the outset the reader is told that he or she has a very poor chance of understanding how society works, since we are dealing with "complex and highly interacting systems," with social arrangements that "belong to the class called multi-loop non-linear feedback systems" and similar arcane "system dynamics" that "the human mind is not adapted to interpreting." Only the highly trained computer specialist can unravel these mysteries. And what revelations does he come up with? "At times programs cause exactly the reverse of desired results." In other words, Joseph de Maistre's vengeful Divine Providence has returned to the stage in the guise of Forrester's "feedback-loop dynamics," and the result is identical: any human attempt to improve society only makes matters worse!

In an influential article, also written in 1971 and entitled "The Limits of Social Policy," Nathan Glazer joined Forrester in invoking the perverse effect, proclaiming, "Our efforts to deal with distress themselves increase distress." [31] In justification Glazer does not appeal to computer models, spelling out instead some plain sociological reasons. Welfare-state policies, so he argues, are meant to deal with distress that used to be taken care of by traditional structures such as the family, the church, or the local community. As these structures break down, the state comes in to take over their functions. In the process, the state causes further weakening of what remains of the traditional structures. Hence the situation is getting worse rather than better.

But Glazer's reasoning was too softly "sociological" for the harder conservative mood that became fashionable during the eighties. Charles Murray's formulation of the perverse effect of social welfare policy returned to the blunt reasoning of the proponents of Poor Law reform in early nineteenth-century England.

---

[31] *Commentary* 52, no. 3 (Sept. 1971): 52.

Inspired, like them, by the simplest economic verities, he argued that public assistance to the poor, as available in the United States, acts as an irresistible incentive to those working or potentially working at low wages or salaries (his famous "Harold" and "Phyllis") to flock to the welfare rolls and to stay there — to become forever "trapped" in sloth and poverty.

CRITICAL REFLECTIONS ON THE PERVERSE EFFECT

Just as earlier I have not controverted Burke or Le Bon, it is not my purpose here to discuss the substance of the various arguments against social welfare policies in the United States and elsewhere. What I have tried to show is how the protagonists of this "reactionary" episode, just as those of the earlier ones, have been powerfully attracted time and again by the same form of reasoning, that is, the claim of the perverse effect. I must apologize for the monotony of my account, but it was deliberate, for in it lies the demonstration of my point that invocation of the perversity thesis is a basic characteristic of "reactionary" thought. This re-iteration of the argument may, however, have had the unfortunate effect of conveying the impression that situations exhibiting perversity are in fact ubiquitous. Actually, my intention is to put forward two propositions of equal weight: (1) the perverse effect is widely appealed to by reactionary thought, *and* (2) it is unlikely to exist "in nature" to anything like the extent that is claimed. I shall now speak — much more briefly — to the second proposition.

One of the great insights of the science of society — found already in Vico and Mandeville and elaborated magisterially during the Scottish Enlightenment — is the observation that, because of imperfect foresight, human actions are apt to have unintended consequences of considerable scope.

The perverse effect is a special and extreme case of the unintended consequence. Here the failure of foresight of the ordinary human actors is well-nigh total as their actions are shown to produce precisely the opposite of what was intended; the social scientists analyzing the perverse effect, on the other hand, experience a great feeling of superiority — and revel in it. Maistre naively said as much when he exclaimed in his gruesome chapter on the prevalence of war in human history, "It is sweet (*doux*) to fathom the design of the Godhead in the midst of general cataclysm." [32]

But the very *douceur* and self-flattery of this situation should put the analysts of the perverse effect, as well as the rest of us, on guard: could they be embracing the effect for the express purpose of feeling good about themselves? In any event, are *they* not suffering from an attack of hubris when they are portraying ordinary humans as wholly groping in the dark, while in contrast they themselves are made to look so remarkably perspicuous? And, finally, are they not rendering their task too easy by focusing on just one privileged and simplistic outcome of a program or a policy — the opposite of the intended one? For it can be argued that the perverse effect, which appears to be a mere variant of the concept of unintended consequences, is in one important respect its denial and even its betrayal. The concept of unintended consequences originally introduced uncertainty and open-endedness into social thought, but the exponents of the perverse effect retreat to viewing the social universe as wholly predictable by means of a rather transparent maneuver.

There is no denying, to be sure, that perverse effects do show up here and there. By intimating that the effect is likely to be invoked for reasons that have little to do with its intrinsic truth value, I merely intended to raise some doubts about its occurring with the frequency that is claimed. I shall now bolster these doubts in a more straightforward way by suggesting that the perverse effect is by no means the only conceivable variety of unintended consequences and side effects.

In the first place, as Adam Smith and Goethe tried to teach us, there are unintended consequences or side effects of human actions

---

[32] *Considérations*, p. 95.

that are *welcome*. But we do not pay much attention to them as they do not pose problems that have to be urgently addressed.

Second, account should be taken of those actions, policies, or inventions that are comparatively devoid of unintended consequences, welcome or otherwise. Given our preoccupation with side effects, these situations tend to be entirely neglected. For example, those who emphasize the perverse incentives contained in unemployment benefits or welfare payments never mention that large areas of social assistance are impervious to the "supply response" that is at the bottom of whatever perverse effect may be at work: people are unlikely to gouge out their eyes, or to mutilate themselves in an industrial accident in order to qualify for the corresponding types of social security benefits.

Finally, we must turn to situations where secondary or side effects *detract* from the intended effect of some purposeful action. In this situation we are getting closer to the perverse case. But the typical outcome here is one where some positive margin survives the onslaught of the negative side effect. A few examples will be useful. The introduction and compulsory use of seatbelts may make some drivers relax their vigilance and in this way be responsible for some accidents that would not have otherwise occurred; but it is quite unlikely that the total number of fatal accidents will actually go up rather than down when this cautionary measure is introduced. Devaluation of the currency, designed to improve the balance of payments, will be more or less effective in this task depending on the extent to which the positive first-order effects of the devaluation are counteracted by its inflationary impact; but once again such second-order effects are unlikely to swamp the first-order ones.

There is in fact something intrinsically plausible about this type of outcome and correspondingly implausible about the perverse effect occurring with considerable frequency. This is so at least to the extent that policy-making is a repetitive, incremental activity: under such conditions yesterday's experiences are continually incorporated into today's decisions, so that tendencies toward perversity stand a good chance of being detected and corrected.[33]

CONCLUSION

The thesis of the perverse effect is probably the most striking, effective, and popular of the three reactive/reactionary theses which I shall deal with in the larger work I have in progress. At the end of that exercise I hope that I will have convinced the reader that it is worthwhile to trace these theses through the debates of the last two hundred years, if only to marvel at certain invariants in argument and rhetoric, just as Flaubert liked to marvel at the invariant *bêtise* of his contemporaries. To show how the participants in these debates are caught by compelling reflexes and lumber predictably through certain set motions and maneuvers — this is perhaps fulfilling enough for the historian of ideas. As for myself, unreconstructed, if modest, *Weltverbesserer* (world improver) that I am, I must confess to having slightly higher ambitions. Once before, I expressed the hope that one conceivable

[33] In a different context I battled the excessive claims of the perversity thesis many years ago. In *Journeys toward Progress* (New York: Twentieth Century Fund, 1963) I studied three protracted policy problems in three Latin American countries. One of them was the process of land-tenure reform in Colombia; an important episode of that process was a land reform law ("Law 200") of 1936 which was aimed at turning tenants into owners and at improving the conditions of rural dwellers in various other ways. According to most local accounts, the effects of the reform were wholly perverse: the passage of the law caused the landowners to eject their tenants from lands they had rented, thereby converting them into landless laborers. I became suspicious of the automatic, knee-jerk way in which such assertions of perversity peppered historical accounts, newspaper articles, and political speeches of both conservatives and radicals. Upon researching the historical record I became certain that Law 200 had been unjustly defamed and that it had a variety of useful accomplishments to its credit (see *Journeys*, pp. 107–13).

This and similar experiences with the way public-policy experiences are assimilated and history is written in Latin America made me suggest (pp. 240–46) that policy analysis and historiography are strongly imprinted there with some deep-set failure complex, and I later coined the term "fracasomania" to denote the trait. I now realize that this geographical or cultural interpretation was too narrow. Arguing along the lines of the perversity thesis, as was done so insistently by the Colombian commentators on Law 200, has many attractions for parties (such as our "reactionaries") who are not necessarily affected by fracasomania.

usefulness of the history of ideas might be, not to resolve issues, but to raise the level of the debate. This could again apply in the present case.

First of all, my account and critique of the lines of argument most commonly used on behalf of reactive/reactionary causes could serve to make advocates of such causes a bit reluctant to trot out these same arguments over again and inclined to plead their case with greater originality, sophistication, and restraint. Second, my exercise could have an even more useful impact on reformers and sundry progressives. They are given notice here of the kinds of arguments and objections that are most likely to be raised against their programs. Hence, they may be impelled to take extra care in guarding against conceivable perverse effects and other problematic consequences, as detailed in my script.

In counterpart to these hopes, my work might have one assuredly unintended consequence: being a treatise of standard objections to progressive moves, it could be used as a textbook of reactionary rhetoric, as a sort of "reaction for beginners." Fortunately I am not much of a textbook writer, nor does my work much appeal to the type, so perhaps I need not worry unduly on that score.

The Pseudodemocratization of the
American Presidency

ROBERT A. DAHL

THE TANNER LECTURES ON HUMAN VALUES

Delivered at
Harvard University

April 11 and 12, 1988

ROBERT DAHL was born in Iowa and received his undergraduate degree from the University of Washington and his doctorate from Yale University. He joined the political science faculty at Yale in 1946. In 1964 he was appointed Sterling Professor. He retired in 1986.

He has been the recipient of two Guggenheim Fellowships, was a fellow of the Center for Advanced Study in the Behavioral Sciences, and is a former president of the American Political Science Association. In 1977 he received that association's James Madison Award for "an American political scientist who has made a distinguished scholarly contribution to political science."

Robert Dahl is the author of several books including *Dilemmas of Pluralist Democracy: Autonomy versus Control* (1982); *A Preface to Economic Democracy* (1985); and *Controlling Nuclear Weapons, Democracy versus Guardianship* (1985).

1. THE MYTH OF THE MANDATE

On election night in 1980 the vice-president-elect enthusiastically informed the country that Ronald Reagan's triumph was "not simply a mandate for a change but a mandate for peace and freedom; a mandate for prosperity; a mandate for opportunity for all Americans regardless of race, sex, or creed; a mandate for leadership that is both strong and compassionate . . . a mandate to make government the servant of the people in the way our founding fathers intended; a mandate for hope; a mandate for hope for the fulfillment of the great dream that President-elect Reagan has worked for all his life" (Kelley 1983, 217). I suppose there are no limits to permissible exaggeration in the elation of victory, especially by a vice-president-elect. The vice-president-elect may therefore be excused, I imagine, for failing to note, as did many others who made comments in a similar vein in the weeks and months that followed, that Mr. Reagan's lofty mandate was provided by 50.9 percent of the voters. Nearly eight years later, it is much more evident, as it should have been then, that what was widely interpreted as Reagan's mandate, not only by supporters but by opponents, was more myth than reality.

In claiming that the outcome of the election provided a mandate to the president from the American people to bring about the policies, programs, emphases, and new directions uttered during the campaign by the winning candidate and his supporters, the vice-president-elect was like other commentators echoing a familiar theory.

ORIGIN AND DEVELOPMENT

A history of the theory of the presidential mandate has not been written and I have no intention of supplying one here. However, if anyone could be said to have created the myth of the presidential mandate, surely it would be Andrew Jackson. Although he never used the word "mandate," so far as I know, he was the first American president to claim not only that the president is uniquely representative of all the people but that his election confers on him a mandate from the people in support of his policy.

Jackson's claim was a fateful step in the democratization of the constitutional system of the United States — or rather what I prefer to call, for reasons I shall explain in the next lecture, the pseudodemocratization of the presidency.

As Leonard White observed, it was Jackson's "settled conviction" that "the President was an immediate and direct representative of the people" (White 1954, 23). In his first presidential message to Congress, he proposed, presumably as a result of his defeat in 1824 in both the electoral college and the House of Representatives, that the Constitution be amended to provide for the direct election of the president, in order that "as few impediments as possible should exist to the free operation of the public will" (James D. Richardson, *A Compilation of the Messages and Papers of the Presidents, 1789–1910*, 2:448 [message of Dec. 8, 1829], cited in White 1954, 23). "To the people," he said, "belongs the right of electing their Chief Magistrate: it was never designed that their choice should, in any case, be defeated, either by the intervention of electoral colleges or by . . . the House of Representatives" (Senate Documents 1, 1829–30, cited in Ceaser 1979, 160 n. 58). His great issue of policy was, of course, the Bank of the United States, which he unwaveringly believed was harmful to the general good. Acting on this conviction, in 1832 he vetoed the bill to renew the bank's charter. It is worth mentioning that like his predecessors he justified the veto as a protection against unconstitutional legislation, but unlike his predecessors in their comparatively infrequent use of the veto he also justified it as a defense of his, or his party's, policies.

Following upon his veto of the bank's charter, the bank became the main issue in the presidential election of 1832. As a
consequence, Jackson's reelection was widely regarded, even among
his opponents (in private, at least), as amounting to "something
like a popular ratification" of his policy (White 1954, 23). When,
in order to speed the demise of the bank, Jackson found it necessary to fire his Treasury secretary, he justified his action on the
ground, among others, that "the President is the direct representative of the American people, but the Secretaries are not" (Richardson 3:90 [April 15, 1834], cited in White 1954, 23).

Innovative though it was, Jackson's theory of the presidential
mandate was less robust than it was to become in the hands of his
successors. In 1848 James Knox Polk explicitly formulated the
claim, in a defense of his use of the veto on matters of policy,
that as a representative of the people the president was, if not
more representative than the Congress, at any rate equally so.

> "The people, by the constitution, have commanded the Presi-
> dent, as much as they have commanded the legislative branch
> of the Government, to execute their will. . . . The President
> represents in the executive department the whole people of the
> United States, as each member of the legislative department
> represents portions of them. . . ." The President is responsible
> "not only to an enlightened public opinion, but to the people
> of the whole Union, who elected him, as the representatives in
> the legislative branches . . . are responsible to the people of
> particular States or districts." (Richardson 4:664–65 [Dec. 5,
> 1848] cited in White 1954, 24)

Notice that in Jackson's and Polk's views, the president, both
constitutionally and as a representative of the people, is on a par
with Congress. They did not claim that in either respect the president is superior to Congress. It was Woodrow Wilson, as we shall
see, who took the further step in the evolution of the theory, by
asserting that in representing the people the president is not merely
equal to Congress but actually superior to it.

Earlier Views

Because the theory of the presidential mandate espoused by
Jackson and Polk has become an integral part of our present-day
conception of the presidency, it may be hard for us to grasp how
sharply that notion veered off from the views of the earlier
presidents.

As James Ceaser has shown, the Framers designed the presidential selection process as a means of improving the chances of
electing a *national* figure who would enjoy majority support. They
hoped their contrivance would avoid not only the populistic competition among candidates dependent on "the popular arts," which
they rightly believed would occur if the president were elected by
the people, but also what they believed would necessarily be a
factional choice if the president were chosen by the Congress,
particularly by the House.[1]

In adopting the solution of an electoral college, however,
the Framers seriously underestimated the extent to which the
strong impulse toward democratization that was already clearly
evident among Americans — particularly among their opponents,
the Anti-Federalists — would subvert and alter their carefully con-
trived constitutional structure. Since this is a theme I shall pick
up in my second lecture, I want now to mention only two such
failures that bear closely on the theory of the presidential mandate. First, the Founding Fathers did not foresee the development of political parties, nor did they comprehend how a two-
party system might achieve their goal of ensuring the election of
a figure of national rather than merely local renown. Second, as
Ceaser (1979) remarks, although the Founders recognized "the
need for a popular judgment of the performance of an incum-
bent," and designed a method for selecting the president that

---

[1] Although Madison and Hamilton opposed the contingent solution of a House
election in the event that no candidate received a majority of electoral votes,
Gouverneur Morris and James Wilson accepted it as not too great a concession
(Ceaser 1979, 80–81).

would, as they thought, provide that opportunity, they "did not see elections as performing the role of instituting decisive changes in policy in response to popular demands" (84). In short, the theory of the presidential mandate not only cannot be found in the Framers' conception of the Constitution; almost certainly it violates that conception.

No president prior to Jackson challenged the view that Congress was the legitimate representative of the people. Even Thomas Jefferson, who adeptly employed the emerging role of party leader to gain congressional support for his policies and decisions, "was more Whig than . . . the British Whigs themselves in subordinating [the executive power] to 'the supreme legislative power.' . . . The tone of his messages is uniformly deferential to Congress. His first one closes with these words: 'Nothing shall be wanting on my part to inform, as far as in my power, the legislative judgment, nor to carry that judgment into faithful execution' " (Corwin 1948, 20).

James Madison, demonstrating that a great constitutional theorist and an adept leader in Congress could be decidedly less than a great president, deferred so greatly to Congress that in his communications to that body his extreme caution rendered him "almost unintelligible" (Binkley 1947, 56) — a quality hardly to be expected from one who had been a master of lucid exposition at the Constitutional Convention. His successor, James Monroe, was so convinced that Congress should decide domestic issues without presidential influence that throughout the debates in Congress on "the greatest political issue of his day . . . the admission of Missouri and the status of slavery in Louisiana Territory," he remained utterly silent (White 1951, 38).

Madison and Monroe serve not as examples of how presidents should behave but as evidence of how early presidents thought they should behave. Considering the constitutional views and the behavior of Jackson's predecessors, it is not hard to see why his opponents called themselves Whigs in order to emphasize his dereliction from the earlier and presumably constitutionally correct view of the presidency.

Woodrow Wilson

The long and almost unbroken succession of mediocrities who succeeded to the presidency between Polk and Wilson for the most part subscribed to the Whig view of the office and seem to have laid no claim to a popular mandate for their policies — when they had any. Even Abraham Lincoln, in justifying the unprecedented scope of presidential power he believed he needed in order to meet secession and civil war, rested his case on constitutional grounds, and not as a mandate from the people.[2] Indeed, since he distinctly failed to gain a majority of votes in the election of 1860, any claim to a popular mandate would have been dubious at best. Like Lincoln, Theodore Roosevelt also had a rather unrestricted view of presidential power and he expressed the view then emerging among Progressives that chief executives were also representatives of the people. Yet the stewardship he claimed for the presidency was ostensibly drawn — rather freely drawn, I must say — from the Constitution, not from the mystique of the mandate.[3]

As I have already suggested, it was Woodrow Wilson, more as political scientist than as president, who brought the mandate theory to what now appears to be its canonical form. Wilson's

---

[2] Lincoln drew primarily on the "war power," which he created by uniting the president's constitutional obligation "to take care that the laws be faithfully executed" with his power as commander-in-chief. He interpreted the war power as a veritable cornucopia of implicit constitutional authority for the extraordinary emergency measures he undertook during an extraordinary national crisis (Corwin 1948, 277–83).

[3] "Every executive officer, in particular the President, Roosevelt maintained, 'was a steward of the people bound actively and affirmatively to do all he could for the people. . . .' He held therefore that, unless specifically forbidden by the Constitution or by law, the President had 'to do anything that the needs of the nation demanded. . . .' 'Under this interpretation of executive power,' he recalled, 'I did and caused to be done many things not previously done. . . . I did not usurp power, but I did greatly broaden the use of executive power'" (Blum 1954, 108).

formulation was influenced by his admiration for the British system of cabinet government. You will recall that in 1879 while still a senior at Princeton he published an essay recommending the adoption of cabinet government in the United States.[4] He provided little indication as to how this change was to be brought about, however, and soon abandoned the idea without yet having found an alternative solution.[5] Nevertheless, he continued to contrast the American system of congressional government, in which Congress was all-powerful but lacked executive leadership, with British cabinet government, in which Parliament, though all-powerful, was firmly led by the prime minister and his cabinet. Since Americans were not likely to adopt the British cabinet system, however, he began to consider the alternative of more powerful presidential leadership.[6] In his *Congressional Government*, published in 1885, he acknowledged that "the representatives of the people are the proper ultimate authority in all matters of government, and that administration is merely the clerical part of government" (Wilson [1885] 1956, 181). Congress is, "unquestionably, the predominant and controlling force, the center and source of all motive and of all regulative power" (31). Yet a discussion of policy that goes beyond "special pleas for special privilege" is simply impossible in the House, "a disintegrate mass

[4] Published in August 1879 in *International Review* as "Cabinet Government in the United States," and republished under that title in 1947 with an introductory note by Thomas K. Finletter (Stamford, Conn.: Overbrook Press).

[5] "He seems not to have paid much attention to the practical question of how so radical an alteration was to be brought about. As far as I know, Wilson's only published words on how to initiate the English system are in the article, *Committee or Cabinet Government*, which appeared in the *Overland Monthly* for January, 1884" (Walter Lippmann, in Wilson [1885] 1956, 14). His solution was to amend Section 6 of Article I of the Constitution to permit members of Congress to hold offices as members of the cabinet, and to extend the terms of the president and representatives (14–15).

[6] His unfavorable comparative judgment is particularly clear in the last two chapters of *Congressional Government* (Wilson [1885] 1956, 163–215; see also 91–98). Just as Jackson had proposed the direct election of the president, in his first annual message Wilson proposed that a system of direct national primaries be adopted (Ceaser 1979, 173).

of jarring elements" while the Senate is no more than "a small, select, and leisurely House of Representatives" (72–73, 145).

By 1908, when *Constitutional Government in the United States* was published, he had arrived at strong presidential leadership as a feasible solution. He faults the earlier presidents who had adopted the Whig theory of the Constitution.

> [T]he makers of the Constitution were not enacting Whig theory. . . . The President is at liberty, both in law and conscience, to be as big a man as he can. His capacity will set the limit; and if Congress be overborne by him, it will be no fault of the makers of the Constitution, — it will be from no lack of constitutional powers on its part, but only because the President has the nation behind him, and Congress has not. He has no means of compelling Congress except through public opinion. . . . [T]he early Whig theory of political dynamics . . . is far from being a democratic theory. . . . It is particularly intended to prevent the will of the people as a whole from having at any moment an unobstructed sweep and ascendancy.

And he contrasts the president with Congress in terms that will become commonplace among later generations of commentators, including political scientists:

> Members of the House and Senate are representatives of localities, are voted for only by sections of voters, or by local bodies of electors like the members of the state legislatures.[7] There is no national party choice except that of President. No one else represents the people as a whole, exercising a national choice. . . . The nation as a whole has chosen him, and is conscious that it has no other political spokesman. His is the only national voice in affairs. . . . He is the representative of no constituency, but of the whole people. When he speaks in his true character, he speaks for no special interest. . . . [T]here is but one national voice in the country, and that is the voice of the President. (Wilson 1908, 67–68, 70, 202–3)

[7] The Seventeenth Amendment, requiring direct election of senators, was not adopted until 1913.

Since Wilson it has become commonplace for presidents and commentators alike to argue that by virtue of his election the president has received a mandate for his aims and policies from the people of the United States. The myth of the mandate is now a standard weapon in the arsenal of persuasive symbols that all presidents exploit. For example, as the Watergate scandals emerged in mid-1973, Patrick Buchanan, then an aide in the Nixon White House, suggested that the president should accuse his accusers of "seeking to destroy the democratic mandate of 1972." Three weeks later in an address to the country Nixon said: "Last November, the American people were given the clearest choice of this century. Your votes were a mandate, which I accepted, to complete the initiatives we began in my first term and to fulfill the promises I made for my second term" (Kelley 1983, 99). If the spurious nature of Nixons' claim now seems self-evident, the dubious grounds for virtually all such pretensions are perhaps less obvious.[8]

A CRITIQUE OF THE THEORY

The Theory

What does a president's claim to a mandate amount to? It is worth noting that the meaning of the term itself is not altogether clear.[9] Fortunately, however, in his excellent book *Interpreting Elections*, Stanley Kelley has "piece[d] together a coherent statement of the theory" (Kelley 1983, 126).

> Its first element is the belief that elections carry messages about problems, policies, and programs — messages plain to all and specific enough to be directive. . . . Second, the theory holds that certain of these messages must be treated as authoritative commands . . . either to the victorious candidate or to the

[8] For other examples of claims to a presidential mandate resulting from the election, see Safire 1978, 398, and Kelley 1983, 72–74, 126–29, 168.

[9] See *OED* 1971, s.v. "mandate"; Safire 1978, 398; Plano and Greenberg 1979, 130; Gould and Kolb 1964, 404; Shafritz 1988, 340.

candidate and his party. . . . To qualify as mandates, messages about policies and programs must reflect the *stable* views both of individual voters and of the electorate. . . . In the electorate as a whole, the numbers of those for or against a policy or program matter. To suggest that a mandate exists for a particular policy is to suggest that more than a bare majority of those voting are agreed upon it. The common view holds that landslide victories are more likely to involve mandates than are narrow ones. . . . The final element of the theory is a negative imperative: Governments should not undertake major innovations in policy or procedure, except in emergencies, unless the electorate has had an opportunity to consider them in an election and thus to express its views. (Kelley 1983, 126–28)

To bring out the central problems more clearly let me extract what might be called the primitive theory of the popular presidential mandate. According to this view, a presidential election can accomplish four things:

1. It confers constitutional and legal authority on the victor.

2. At the same time, it also conveys information. At a minimum it reveals the first preferences for president of a plurality of voters.

3. However, according to the primitive theory the election, at least under the condition Kelley describes, conveys further information: namely that a clear majority of voters prefer the winner because they prefer his policies and wish him to pursue his policies.

4. Because the president's policies reflect the wishes of a majority of voters, when conflicts over policy arise between president and Congress, the president's policies ought to prevail.

Now you will notice that while we can readily accept the first two propositions the third, which is pivotal to the theory, might be false. But if the third is false, then so is the fourth. So the question arises, Beyond revealing the first preferences of a plurality of voters, do presidential elections also reveal the additional information that a plurality (or a majority) of voters prefer the policies of the winner and wish the winner to pursue those policies?

A Critique

In appraising the theory I want to distinguish between two different kinds of criticisms. Some critics contend that even when the wishes of constituents can be known, they should not be regarded as in any way binding on a legislator. I have in mind, for example, Edmund Burke's famous argument that he would not sacrifice to public opinion his independent judgment of how well a policy would serve his constituents' interests, and the argument suggested by Hanna Pitkin that representatives bound by instructions would be prevented from entering into the compromises that legislation usually requires (Pitkin, cited in Kelley 1983, 133).

Some critics, on the other hand, may hold that when the wishes of constituents on matters of policy can be clearly discerned, they ought to be given great, and perhaps even decisive, weight. But, these critics contend, constituents' wishes usually cannot be known, at least when the constituency is large and diverse, as in presidential elections, for example. In expressing his doubts on the matter in 1913, A. Lawrence Lowell quoted Sir Henry Maine: "The devotee of democracy is much in the same position as the Greeks with their oracles. All agreed that the voice of an oracle was the voice of god, but everybody allowed that when he spoke he was not as intelligible as might be desired" (A. Lawrence Lowell, *Public Opinion and Popular Government*, 1913, 73, cited in Kelley 1983, 134).

It is exclusively the second kind of criticism that I want now to consider. Here again I am indebted to Stanley Kelley for his succinct summary of the main criticisms. "Critics allege that 1. some particular claim of a mandate is unsupported by adequate evidence; 2. most claims of mandates are unsupported by adequate evidence; 3. most claims of mandates are politically self-serving; or 4. it is not possible in principle to make a valid claim

of a mandate, since it is impossible to sort out voters' intentions"
(Kelley 1983, 136). Kelley goes on to say that while the first
three criticisms may well be valid, the fourth has been outdated by
the sample survey, which "has again given us the ability to discover the grounds of voters' choices" (Kelley 1983, 136). In
effect, then, Kelley rejects the primitive theory and advances the
possibility of a more sophisticated mandate theory according to
which the information about policies is conveyed not by the election outcome but instead by opinion surveys. Thus the two functions are cleanly split: presidential elections are for electing a
president; opinion surveys provide information about the opinions,
attitudes, and judgments that account for the outcome.

However, I would propose a fifth proposition, which I believe
is also implicit in Kelley's analysis: while it may not be strictly
impossible *in principle* to make a reasoned and well-grounded
claim to a presidential mandate, to do so *in practice* requires a
complex analysis that in the end may not yield much support for
presidential claims.

But if we reject the primitive theory of the mandate and adopt
the more sophisticated theory, then it follows that prior to the
introduction of scientific sample surveys, no president could reasonably have defended his claim to a mandate. To put a precise
date on the proposition, let me remind you that the first presidential election in which scientific surveys formed the basis of an
extended and systematic analysis was 1940 (see Lazarsfeld, Berelson, and Gaudet 1948).

I do not mean to say that no election before 1940 now permits
us to draw the conclusion that a president's major policies were
supported by a substantial majority of the electorate. But I do
mean to say that for most presidential elections before 1940 a
valid reconstruction of the policy views of the electorate is impossible or enormously difficult, even with the aid of aggregate
data and other indirect indicators of voters' views. When we consider that presidents ordinarily asserted their claims soon after

their election, well before historians and social scientists could have sifted through reams of indirect evidence, then we must conclude that before 1940 no contemporary claim to a presidential mandate could have been supported by the evidence available at the time.

While the absence of surveys undermines presidential claims to a mandate before 1940, the existence of surveys since then would not necessarily have supported such claims. Ignoring all other shortcomings of the early election studies, the fact is that the analysis of the 1940 election I just mentioned was not published until 1948. While that interval between the election and the analysis may have set a record, the systematic analysis of survey evidence that is necessary (though perhaps not sufficient) to interpret what a presidential election means always comes well after presidents and commentators have already told the world, on wholly inadequate evidence, what the election means.[10] *The American Voter*, perhaps the most famous voting study to date, drew primarily on interviews conducted in 1952 and 1956, and did not appear until 1960 (Campbell et al. 1960). The book by Stanley Kelley published in 1983 that I have drawn on so freely here interprets the elections of 1964, 1972, and 1980.

A backward glance quickly reveals how empty the claims to a presidential mandate have been in recent elections. Take the year 1960. If more than a bare majority is essential to a mandate, then surely John F. Kennedy could have received no mandate, since he gained less than 50 percent of the total popular vote by the official count — just how much less by the unofficial count varies with the counter. Yet "on the day after election, and every day thereafter," Theodore Sorenson tells us, "he rejected the argument that the country had given him no mandate. Every election has a winner and a loser, he said in effect. There may be difficulties with the

---

[10] The early election studies are summarized in Berelson and Lazarsfeld 1954, 33–47.

Congress, but a margin of only one vote would still be a mandate" (quoted in Safire 1978, 398).

By contrast, 1964 was a landslide election, as was 1972. From his analysis, however, Kelley (1983) concludes that "Johnson's and Nixon's specific claims of meaningful mandates do not stand up well when confronted by evidence." To be sure, in both elections some of the major policies of the winners were supported by large majorities among those to whom these issues were salient. Yet "none of these policies was cited by more than 21% of respondents as a reason to like Johnson, Nixon, or their parties" (139–40). So, on Kelley's showing, no mandates there.

In 1968, Nixon gained office with only 43 percent of the popular vote. No mandate there. Likewise in 1976, Carter won with a bare 50.1 percent. Once again, no mandate.

When Reagan won in 1980, thanks to the much higher quality of surveys undertaken by the media a more sophisticated understanding of what that election meant no longer had to depend on the academic analyses that would only follow some years later. Nonetheless, many commentators, bemused as they so often are by the arithmetical peculiarities of the electoral college, immediately proclaimed both a landslide and a mandate for Reagan's policies. What they often failed to note was that Reagan gained just under 51 percent of the popular vote. Despite the claims of the vice-president-elect, surely we can find no mandate there. Our doubts are strengthened by the fact that in the elections to the House, Democratic candidates won just over 50 percent of the popular vote and a majority of seats. However, they lost control of the Senate. No Democratic mandate there, either.

These clear and immediate signs that the elections of 1980 failed to confer a mandate on the president or his Democratic opponents were, however, largely ignored. For it was so widely asserted as to be commonplace that Reagan's election reflected a profound shift of opinion away from New Deal programs and toward the new conservatism. However, from his analysis of the survey evidence, Kelley (1983) concludes that the commitment of voters to candidates was weak; a substantial proportion of Reagan voters were more interested in voting against Carter than for Reagan; and despite claims by journalists and others, the New Deal coalition did not really collapse. Nor was there any profound shift toward conservatism. "The evidence from press surveys . . . contradicts the claims that voters shifted toward conservatism and that this ideological shift elected Reagan." In any case, the relation between ideological location and policy preferences was "of a relatively modest magnitude" (170–72, 174–81, 185, and Warren E. Miller and Theresa Levitin [1979], 766, cited in Kelley, 1983, 187).

In winning by a landslide of popular votes in 1984, Reagan achieved one prerequisite to a mandate. Yet in that same election, Democratic candidates for the House won 52 percent of the popular votes. Two years earlier, they had won 55 percent of the votes. On the face of it, surely, the 1984 elections gave no mandate to Reagan.

Before the end of 1986, when the Democrats had once again won a majority of popular votes in elections to the House and had also regained a majority of seats in the Senate, it should have been clear, and it should be even clearer now, that the major social and economic policies for which Reagan and his supporters had claimed a mandate have persistently failed to gain majority support. Indeed, the major domestic policies and programs established during the thirty years preceding Reagan in the White House have not been overturned in the grand revolution of policy that his election was supposed to have ushered in. For nearly eight years, what Reagan and his supporters have claimed as a mandate to reverse those policies has been regularly rejected by means of the only legitimate and constitutional processes we Americans have for determining what the policies of the United States government should be.

CONCLUSION

What are we to make of this long history of unsupported claims to a presidential mandate?

The myth of the mandate would be less important if it were not one element in the larger process of the pseudodemocratization of the presidency — the creation of a type of chief executive that in my view should have no proper place in a democratic republic. I shall say more about that development in my next lecture.

Yet even if we consider it in isolation from the larger development of the presidency, the myth is harmful to American political life. By portraying the president as the only representative of the whole people and Congress as merely representing narrow, special, and parochial interests, the myth of the mandate elevates the president to an exalted position in our constitutional system at the expense of Congress. The myth of the mandate fosters the belief that the particular interests of the diverse human beings who form the citizen body in a large, complex, and pluralistic country like ours constitute no legitimate element in the general good. The myth confers on the aims of the groups who benefit from presidential policies an aura of national interest and public good to which they are no more entitled than the groups whose interests are reflected in the policies that gain support by congressional majorities. Because the myth is almost always employed to support deceptive, misleading, and manipulative interpretations, it is harmful to the political understanding of citizens.

It is, I imagine, now too deeply rooted in American political life and too useful a part of the political arsenal of presidents to be abandoned. Perhaps the most we can hope for is that commentators in public affairs, in the media, and in academic pursuits will dismiss claims to a presidential mandate with the scorn they usually deserve.

But if a presidential election does not confer a mandate on the victor, some of you may wonder, what does a presidential election mean, if anything at all? The answer is, I think, that while a presidential election does not confer a popular mandate on the president — nor, for that matter, on congressional majorities — it confers the legitimate authority, right, and opportunity on a president to try to gain the adoption, by constitutional means, of the policies the president supports. In the same way, elections to Congress confer on a member of Congress the authority, right, and opportunity to try to gain the adoption by constitutional means of the policies he or she supports. Each may reasonably contend that a particular policy is in the public good or public interest and, moreover, is supported by a majority of citizens.

I do not say that whatever policy is finally adopted following discussion, debate, and constitutional processes necessarily reflects what a majority of citizens would prefer, or what would be in their interests, or what would be in the public good in any other sense. What I do say is that no elected leader, including the president, is uniquely privileged to say what an election means — nor, certainly, to claim that the election has conferred on the president a mandate to enact the particular policies the president supports.

II. AFTER THE BICENTENNIAL:
THE CONSTITUTION RECONSIDERED

The bicentennial of the writing of the American Constitution was animated by a spirit of celebratory glorification, congratulation, and complacency that the Framers themselves, I sometimes thought, would have found embarrassing and perplexing. But perhaps I am only reflecting my own response. I feel about the Framers and their handiwork somewhat the same way I feel about the Wright brothers. What the Wright brothers achieved in developing powered flight should forever merit our unstinting admiration. But much as I admire their achievement, I would not want to fly in the machine that Orville flew for fifty-nine seconds at Kitty Hawk on that momentous day in 1903.

Considered against the background of world history, both
earlier and later, what was achieved by the Framers of the American Constitution unquestionably warrants our praise. But considered in the context of its present difficulties, we are entitled to
wonder whether the constitutional system that has evolved from
their design is, two centuries later, adequate for governing a
modern country.

The heart of the problem of the Constitution, as I see it, is this.
The Framers created a political system that in important respects
would not and was not intended to fit comfortably with the strong
impulse toward democracy that by 1787 had already developed
among many Americans and that was to grow stronger with the
passage of time. As a consequence of this democratic impulse,
from time to time efforts were made to democratize the original framework of government. Yet though these efforts suc-
cessfully eliminated or altered certain features thought to be
insufficiently democratic, democratization sometimes produced unforeseen consequences.

It is the unforeseen consequences of the democratization of
the presidency that should most concern us. The long effort to
democratize the presidency not only violated the clear intentions
of the Framers — a consequence I confess I do not find particularly disturbing, though doubtless others will — but, in one of the
ironies for which history is famous, has come to endanger the
democratic process itself. This is why I want to call it the pseudodemocratization of the presidency.

The Design

Some features of the Constitution that advocates of democratization found objectionable, at the time or in later years, were
deliberately designed, as we know, to serve as impediments to
popular rule. The aims of the Framers in this respect are a well-
worn theme, much discussed, sometimes played down, more often

exaggerated, and in important details still a matter of scholarly controversy.

What is often forgotten, however, is that the Constitution that emerged from the convention in 1787 and was adopted in 1789 — let me call it the 1789 Constitution — was not, bicentennial mythology to the contrary, the product of a single, coherent theory of government. The 1789 Constitution was also a product of compromises, of logrolling, and of ignorance. Compromises were necessary, among other reasons, because of conflicts between advocates and opponents of greater national power; because of ideological differences among the delegates, notably differences between the more aristocratic republicans and the more democratic republicans; because of the ultimately uncompromisable institution of slavery; and because of the deep and protracted dispute over the relative weight in the federal system that was to be given to larger and smaller states, a difference that was of far greater importance to the delegates than it has ever actually been in American political life. Logrolling was facilitated by the small number of delegates, the even smaller number who ordinarily attended, and the fact that votes were assigned not to delegates but to states — one vote to each state.

Finally, we must not underestimate the importance of ignorance. Ignorance was inherent in the situation of the Framers, simply because in all prior history, no people other than the Americans themselves during their brief period of government under the Articles of Confederation had ever attempted the daunting task of operating a large representative republic. Although the delegates drew readily on the history of earlier democratic and republican governments, they could find none, not Athens, Rome, Venice, Holland, Switzerland, or any other, that provided truly comparable experiences. Probably in no respect did history provide less guidance than on the matter of the executive. It is no wonder that on this question, perhaps more than on any other, the delegates floundered, adopting one solution after another, until they finally settled, for reasons that are by no means clear, on the executive they provided for in Article II.

Before we fault them for their ignorance, I suggest we try to imagine ourselves as delegates to a convention today, called for the purpose of designing a new constitution for the United States. After two centuries of experience with our own political system, which is far and away the most fully studied political system in the history of the world, and the invaluable addition of substantial comparative evidence from a very large number of other countries, I wonder how much better we would be at predicting — or better, guessing — how new political institutions would actually work in practice.

The Constitution Judged by Democratic Standards

Whether as a result of deliberate purpose, compromises, or an inability of the delegates to foresee what would actually develop out of their initial framework, the Constitution of 1789 failed to satisfy democratic standards in a number of ways. By democratic standards I mean standards that existed to a considerable degree at the time in some quarters. They existed among Anti-Federalists, for example, many of whom advocated a much more democratic doctrine than did most of the delegates to the convention. But I also mean the democratic standards that would develop in the course of the next two centuries, not only in the United States but in other democratic countries.

Are Democratic Standards Relevant?

Let me anticipate an objection to evaluating the work of the Framers by democratic standards. You might say that they did not intend to create a democratic government and therefore it is anachronistic or otherwise mistaken to judge them by standards they did not themselves adhere to. But this objection is either trivial, wrong, irrelevant, or all of these. One common and trivial argument in this vein is that what they intended to create and did create was not a democracy but a republic. To the Framers and their contemporaries, the argument runs, "democracy" meant direct government by a citizen assembly, whereas by "republic" they meant a representative government; since their Constitution put forth a representative government it obviously was not intended to be a democracy. But if this argument is meant to be an objection to our employing democratic standards to judge their work, it is simply trivial. For even if the terms "democracy" and "republic" were so distinguished in the eighteenth century, that distinction rapidly disappeared from ordinary usage, and what we mean by "democracy" today obviously includes the possibility of representative government.

However, that particular objection is not only trivial but it is also wrong. Despite Madison's insistence to the contrary in *The Federalist Papers*, it is simply not true that "democracy" was consistently used to mean direct assembly government and "republic" to mean representative government. In his excellent study, Willi Paul Adams (1980) remarks that "even today one still encounters the pseudo-learned argument that the founding fathers intended the United States to be a republic but not a democracy" (117). Adams quotes, among others, the *Providence Gazette* for August 9, 1777: "By a *democracy* is meant, that form of government where the highest power of making laws is lodged in the common people, or persons chosen out from them. This is what by some is called a republic, a commonwealth, or free state, and seems to be most agreeable to *natural right and liberty*" (99; and see pp. 99–117).[11]

Yet even if objections like these were not trivial or wrong

---

[11] Robert W. Shoemaker (1966) agrees that "the terms were used in a variety of ways. Often, for example, they were used synonymously," but he concludes that "representation was much more often associated with republicanism than with democracy, and thus serves as a legitimate criterion to distinguish the two" (83 and 89). His conclusion seems to me unwarranted. He does not convincingly demonstrate that "representation was much more often associated with republicanism than with democracy." In any case, given the fact that the terms were used "in a variety of ways" and often synonymously, it is arbitrary to say that representation "serves as a legitimate criterion to distinguish the two."

they would still be irrelevant to our needs. It is we after all, not the Framers, who live under the American Constitution. Just as we are entitled to employ our own standards, and not those of the Wright brothers or other Americans in 1903, in judging the desirability of using their 1903 airplane to fly from Boston to Los Angeles or London, surely we are entitled to bring our own standards to bear on the task of evaluating that Constitution. The question is not whether the Framers and the Wright brothers were great men and made great contributions. The question is whether their concrete historical contributions now serve our needs. In answering this question with respect to the concrete work of the Framers, we are entitled to consider how well or how poorly the Constitution now meets democratic criteria. Even if democratic standards are not the only ones we might reasonably employ to judge the present suitability of our Constitution, to Americans they are among the most relevant standards for judging the worth of political institutions.

Undemocratic Aspects of the Constitution

In a number of respects the 1789 Constitution was inconsistent with the commitment to the democratic process that was evolving among Americans, or at least elements of the politically active stratum sufficiently numerous and influential to bring about changes both in the formal Constitution itself and in the political processes by which Americans were governed.

As everyone knows, the 1789 Constitution contained no explicit guarantee of political and civil rights. The omission was of course one of the principal targets of the Anti-Federalists, whose objections at the state ratifying conventions, particularly in Virginia and New York, persuaded Madison and others to agree to add a Bill of Rights.

The omission was so swiftly corrected, then, that we can properly think of the first ten amendments as integral with the original Constitution. But other omissions proved less easy to correct. As we all know, the Constitution not only lacked any prohibition against slavery, in effect it authorized slavery for the near future and arguably for longer.[12] Because even free citizens, of whatever race or color, were not guaranteed the right to vote, the states were authorized to exclude whomever they chose from the suffrage. Women were excluded from the suffrage almost everywhere.[13] For generations many states, north and south, continued by law to exclude free blacks (Elliott 1974, 40). Native Americans — Indians — were not only excluded from the suffrage but often treated as enemies without rights of any kind. Thus the republic founded by the Constitution was at most a white male republic.

The 1789 Constitution also deliberately limited popular sovereignty by its indirect system for choosing senators and the president. In addition, it placed significant restrictions on the power of national majorities to govern. This it accomplished by its limits on congressional authority in Article I; by the guarantee resulting from the famous Connecticut Compromise that each state was entitled to equal representation in the Senate without respect to population; by a complex procedure for amendment that would allow tiny but strategically located minorities to block changes;[14] by vesting federal judicial power in judges who were not subject to popular election or recall; and by sufficient vagueness in Article III about the powers of the judiciary to permit the development of a

[12] Article I, Section 9, denied Congress the power to prohibit until 1808 "The Migration or Importation of Such Persons as any of the States now existing shall think proper to admit" (i.e., slaves) and Article V prohibited any amendments to this provision before 1808. Article IV, Section 2(3), required that fugitive slaves escaping to another state "shall be delivered up on Claim of the Party to whom such Service of Labour may be due."

[13] My colleague Rogers Smith has called my attention to one exception: The constitution of New Jersey permitted women to vote until 1807.

[14] Based on 1980 state populations, it would be theoretically possible for a proposed amendment to be blocked by thirty-four senators from the seventeen smallest states with 7.1 percent of the population of the United States. Since it is extremely unlikely that opinion in these seventeen states would be unanimous, a veto bloc could consist of less than 7 percent; in principle, a bit less than 4 percent would be sufficient. Admittedly this theoretical outcome is most unlikely.

Supreme Court empowered in effect to exercise a veto over laws enacted by Congress and the president.

Democratizing the Constitution

Some of these exclusions from full citizenship, limits on popular sovereignty, and limits on majority rule evidently violated beliefs about government that were expressed in the democratic attitudes and ideas that, as best one can tell, formed the public ideology of a substantial majority of political activists. Many Anti-Federalists became Jeffersonian Republicans and they now extended their already existing commitments to popular sovereignty over state and local governments to the national government. In the long run it was the democratic elements of Anti-Federalist thought, applied, however, to governments at all levels, that prevailed among political activists and probably the general public as well.

As a consequence, many important features of the American political system, including the Constitution of 1789, were altered to make them conform more closely to the evolving democratic ideology. It is striking that nearly all the amendments to the Constitution since 1791 — that is, after the adoption of the Bill of Rights — have further democratized it.[15] Of the sixteen amendments after the Bill of Rights, three were mainly to cure flaws that had little or nothing to do with democracy. Two restricted majority rule and popular sovereignty in certain respects. But the remaining eleven can properly be counted as expanding democracy by reducing or eliminating exclusions from the full rights of citizenship, limits on popular sovereignty, or limits on majority rule (tables 1 and 2; for more detail, see Grimes 1979, 157–67 and passim).

It was not only by constitutional amendments that the prevailing democratic ideology worked its influence on political struc-

---

[15] "In large measure, the progress of democratic rights is recorded in the amendments to the Constitution" (Grimes 1979, 163).

TABLE 1. DEMOCRATIZING THE CONSTITUTION BY AMENDMENT

Art. No.	Original provision	Amend. No.	Date	Subject
	No explicit guarantee of political and civil rights	1	1791	Bill of rights
		14	1868	Citizenship, due process, equal protection
	Exclusions from rights			
	Slaves			
	Slavery not prohibited	13	1865	Slavery prohibited
IV,2	Fugitive slaves			
I,9	Importation authorized		1808	Authoriz. lapses
	Slaves not citizens	14	1868	Citizenship
	Suffrage			
I,2	No guarantees, left to states			
I,3		15	1870	Race
I,4		19	1920	Sex
		23	1961	Poll tax outlawed
		24	1964	D.C. residents
		26	1971	Age
	Limits on Pop. Sovereignty			
	Indirect elections			
II	President			Popular election of electors (1789–1868)
I,3	Senators	17	1913	Direct election
III	Judiciary: life appt.[a]			Unchanged
	No referenda[b]			Unchanged
	Limits on majority rule			
I	Limited cong. powers	16	1913	Income tax
				Judicial interpretation
I,3	Compos. of Senate			Unchanged
V	Amending process			Unchanged
	Supreme Court: judicial review			Unchanged

Note: Amendments 11, 18, 20, 21, and 25 are not germane.

[a] Some democratic countries provide limited terms of office for members of the highest court.

[b] The United States "is one of only four of the long-term democracies — the others are Israel, Japan, and the Netherlands — in which a national referendum has never been held" (Lijphart 1985, 21).

TABLE 2. THE TENDENCY OF CONSTITUTIONAL AMENDMENTS AFTER 1791

Subject	No.	Expanding	Restricting	Other
Suits vs. states	11			x
Pres. election	12	x		x
Abolition	13	x		
Rights	14	x		
Suffrage	15	x		
Income tax	16	x		
Dir. elec. of senators	17	x		
Prohibition	18		x	
Suffrage (gender)	19	x		
Terms (succession)	20			x
Repeal	21	x		
Pres. (two terms)	22		x	
Suffrage (poll tax)	23	x		
Suffrage (D.C. res.)	24	x		
Succession	25			x
Suffrage (18 yrs.)	26	x		

tures and processes but also in extra-constitutional ways. Let me briefly mention two familiar developments of exceptional importance. One, which began soon after the political machinery of the Constitution was in place, was the emergence of political parties. The other, which we have witnessed in operation quite recently, was the exertion of political influence over judicial appointments, particularly appointments to the Supreme Court. The effect was to limit the antidemocratic potential of judicial review by ensuring that the Court would not hold out for long against national majorities that were large and enduring enough to capture the Congress, particularly the Senate, and the presidency.

Each of these developments helped to democratize the constitutional and political processes in substantial ways. But each is a large and complex topic in itself, and while they greatly reinforced that general process, I shall say little about them here.

THE DEMOCRATIZATION OF THE PRESIDENCY

Let me turn instead to the presidency. It was inevitable that the executive designed by the Framers would be fundamentally altered in response to the powerful influence of democratizing impulses. If the Framers had intended a chief executive whose selection and capacity for governing would not require him to compete for popular approval and who therefore would not depend on "the popular arts" of winning public support (Ceaser 1979, 47), they seriously underestimated both the strength of the democratic impulses among their fellow citizens and its effects on the presidency. Nothing reveals this more clearly than the amazing speed with which their design for the executive was replaced by a presidency dependent on popular election and popular approval.

The consequences of democratization were evident almost at once and gained strength with the passage of time. I have already described one aspect of this process of democratization in some detail: the invention of the theory of the presidential mandate. Jackson's invention was, however, preceded by decades of democratization that gave plausibility to the theory.

By Jackson's time the presidency had long since become an office sought by partisan candidates in popular elections. Earlier I alluded to the creation of political parties. Though political parties had existed in Britain and Sweden as elite organizations in systems with a severely limited suffrage, under the leadership of Jefferson and Madison the Republican party became an instrument by which popular majorities could be organized, mobilized, and made effective in influencing the conduct of government. Henceforth a president would combine his role as a presumably nonpartisan chief executive with his role as a national leader of a partisan organization with a partisan following.[16]

[16] As Ceaser (1979) remarks, "The nonpartisan selection system established by the Founders barely survived a decade. By the election of 1796, traces of partisanship were already clearly in evidence, and by 1800 the contest was being fought on strictly partisan lines" (88). Like many other innovations, Jefferson's had unintended consequences. "Jefferson . . . had an abiding distrust of national elections and, except in the case of his own election, never regarded them as the proper forum for making decisive changes. . . . The paradox of Jefferson's election in 1800 was that while he was chosen for partisan reasons, he did not intend to institute a system of permanent party competition (90).

If the presidential office was to be attained by partisan contestation, then in order to reach that office a serious presidential candidate would ordinarily need to gain the endorsement and support of a political party. Though the story of the evolution of the presidential nominating process has often been told, it so vividly reveals the impact of democratizing impulses that I want to summarize it briefly.

The Nominating Process

The first organized system for nominating candidates for president and vice-president was the congressional caucus, which both the Republicans and the Federalists introduced in 1800 (Cunningham 1957, 163–65). Yet given the emerging strength of democratic ideology, a system so obtrusively closed to participation by any but a small group of congressional politicians was clearly vulnerable. Democratic sentiments we would find familiar in our own time were expressed in a resolution passed in the Ohio legislature in 1823: "The time has now arrived when the machinations of the *few* to dictate to the *many* . . . will be met . . . by a people jealous of their rights. . . . The only unexceptional source from which nominations can proceed is the people themselves. To them belongs the right of choosing; and they alone can with propriety take any previous steps" (Ostrogorski 1926, 12 n. 1).

By 1824, when the candidate of the congressional caucus of Democratic Republicans trailed a bad fourth in the election behind Jackson, John Quincy Adams, and Henry Clay, who all ran without benefit of a blessing by the caucus, the outrage to democratic sentiments was easily exploited, most notably by Jackson and his supporters, and the congressional nominating caucus came to an end.[17]

In an obvious extension of democratic ideas, which by then had thoroughly assimilated the concept of representation, in 1831

---

[17] Though Jackson gained more votes than Adams, both popular and electoral, he was denied victory in the House of Representatives.

and 1832 the nominating convention came into existence. But in due time, "just as once the democratic passions of the people were roused against the Congressional caucus, so now they were turned against the convention system. . . . Away therefore with the delegates, who can never be trusted, and back to the people!" Ostrogorski 1926, 342).

So in a further obvious extension of democratic ideas to the nominating process, from 1901 onward the direct primary was introduced, initially for state and congressional nominations, and soon for presidential candidates. The presidential primary system was in turn subjected to the democratizing impulse. "By the election of 1972," Ceaser remarks, "the election process had been transformed into what is essentially a plebiscitary system." [18]

Reducing "Intermediation"

The democratization of the nominating process is instructive for many reasons — among others because after almost two centuries of trials employing three major forms with many variations, a sensible method of nominating presidential candidates still seems beyond the reach of Americans. The present system has its defenders, no doubt, but they seem to be rapidly diminishing.

The democratization of the nominating process is also instructive because it shows how the relations between the public and presidents or presidential candidates have become increasingly direct. Jeffrey Tulis has recently described the enormous change that has taken place in the way presidents address the public — presidential speech, if you like. The view that prevailed during the early years of the republic, and for much of the nineteenth century, tended to follow "two general prescriptions for presidential speech." First, proposals for laws and policies would be

[18] Ceaser (1979) describes three phases in the evolution of the presidential selection process since the introduction of the primaries: 1912–20, a period of the expansion of the primaries and the "plebiscitary model"; 1920–60s, which saw the decline of primaries and the resurgence of parties; and the period since 1972 (215).

written and directed principally to Congress, and though public
they would be fashioned for congressional needs and not necessarily for general public understanding or approval. Second, when
presidential speech was directed primarily to the people at large
it would address general principles rather than specific issues.
"The inaugural address, for example, developed along lines that
emphasized popular instruction in constitutional principle and the
articulation of the general tenor and direction of presidential
policy, while tending to avoid discussion of the merits of particular policy proposals" (Tulis 1987, 46–47).

Presidents rarely directly addressed the general public, except
possibly on official occasions. From George Washington through
Andrew Jackson, no president gave more than five speeches a year
to the general public, a total that was not exceeded by half the
presidents from Washington through William McKinley. When
they did address the general public the early presidents rarely employed popular rhetoric or discussed their policies (Tulis 1987,
tables 3.1 and 3.2).[19] Moreover, Gil Troy (1988) has recently
discovered that until Woodrow Wilson no president had ever
"stumped on his own behalf." Until the 1830s, even presidential
candidates did not make stump speeches. "Such behavior," Troy
has written, "was thought undignified — and unwise. Presidential
candidates, especially after nomination, were supposed to stand,
not run, for election."

What we now take as normal presidential behavior is a product
of this century. The innovators were Theodore Roosevelt and,
to an even greater extent, Woodrow Wilson.[20] Since their day,
and particularly in recent decades, the task of shaping presidential
speech to influence and manipulate public opinion, if necessary
by appeals made over the heads of Congress in order to induce the

[19] The great exception was Andrew Johnson, who, however, scarcely served as
a model for his successors (Tulis 1987, 87–93).

[20] On Theodore Roosevelt, see Tulis 1987, 95–116, on Wilson, 118–37.

Congress to support the president's policies, has become a central element in the art and science of presidential conduct.

THE PRESIDENT AND THE CONSTITUTIONAL SYSTEM

Thus the presidency has developed into an office that is the very embodiment of the kind of executive the Framers, so far as we can discern their intentions, strove to avoid. They did not wish an executive who would be a tribune of the people, a champion of popular majorities; who would gain office by popular election; who as a consequence of his popular election would claim a mandate for his policies; who in order to mobilize popular support for his policies would appeal directly to the people; who would shape the language, style, and delivery of his appeals so as best to create a public opinion favorable to his ambitions; and who whenever it seemed expedient would bypass the members of the deliberative body in order to mobilize public opinion and thereby induce a reluctant Congress to enact his policies. That is, however, a fair description of the presidency that emerged out of the intersection of the Framers' design with the strongly democratic ideology that came to prevail among politically active Americans.

Other democratic countries have rejected the American presidency as a model. Of the twenty-two countries that have been democratic since 1950, seventeen possess parliamentary governments in which the chief executive is dependent on the confidence of the legislature. One, Switzerland, has a unique plural executive, a Federal Council of seven members elected by parliament for fixed four-year terms. Only four democratic countries have a president who is vested with significant authority and not dependent on the legislature's confidence. These, in addition to the United States, are Finland, France since 1958 under the Fifth Republic, and Costa Rica (which has been continuously democratic since the restoration of civilian rule and the abolition of its military in 1950 following a coup in 1948). In both Finland and France, however, the president shares with a prime minister both formal constitutional authority and a great deal of actual control over policies. The American system for selecting candidates and presidents, indeed any general system of direct primaries for choosing candidates for public office, is unique.[21] The Latin American republics have been most prone to adopt a strong presidential system — with, on the whole, most unhappy results. It is worth noting that the authors of the preliminary draft of the new constitution for Argentina explicitly recognized the dangers of presidential government and have proposed to reduce them by a solution like the French Fifth Republic, that is, a popularly elected president and a prime minister and cabinet dependent on Parliament.[22]

One response to this kind of presidency is to argue that these developments are, on the whole, good. They are good, it might be said, because democracy is good, more democracy is better than less democracy, and a more democratized presidency is better than a less democratized presidency. In the immortal cliché of the McGovern-Fraser Commission, "the cure for the ills of democracy is more democracy" (cited in Ceaser 1979, 275). Yet this response does not seem to quiet the fears of a growing number of critics. In Arthur Schlesinger's now popular term, the presidency was transformed into the imperial presidency (1973); James Ceaser, Theodore Lowi, and others have referred to the development of the plebiscitary presidency (Ceaser 1979, 5, 17, 214; Lowi 1985, 97–175); Lowi has also dubbed it the personal presidency, remarking that "the new politics of the president-centered Second

[21] For the twenty-two democratic countries, see Lijphart 1984, table 5.1. Lijphart's list counts both the Fourth and Fifth Republics in France and does not include Costa Rica. I have counted only the Fifth Republic and have included Costa Rica. In an article appropriately entitled "The Pattern of Electoral Rules in the United States: A Deviant Case among the Industrialized Democracies" (1985), he remarks that "there are a few non-American examples that resemble . . . primaries . . . but primaries according to [Austin] Ranney's strict definition occur not only exclusively but pervasively in the United States" (20).

[22] These proposals were submitted in 1986 by The Council for the Consolidation of Democracy and the Reform of the Constitution. See *El Consejo*, 1986, 49–57.

Republic can best be described as a plebiscitary republic with a personal presidency" (xi) ; in his recent book, Jeffrey Tulis (1987) calls the presidency that was seeded by Wilson and cultivated by his successors the rhetorical presidency.

In criticisms of the modern presidency I want to distinguish several different perspectives. From one perspective, what is lamentable is the break with the doctrines, intentions, and designs of the Founders. A rather different perspective, one more pragmatic and functional, emphasizes that the presidency is simply no longer working satisfactorily in its existing constitutional setting. For example, a president claiming a mandate for his policies may be blocked in one or both houses of Congress by a majority of members who, in effect, also claim a mandate for their policies. The result is not constructive compromise but deadlock or contradictions in policies. Examples are the recent conflicts over the deficit and over American policies in Central America.

From a third perspective, however, the presidency has come to endanger the operation of democratic processes. It is this perspective that I want to emphasize here.

I have alluded to the developments over the past two centuries as the *pseudodemocratization* of the presidency. I have no wish, much less any hope, of adding to the other Greco-Latin epithets another even more cumbersome and more ugly, but the term does speak directly to my concerns. By pseudodemocratization I mean a change taken with the ostensible, and perhaps even actual, purpose of enhancing the democratic process that in practice retains the aura of its democratic justification and yet has the effect, intended or unintended, of weakening the democratic process.

In the case of the presidency, I have two adverse consequences in mind. One, the more obvious, is a loss of popular and congressional control, direct and indirect, over the policies and decisions of the president. A president endowed with the mystique of a mandate, a mystique that may sometimes be deepened in a demo-

cratic country by the majesty and mystery generated by his popu-
larity and his capacity to evoke and reflect popular feelings, yearn-
ings, and hopes, may encounter resistance to a particular policy —
resistance from Congress, perhaps even from the public. So he
exploits all the resources of his office to overcome that resistance:
his rhetorical resources, his unique capacity to influence or even
manipulate public opinion, and all the power and authority derived
properly or factitiously from the Constitution, including his power
as commander-in-chief, his unique authority over foreign affairs,
his right or claim to executive privilege and secrecy, his authority
and influence over officials in the executive branch, over the objectives they are obliged or induced to seek, and over the moneys
and other resources necessary to reach those objectives. Whatever
term we may wish to apply to an executive like this, we can hardly
call it democratic.

The other consequence, though more elusive and not wholly
independent of the first, is equally important. Now in one view —
which I would describe as either simplistic or hostile — democracy
means rule by public opinion. This view is, I believe, mistaken
both historically and theoretically. Democracy cannot be justified,
I think, and its advocates have rarely sought to justify it, as no
more than the triumph of raw will. It can be justified, and I
believe it is justified, because more than any feasible alternative
it provides ordinary people with opportunities to discover what
public policies and activities are best for themselves and for others,
and to ensure that collective decisions conform with — or at least
do not persistently and fundamentally violate — the policies they
believe best for themselves and for others.

I cannot undertake to explicate the complexities in the notion
of discovering what is best for themselves and for others, nor,
I think, do I need to. For it is obvious that discovering what is
best for oneself or others requires far more than announcing one's
raw will or surface preferences. Imagine this extreme situation.
Suppose we were called upon to vote in a national plebiscite on a

proposed treaty governing nuclear weapons that had been secretly negotiated between the president and the leader of the Soviet Union. Suppose further that the plebiscite is to be held one day after the agreement between the two leaders, and that we are to vote yes or no. The very perversity of this example serves to emphasize the crucial importance of opportunities for *understanding* as a requirement in the democratic process and illustrates why in the absence of such opportunities we should speak instead of a pseudodemocratic process.

Many writers have stressed the importance of *deliberation*. While some of them associate it with classical republicanism, deliberation is surely central to the idea of democratic decision making. What I have referred to elsewhere as enlightened understanding is, I believe, an essential criterion for the democratic process. Deliberation is one crucial means, though I think not the only means, to enlightened understanding. Others include systematic research and analysis, experimentation, consultation with experts, orderly discussion, casual and disorderly discussion, daydreaming, and self-inquiry.

The modern presidency, I believe, all too often impairs not only deliberation but also other means to a more enlightened understanding by citizens and the Congress. Nelson Polsby's conclusions about the presidential selection process should, I think, be extended to the presidency as a whole. The increasing directness of relationships between a candidate or president and the public means that the traditional "intermediation processes," to use his term, have become less effective. Face-to-face groups, political parties, and interest groups are less autonomous and now rely heavily on the mass media (Polsby 1983, 134, 170–72). For example, some nice experiments have recently shown that in assessing the relative importance of different issues, citizens are strongly influenced by television news (Iyengar and Kinder 1987). I share Polsby's judgment that not only are deliberate processes weak in the general public's consideration of candidates and presidents, but they are also insufficiently subject to extensive review and appraisal by their peers (Polsby 1983, 134, 170–72). I also share his judgment that "the directness of direct democracy in a very large scale society seems . . . illusory" (147).

CONCLUSION

How serious a matter is the pseudodemocratization of the presidency, and what, if anything, can and should we do about it?

To answer those questions responsibly would obviously take us far beyond the slender limits of these lectures. Among friends and colleagues I think I detect rather sharply differing perspectives. Let me list several.

1. The problem is not serious.

2. Though the problem is serious, the solution is to elect one more great president.

3. The problem is serious but there isn't much we can do about it.

4. The problem is serious but can be corrected by fairly modest incremental changes, possibly including a constitutional amendment, say one providing for an American equivalent to the question hour.

5. The problem is so profoundly built into the interaction between the constitutional framework and democratic ideology that it cannot be solved without a fundamental alteration in one or the other.

The last view is the one to which I find myself increasingly drawn. However, given that conclusion, a solution, assuming one is attainable, could require that we Americans either transform our constitutional framework or instead give up our democratic beliefs. I think some critics may hope that Americans will reject their democratic ideology in favor of what these critics believe to be eighteenth-century republican doctrines that would restore the Constitution to its pristine condition in the form the Framers presumably intended. I think this alternative is not only morally wrong but politically and historically illusory.

A goal more suitable to the democratic beliefs of Americans would be for us to begin the arduous task of rethinking our constitutional needs in order to determine whether we may not design a form of government better adapted to the requirements of democracy and less conducive to pseudodemocratization. Among other rethinking we need to consider how to create better opportunities for deliberation and other means by which citizens might gain a more enlightened understanding of their political goals.

To achieve the daunting goal of rethinking our Constitution will not be easy and no one should believe that, properly done, it can be accomplished quickly. But begun now, we might yet achieve it before this century is over. It would be an appropriate undertaking to commence during the year following the bicentennial of the American Constitution.

WORKS CITED

Adams, Willi Paul. *The First American Constitutions; Republican Ideology and the Making of the State Constitutions in the Revolutionary Era.* Chapel Hill: University of North Carolina Press, 1980.

Berelson, Bernard R., and Lazarsfeld, Paul F. *Voting.* Chicago: University of Chicago Press, 1954.

Binkley, Wilfred E. *President and Congress.* New York: Knopf, 1947.

Blum, John Morton. *The Republican Roosevelt.* New York: Atheneum, 1954.

Campbell, Angus; Converse, Philip E.; Miller, Warren E.; and Stokes, Donald E. *The American Voter.* New York: Wiley, 1960.

Ceaser, James W. *Presidential Selection: Theory and Development.* Princeton: Princeton University Press, 1979.

El Consejo para la consolidacion de la democracia y la reforma constitucional. Reforma constitucional: Dictamen preliminar. Buenos Aires: Editorial Universitaria de Buenos Aires, 1986.

Corwin, Edward S. *The President: Offices and Powers, 1787–1948.* 3d ed. New York: New York University Press, 1948.

Cunningham, Noble E., Jr. *The Jeffersonian Republicans: The Formation of Party Organization, 1789–1801.* Chapel Hill: University of North Carolina Press, 1957.

Elliott, Ward E. Y. *The Rise of Guardian Democracy: The Supreme Court's Role in Voting Rights Disputes, 1845–1896.* Cambridge, Mass.: Harvard University Press, 1974.

Gould, Julius, and Kolb, William L. *A Dictionary of the Social Sciences.* New York: Free Press, 1964.

Grimes, Alan P. *Democracy and the Amendments to the Constitution.* Lexington, Mass.: Lexington Books, 1979.

Iyengar, Shanto, and Kinder, Donald R. *News That Matters: Television and American Opinion.* Chicago: University of Chicago Press, 1987.

Kelley, Stanley, Jr. *Interpreting Elections.* Princeton: Princeton University Press, 1983.

Lazarsfeld, Paul F.; Berelson, Bernard; and Gaudet, Helen. *The People's Choice.* New York: Columbia University Press, 1948.

Lijphart, Arend. *Democracies.* New Haven: Yale University Press, 1984.

———. "The Pattern of Electoral Rules in the United States: A Deviant Case among the Industrialized Democracies." *Government and Opposition* 20 (Winter 1985): 18–28.

Lowi, Theodore J. *The Personal President: Power Invested, Promise Unfulfilled.* Ithaca: Cornell University Press, 1985.

Ostrogorski, M. *Democracy and the Party System in the United States.* New York: Macmillan, 1926.

Oxford English Dictionary. Compact edition. Oxford: Oxford University Press, 1971.

Plano, Jack C., and Greenberg, Milton. *The American Political Dictionary.* New York: Holt, Rinehart and Winston, 1979.

Polsby, Nelson W. *Consequences of Party Reform.* Oxford: Oxford University Press, 1983.

Safire, William. *Safire's Political Dictionary.* New York: Random House, 1978.

Schlesinger, Arthur, Jr. *The Imperial Presidency.* Boston: Houghton Mifflin, 1973.

Shafritz, Jay M. *The Dorsey Dictionary of American Government and Politics.* Chicago: Dorsey Press, 1988.

Shoemaker, Robert W. " 'Democracy' and 'Republic' as Understood in Late Eighteenth Century America." *American Speech* 41 (May 1966): 83–95.

Troy, Gil. "Candidates Take to the Stump, Then and Now." Letter. *New York Times*, January 17, 1988, 26E.

Tulis, Jeffrey K. *The Rhetorical Presidency.* Princeton: Princeton University Press, 1987.

White, Leonard D. *The Jacksonians: A Study in Administrative History, 1829–1861.* New York: Free Press, 1954.

———. *The Jeffersonians: A Study in Administrative History, 1801–1829.* New York: Free Press, 1951.

Wilson, Woodrow. *Cabinet Government in the United States.* Stamford: Overbrook Press, 1947.

———. *Constitutional Government in the United States.* New York: Columbia University Press, 1908.

———. *Congressional Government: A Study in American Politics.* 1885. Reprint. Introduction by Walter Lippman. New York: Meridian Books, 1956.

The Alternative of Dissent

JAVIER MUGUERZA

Translated by Philip Silver

THE TANNER LECTURES ON HUMAN VALUES

Delivered at

The Instituto de Derechos Humanos
of
The Universidad Complutense de Madrid

April 19 and 20, 1988

JAVIER MUGUERZA, a Spaniard, holds a doctorate in philosophy from the Universidad Complutense de Madrid. He has been Professor of Ethics and Sociology at the Universities of La Laguna (Tenerife), Barcelona, and Madrid, and Visiting Professor at the Universidad Nacional Autónoma de México, as well as Visiting Fellow at the National Humanities Center in North Carolina. At present he holds the Chair of Philosophy of Law and of Moral and Political Philosophy at the Universidad Nacional de Educación a Distancia and is a member of the Instituto de Filosofía of the Consejo Superior de Investigaciones Científicas. His works include *La concepción analítica de la filosofía* (Madrid, 1974), *La razón sin esperanza* (Madrid, 1980), and *Desde la perplejidad* (Madrid, in press).

Despite the fact that our century measures itself by events as ominous as Auschwitz, Gulag, or Hiroshima — and the list could of course be extended to include other similar ones of yesterday or even today — writers on the subject of our topic have occasionally yielded to the temptation to express a comprehensible optimism. Indeed, never before have human rights enjoyed as much legal recognition throughout the world as they do today. And this degree of recognition transforms those rights into something like incontrovertible fact — beyond or beneath their not infrequent violation where they are in effect and their pervasive lack of application where they are only nominally in force.

That the law is a fact — to use a famous and cherished example — does not excuse us from reflecting, and especially from reflecting philosophically, on that fact. As Kant taught, the mission of philosophy is indeed no other than to provide a rationale for these seemingly incontrovertible "facts." In an attack on what they term "the ideology of human rights," Alain de Benoist and Guillaume Faye — themselves ideologues of the so-called French "New Right" — once reproduced, with malicious delight, a well-known anecdote told — with no hint of malice, but with a certain sorrow — by Jacques Maritain years ago in his introduction to a collective volume, *The Rights of Man*, published by UNESCO: when, in a commission of that body, someone expressed surprise at the ease with which members of clearly opposing ideologies were able to agree on a list of rights, he was told that "they were in agreement as to the rights on the list, but on condition they not be asked why." However, this is a typical question that philosophers, ex officio, may not avoid asking, inasmuch as "providing a rationale" is simply an attempt to respond to this query about why. In all likelihood philosophy, which is far from a science, cannot pride itself on being beyond ideology, whether of the Right or the Left, but if it cannot be reduced to mere ideology, this is certainly due to its impenitent habit of demanding reasons.

And if a given philosopher, as in my case, almost claims — with appropriate modesty, but with conviction — to be a "rationalist," clearly these will have to be reasons to the second power, in other words, will have to be *reasonable reasons* and not just Pascalian "reasons of the heart." The subject of human rights is one in which the latter reasons may well be unavoidable. Thus, one might declare himself a fervent supporter of human rights and be irretrievably skeptical about providing a grounding for them, which to me seems not only perfectly respectable but undoubtedly preferable to its opposite: the position held by those who, considering rights grounded in theory, do not hesitate to infringe them in practice. Still, no matter how deep their respect for reasons of the heart, philosophical rationalists will never be satisfied with them. Whenever I speak in what follows of "the ethical founding of human rights," understand that I mean their *rational foundation* or, rather, the attempt to found them rationally, so that we will be concerned about this class of "reasonable reasons" — rather difficult to find, by the way, which hardly assures me of success.

But, to begin in earnest, what are we to understand henceforth by "human rights" ? For the purposes of this lecture I want to begin by subscribing to a definition that a philosopher of law, Professor Antonio E. Pérez Luño, has given us in an authoritative book on the subject.[1] In his view, human rights are "a group of faculties and institutions that, in each historical moment, embody those *demands* of human dignity, liberty and equality, that *ought to be* positively recognized in the legal statutes both nationally and internationally." [2] Here is a brief, concise definition that

[1] A. E. Pérez Luño, *Derechos humanos, estado de derecho y constitución* (Madrid, 1984).

[2] Ibid., 48.

admirably focuses on the heart of the matter and which is prefaced by the author with some twenty-odd pages dedicated to guaranteeing its plausibility.[3] Thus, although it amounts to a stipulation, his proposal is by no means a "Humpty-Dumpty definition," since it rests both on a lexicographical study of the linguistic limits of the defined term and on something even more important, that is, a conceptual circumscription of its context.

In addition, Pérez Luño is well aware of the merits of his definition, which he believes avoids some of the more qualified charges against the very attempt to define human rights.[4] In the first place his definition is not "tautological," as a definition would be that read: "the rights of man are those that belong to him by virtue of his being a man," since his definition not only specifies a series of human "requirements" but also mentions the historical character of this "specificity." Second, neither is it a "formalist" definition, for example, "the rights of man are those that belong or ought to belong to all men, and of which no man may be deprived," since Pérez Luño's definition, in referring to the active recognition of such rights in the legal statutes, leaves enough margin for both the normative aspects of the "process of positive support in laws," or legal recognition, and the techniques of protection and guarantees as to their actual implementation. Third and last, the definition means to avoid being "teleological," as would be the case with definitions that allude to preserving ultimate values, ones ordinarily susceptible to diverse and contested interpretations, of the kind: "the rights of man are those necessary for the perfecting of human beings, for social progress or the development of civilization, and so on." However, in my view it is by no means clear that Pérez Luño's definition manages to avoid this third charge, if that is what it is, with as much ease or as

[3] Ibid., chap. 1.

[4] On p. 25 the author draws on Norberto Bobbio's "L'illusion du fondement absolu," in the joint volume, *Les fondement des droits de l'homme* (Florence, 1966), 3–9; see also 49ff.

much success as the previous ones.[5] That is, I do not think that "dignity," "liberty," and "equality" are values any less susceptible to diverse interpretations, or any less contested, than "the perfecting of the human being," "social progress," or "the development of civilization," although, as we will see, I believe that from an ethical point of view they are rather more fundamental than the latter.

But my major disagreement with Pérez Luño's definition has to do with the general meaning he attributes to it. In his opinion, "the proposed definition is intended to unite the two main dimensions of the general notion of human rights, that is, the jusnaturalist requirement as to their grounding and the techniques of its positive support in law and protection that assure their enjoyment." [6] Of course, Pérez Luño has every right, natural or not, to extract jusnaturalist implications from his definition, but not all of us who accept his definition can be expected to accept the burden of those implications.

From his definition it follows — or, more exactly, it is understood — that the demands of human dignity, liberty, and equality alluded to are prior to the process of positive support in law and that the reason why they ought to be legally recognized provides the grounding for the rights in question. But is that all? Jusnaturalism, as we will see, is nowhere in view, or at least not unless one acknowledges beforehand — as a jusnaturalist would undoubtedly be inclined to do — that the fact that those demands are prior to the process of legal recognition makes them natural rights.

To me such a presupposition seems gratuitous. But before taking up this point, I want to deal with another, less important, one. That is, the presupposition that values such as dignity,

[5] In any case the supposed charge was not so much leveled at the "teleological" character of the definition — that is, at its goal of saving ultimate values — as at the vagueness and imprecision of the values in question.

[6] Pérez Luño, *Derechos humanos*, 51.

liberty, or equality are the exclusive patrimony of the jusnaturalist tradition.

To concentrate for the moment on the first of these, who would assert that the jusnaturalist tradition and the tradition of human rights are coextensive? Pérez Luño adduces the case of Samuel Pufendorf, whose system of human rights indeed rests on the idea of the *dignitas* of man.[7] And there is no doubt about Pufendorf's representing an important stage in the history of modern natural law. But, on the other hand, it is not as clear that we can discern the same jusnaturalist filiation in the Kantian notion of *Würde*, nor in Kant's philosophy of law.[8] And the case of Kant is of particular interest to us here.

No one would deny that there are abundant traces of jusnaturalist influence in Kant, just as it is impossible to deny that the general division of the *Rechtslehre*, or "system of the principles of law," that he espouses opposes natural law (*Naturrecht*), which is based on a priori principles, to positive, or statutory, law (*statutarisches Recht*), which depends on the will of the legislator.[9] But Kant's so-called "rational law" (*Vernunftrecht*) cannot simply be identified with traditional natural law, even of a rationalist lineage, not even if we find that it does not mind assuming — on the basis of quite different suppositions — some of the latter's functions, which it consequently inherits.[10] And, especially, I do not believe we can or should interpret in a jusnatu-

---

[7] Ibid. In this connection see Hans Welzel's classic *Die Naturrechtslehre Samuel Pufendorfs*, 2d ed. (Berlin, 1958).

[8] On this subject, see J. G. Murphy, *Kant: The Philosophy of Right* (London, 1970); S. Goyard-Fabre, *Kant et le problème du droit* (Paris, 1975); Z. Batscha, ed,. *Materialien zu Kants Rechtsphilosophie* (Frankfurt am Main, 1976); F. Kaulbach, *Studien zur späten Rechtsphilosophie Kants* (Würzburg, 1982); H.-G. Deggau, *Die Aporien der Rechtslehre Kants* (Stuttgart, 1983).

[9] I. Kant, *Metaphysik der Sitten. I. Metaphysische Anfangsgründe der Rechtslehre*, Werke, Akademie Ausgabe, vol. 6, p. 237. All references to Kant's works are to this edition.

[10] See below, in connection with Jürgen Habermas's interpretation of Kant's "rational law."

ralistic sense Kant's fundamental distinction between "morality" (*Moralität* and also *Sittlichkeit*), on the one hand, and "legality" (*Gesetzmässigkeit* or *Legalität*), on the other, a distinction to which we will presently return.[11]

In my view, Pérez Luño has too generous a notion of *jusnaturalism*, which leads him to swell unnecessarily the number of its adepts, even though he does indeed mention that the "open" definition of it that he holds helps him avoid the danger of making a "Procrustean bed" of his conception:[12] it is not such a bed — if this is understood in the sense intended by that legendary bandit, who, in order to fit his victims exactly to the bed, would shorten the protrusions of the taller ones or violently stretch the limbs of the shorter ones until he dislocated them; but, "generously understood," this Procrustean bed could contain a device that, as the occasion demanded, allowed the bed itself, and not the victims, to be made larger or smaller, so that whoever laid himself down there would run the risk of waking up a "jusnaturalist."

But I do not want my friendly discussion with Pérez Luño to seem an obsessive tirade. My aim is simply that my defense of ethics — the declared object of this lecture — not be in any way confused with the defense of a supposed *natural law*, a confusion I fear he is guilty of himself, since he writes that "only from the jusnaturalist point of view does it make sense to pose the problem of the grounding of human rights."[13] This confusion in fact is not infrequent in the panorama of contemporary philosophy, as the case of Ernst Bloch makes clear in an exemplary way, which forces me to concede that Pérez Luño is ultimately in very good company.

From the title of Bloch's *Naturrecht und menschliche Würde* to its last page, we are always impressed, even deeply so, by the

---

[11] Kant, *Metaphysik der Sitten*, 219.

[12] Pérez Luño, *Derechos humanos*, 136–37.

[13] Ibid.

undoubted ethical pathos of his thought,[14] even though Bloch never speaks there of "ethics," but always of "natural law," perhaps, it seems to me, because, in the Marxist tradition, it is easier to fly in the teeth of Marx's "prejudices" about human rights[15] than to overcome the embarrassment, disguised as *akribeia*, that kept him and his followers from acknowledging that at times what he was doing was *simply ethics*.

For my part I would say, in synthesis, that the "demands" of dignity, liberty, and equality included in Pérez Luño's definition of human rights — demands that, according to his definition, "ought to be" legally recognized — are "moral demands," and I would add that they should be awarded full status as human rights when they have passed the extra test of their legal recognition. In my case, I am not sure such a coarse and crude duality would be willingly accepted under the banner of the highly regarded "dual theory" of those rights.[16] Like all dualisms that are too abrupt, perhaps mine too gives the impression of suffering from an obvious schizophrenia, the same one — consisting of separating *morality* and *legality* — that Hegel once accused Kant of, following which he reduced ethics, now changed to "ethicity," to his philosophy of law (which, in any case, proves that Kant's schizophrenia is preferable to Hegel's paranoia, which was capable of swallowing up and "going beyond" in his philosophical system what Hegel was in the habit of referring to disdainfully as "mere

[14] E. Bloch, *Naturrecht und menschliche Würde*, Gesamtausgabe, vol. 6 (Frankfurt am Main, 1961).

[15] See in this regard Manuel Atienza, *Marx y los derechos humanos* (Madrid, 1983).

[16] The "dualistic conception" of human rights, which — as opposed to jusnaturalists and juspositivists — attempts to "integrate" their condition as "values" (prior to their recognition in any legal text) with their condition as valid "legal norms" (once legally recognized), has been maintained by Gregorio Peces-Barba in his *Derechos fundamentales* (Madrid, 1983), 24–27, 28ff.; in connection with our subject see also, by the same author, *Introducción a la filosofía del derecho* (Madrid, 1983), esp. 305–30; *Los valores superiores* (Madrid, 1984); and *Escritos sobre derechos fundamentales* (Madrid, 1988), esp. 215–26.

morality.")[17] Be that as it may, the *moral demands* in question would be "potential" human rights, whereas the human rights would in their turn be moral demands, "satisfied" from a legal point of view. And I would not give too much importance to purely verbal questions, since I am well aware that "human rights," especially with this name, are such a powerful weapon today that it would be foolish to reduce their effectiveness by giving them the less usual name of "moral demands."[18] If we must, therefore, be confronted by the Janus face of human rights—one of whose sides has an ethical profile and the other a legal profile — I would be content simply to request that, in the first case, we consider them "rights" in a merely metaphorical sense, just as, for that matter, jusnaturalism has always done in speaking of "natural rights."

What I would not so readily agree to is the ambiguous and confusing name of "moral rights" that they are so often given

[17] See on this point Amelia Valcárcel, *Hegel y la ética (Sobre la superación de la "mera moral")*, prologue by J. Muguerza (Barcelona, 1988).

[18] Another reason not to do this is the insistence with which the detractors of human rights — and not just their ideology — reject even the name, by invoking against them the well-known statement of such an illustrious reactionary as Joseph de Maistre: "There is no man in the world. In my lifetime I have seen Frenchmen, Italians, and Russians. I also know, thanks to Montesquieu, that one can be Persian: but as to man, I swear I have never met one in my life" (this text, which comes from his *Considérations sur la France* of 1791, is quoted by A. de Benoist and G. Faye in the dossier on *Les droits de l'homme* that appeared in *Eléments* 37 [1981]: 5–35. This "national-communitarian" point of view would allow for "the rights of [certain] men" (French, Italian, Russian, etc.) but not "the rights of man," which, nevertheless, need not be — in contrast to what de Maistre believed — an abstract "universal man," but rather Tom, Dick, or Harry, that is, a concrete "individual," whose concreteness always outweighs his membership in a specific community, whether national or not. For a criticism of what he correctly calls the "fallacy of the concrete man" of de Maistre and his outdated contemporary followers, see Leszek Kolakowski, "Warum brauchen wir Kant?" *Merkur* 9–10 (1981): 915–24. In his turn, and from a position not at all sympathetic to human rights understood as "subjective rights," Michel Villey has argued interestingly for the "nominalist" and individualistic origin of this latter notion in "La genèse du droit subjectif chez Guillaume de Occam," *Archives de Philosophie du Droit* 9 (1964): 97ff., and *La formation de la pensée juridique moderne* (Paris, 1968), chaps. 4 and 5, a thesis I would have no trouble subscribing to if only I were allowed to see virtue wherever the author sees vice.

today, which is something I want to deal with apart from the question of jusnaturalism. I prefer to do it this way because not all who use the name are in debt to, nor would accept the designation of, jusnaturalists.[19] And it seems to me at least questionable that a contemporary champion of "moral rights" like Ronald Dworkin, so often catalogued this way, should or could be included in the list.

I will not say, as Jeremy Bentham did of natural rights, that "moral rights" are a *nonsense upon stilts,*[20] but I will say that they are at least a contradiction.[21] Perhaps neither syntactic nor semantic, as when one speaks of "a square circle" or of "wooden iron," but rather pragmatic, like the one that would pertain if we were to speak, let us suppose, of "laws of traffic" without there being any actual highway code. Before such existed, it would make no sense to say that the small sedan traveling the road "has the right" to cross ahead of a big truck approaching from the left. Yet the truth is that according to certain current interpretations, moral rights are conceived of precisely as "prior to" any possible recognition of them in legal statutes. Is such an interpretation defensible? Whether it is or not, one must acknowledge that it has in its favor our use of such expressions as "I have a right to . . ." in ordinary language, expressions that we most often use without intending an appeal to any article of the legal statutes. And, despite old Bertrand Russell's warning about the ordinariness of being bound by analyses of ordinary language, perhaps it would

19 I am not certain, to quote a few examples of philosopher-compatriots, if Professor Eusebio Fernández would at all approve of such a cataloguing (see his *Teoría de la justicia y derechos humanos* [Madrid, 1984], esp. 104ff.), but I know that Professor Francisco Laporta (see his "Sobre el concepto de derechos humanos," in *Actas de las X Jornadas de Filosofía Jurídica y Social, Alicante, December 1987,* [in press]) would be vexed with me if I listed him as a jusnaturalist.

20 [The words "*nonsense upon stilts*" were in English in the original; J.M.'s italics.]

21 J. Bentham, *Anarchical Fallacies, Being an Examination of the Declaration of Rights Issued during the French Revolution,* in *Works,* ed. John Bowring (Edinburgh, 1838; repr. New York, 1962), 2:500.

not be beside the point to notice what we usually mean when we say, "I have a right to an explanation (a satisfaction, a redress, or anything else)." In many instances, "I have a right to something" is simply another way of saying that "I require (demand, ask for, etc.) that something," where the notion of right plays no part. But of course on occasion the first expression, "I have a right to something," would require a paraphrase like "I deserve that something" or "I am owed such and such a thing," where the paraphrase might cause difficulties if we took *ad pedem litterae* the so-called thesis of the "correlativity of rights and duties" held by Wesley Hohfeld among others.[22]

To put it in too sketchy terms, the thesis of correlativity can be summed up in the assertion that the idea of a "right-holder" (*sujeto de derecho*) and that of a "duty-bearer" (*sujeto de [el correspondiente] deber*) are coimplicating ideas. Now then, this sort of correlation seems to function more clearly in the case of institutional rights and duties — for example, with legal rights and duties — than in the case of noninstitutional ones, as would presumably be the case with moral rights and duties. If it is my legal right that Peter fulfill what is stipulated in a contract we have signed, Peter has a legal duty or obligation to fulfill it. And vice versa. But the relevancy of the "vice-versa" clause here becomes less clear when we move from the legal plane to the moral one. I am not sure that the preceding description would also serve to describe the reciprocal pacts Robinson Crusoe and Friday agreed to, so that Friday would be authorized to infer that he "has a right to such and such" from the declaration that "Robinson owes him such and such." At least I am not certain that this inference would be of much use to him in the absence of a judge on the island to oversee compliance with such pacts. But, in any case, it does seem clear that the phrase "X owes Y such and such"

[22] For a review and an up-to-date discussion of Hohfeld's thesis, see Carl Wellman, *A Theory of Rights: Persons under Laws, Institutions, and Morals* (Totowa, N.J., 1985).

does not always imply that "Y has the (moral) right to receive such and such from X." For example, I am absolutely convinced that we humans have "moral duties" regarding animals and would welcome their having "legal rights" that were recognized in a society that considers itself civilized. But I would not allow that from the fact that we humans have moral duties regarding animals it follows that the latter have moral rights. An animal may well be a right-holder in the legal sense when humans bestow this condition on it, but no animal will ever be a moral subject. Morality is the prerogative of men and, of course, women — that is, of human beings — and I do not believe the partisans of moral rights would be willing to consider animals holders of such rights, as they would have to be, however, if those partisans wished to pursue the questionable thesis of the correlativity of duties and rights to its final consequences. But one never knows: in a heated discussion I once heard an American friend, who was a member of the Animal Liberation Front, speak of "animals' human rights" (*derechos humanos de los animales*).

But, in concluding our excursus into ordinary language, I would only like to mention an expression that on the contrary seems to me extremely revealing of certain aspects of the moral phenomenology involved here, an expression that is furthermore an integral, and colloquial, turn of phrase. I refer, of course, to the expression "You've no right," which we so often use independently of any legal context: the expression "You've no right (for example, to treat someone in a manner we judge reprehensible)" is usually accompanied by a feeling of moral indignation which in our example might be a translation of the conviction that "it is denigrating to treat anyone that way" or that "such treatment violates his dignity." But I already warned a moment ago that we would do well to separate the treatment of human dignity from that of the supposed natural rights, and I feel the same about supposed moral rights, which counsels that we postpone that subject until the proper time comes.

Nevertheless, all we have said thus far regarding moral rights fails to do complete justice — I hasten to say — to the aforementioned position of Dworkin. For Dworkin speaks not only of *moral rights* but of *moral principles*, which is something quite distinct and of a much higher ethical caliber. In his work one notices a determined effort to bring law (and not only its philosophy, the philosophy of law) closer to ethics, an effort I can only fervently applaud.[23] And on each occasion one notices a criticism of positivism with which, minor differences aside, I confess I also fundamentally agree. In connection with his critique it has been observed, and not without reason, that the former targets a concept of legal positivism that is too narrow, as in the case of the so-called "positivism of the law" so magnificently summed up in K. Bergbohm's frightening sentence: "The most infamous law must be deemed applicable provided it was promulgated in a formally correct manner." But it is nevertheless true that Dworkin goes somewhat beyond that restricted concept of positivism, as his polemic with Professor Herbert Hart over the role of *key norm* of the so-called "rule of recognition" shows.[24] If I refer here to this often-mentioned question it is because I am convinced that its import is much greater than is usually thought. In his criticism of what he calls the "model of norms," Dworkin criticizes the positivists for their inability to distinguish between "a law" (*una ley*) and "the law" (*el derecho*), but the point of his reproach is to show the insufficiency of a conception of the law as a system of laws or norms the identity of whose parts would be due to the functioning of the aforesaid "key norm." Taken as such a key norm, Hart's *rule of recognition* would have the task of laying down which laws or norms would make up the law, just as Article 1 of our Civil Code determines what laws and norms

[23] R. Dworkin, *Taking Rights Seriously* (Cambridge, Mass., 1977); *A Matter of Principle* (Cambridge, Mass., 1985); *Law's Empire* (Cambridge, Mass., 1986).

[24] See H. L. A. Hart, *The Concept of Law* (Oxford, 1961), 89ff., and R. Dworkin, *Taking Rights Seriously*, chaps. 2 and 3.

belong to that current legal or normative system.[25] Now then, this sort of criterion of identification might well seem inane when faced with what Dworkin calls "difficult cases," where we come up against the problem of finding a norm that is applicable. In such cases of legal indeterminacy, it is Hart's opinion that the case would have to be left to the discretion of the judge, whereas for Dworkin this would amount to conceding him the undesirable power of "creating law," with the added difficulty that the judge would be empowered to legislate retroactively. In his opinion what the judge would have to do in such cases, and what he in fact does in such cases, is to go beyond the norms — that is, the *normative model* — and turn to principles (or, alternatively, to "political directives"), principles — this would be Dworkin's choice — that contain the requisites of justice, equity, or other moral requirements. In the example Dworkin himself so often uses,[26] a judge rejects the perfectly legal bequest of an inheritance because of the fact that the testator was murdered by the inheritor and by appealing to the principle — legally unstated, but valid in the judge's view — that "no one may (strictly speaking, ought to) benefit from their own crime." Personally I wonder, however, if Dworkin's recourse to principles does not allow the judges at least as much "discretionality" as Hart does in the absence of any exact norm. Not to mention the possibility that those judges take as principles the *political directives* relative to objects held to be socially beneficial (utilitarianism seems to me just as detestable a moral philosophy as it does to Dworkin, but one cannot discard the possibility that some utilitarian judge might discover a vein of moral principles in it) or that judges might simply disguise the strangest and most varied *ideological prejudices* as principles. For example, one could adduce in this regard an old bit of court reporting in a Madrid newspaper that — the differences between

[25] Dworkin, *Taking Rights Seriously*, chap. 3, § 6.

[26] I refer to the well-known case of *Riggs versus Palmer*, which Dworkin examines in *Taking Rights Seriously*, chap. 2, § 3, and elsewhere.

our judicial system and the Anglo-Saxon one aside — will illustrate what I'm saying. If I remember correctly, a dead husband
left a will — our examples run to wills — making his wife sole
heir on the condition that she never remarry (in truth the kindest
thing one can say about certain testators is that they are better
dead); but one day the wife, who for a number of years had
scrupulously adhered to this condition of the will, was discovered
to be pregnant (which, naturally, provoked a suit on the part of
the dead man's nearest relatives); the tribunal charged with deciding the case declared the will null and void, since it found that, if
the last will of the testator had been to guarantee his wife's fidelity
after his death, he would have disapproved a fortiori a situation
like the present one that added licentious conduct to infidelity
(since I cannot imagine that such an extraordinary decision could
be literally based on any legal text, no matter how peculiar its
content, I am inclined to attribute the tribunal's action to the
repository of their "moral principles").[27] But of course this unfortunate anecdote doesn't reduce the importance of Dworkin's
invocation of moral principles. For, as has been correctly pointed
out,[28] that invocation is not so much directed at Hart's normative
model and its rule of recognition as it is at the latter's condition
as key norm. And, in this sense, against any other key norms of
the same family, whether Hans Kelsen's *fundamental norm* or
John Austin's *sovereign's command*, that is, against the supposed
positivist self-sufficiency of the law, which can hardly contain its
own grounding.

For our purposes the preceding conclusion is important. For
a good positivist would never lose sleep over the question of an

[27] Although I cannot document this reference now, I seem to remember reading this article in the Madrid daily *ABC* back in the fifties, when I was just entering a now-distant adolescence, during the heyday of the Franco regime, which undoubtedly explains many details of the case.

[28] See Albert Calsamiglia, "Ensayo sobre Dworkin" (prologue to the Spanish
translation of *Taking Rights Seriously* [*Los derechos en serio*], Barcelona, 1984,
7–29), and "¿Por qué es importante Dworkin?" *Doxa* 2 (1985): 159–66.

extralegal grounding of the law, even in the case of human rights. Once incorporated into the legal statutes — for example, in the form of *fundamental rights* or anything similar — why inquire further into their "grounding" or foundation? But, as I said, human rights offered us a Janus face and were moral demands before being recognized as such rights. As moral demands they constituted *presumed rights* — something quite different from supposed rights, where the adjective would serve to disqualify rather than just to qualify — or, if one prefers, they might be considered *assumed rights*, that is, demands assumed "as if" they were rights. But how justify our assumption or presumption of these rights without inquiring into their grounding? Whatever the positivist may say, questions about this grounding are far from idle and we must continue to ask them.

But, despite my insistence on ethics, I intend that our treatment of grounding or foundation be as realistic as possible. And, when I speak of realism, I also mean this in the sense of *legal realism*, which, as we know, need not be a dirty realism — unlike the latest United States novels. At least, Judge Oliver Wendell Holmes's scandalous definition, according to which law is nothing but the set of "the predictions about what the judges will do in fact," a definition that amounted to the birth notice of American legal realism, has never seemed scandalous to me, nor has the circumscription of legal validity to the judges' conduct, which Alf Ross and the Scandinavian realists contributed to the theorizing about "law in force," ever seemed scandalous to me either.[29] To put it in the briefest terms, it is a question of recognizing, in contrast to any doctrinaire view of jurisprudence, that judges may sometimes decide — although they will not always, or necessarily, do so — not by virtue of reasons that allow them to adduce an appropriate legal rule for their decision, but just the reverse, that is, by first deciding and then choosing — as with a "rationaliza-

[29] See Dworkin, *Taking Rights Seriously*, chap. 1, and Liborio Hierro, *El realismo jurídico escandinavo* (Valencia, 1981).

tion" — the aforementioned rule. In the classical model of prediction attributed to Hempel and Popper, the prediction of a
phenomenon is merely an explanation of it before it happens.
This calls for one or more general laws, as well as the specification of a series of relevant conditions, and, based on these premises, the prediction of the phenomenon, or its explanation in
advance, would then be derived as the conclusion of a deductive
or inductive-probabilistic argument. For example, the law that
"all metals enlarge when heated," together with a specification
of the conditions of temperature being applied to a metal object
and of the coefficient of enlargement of the metal in question,
will enable us ultimately to predict that said object will become
enlarged at a given moment (or explain why it became enlarged
the instant following its having done so, since the explanation of
a phenomenon, in its turn, is nothing other than its prediction
post eventum, or its retrodiction). And the same thing that
happens with this phenomenon could occur, *mutatis mutandis*,
with another phenomenon like a judge's decision, despite the fact
that in this case we have an individual and, therefore, an inten-
tional action, which would tend to put in question the Hempel-
Popper model as well as the symmetry of "explanation-prediction"
that their model supports.[30] Be that as it may, the only thing that
legal realism urges us to do, and it is quite a worthy recommendation, is not to look exclusively for the premises of our explanations and/or predictions in legal texts but in the real social life of
the judiciary, which is the reality most likely to provide us with
the repertory of more or less general laws and more or less relevant conditions that we will need in order not to lose sight of the
latter. (I would not even like to imagine, for example, the "relevant conditions" that would have to be specified in order to explain
and/or predict the conduct of judges like the magistrates in the

---

[30] See on this subject my paper "La versatilidad de la explicación científica,"
in *A ciencia incierta* (in preparation).

"Bardellino case.")[31] From this point of view, it would be no exaggeration to affirm that, in its description of the law, legal realism is merely guilty of realism and that the reasons judges use to back up their decisions are often — or, at least, occasionally — no more than *rationalizations*.[32] At least, there is no point in denying that the above reasons might be, and occasionally will be, extrajuridical ones — political, for example, and also moral, as Dworkin would wish.

In other words, there could well be reasons of an ethical nature along with the others. But what has been said regarding the judges ought to be applied to the other legal figures — for example, to legislators, who in a political regime such as ours more or less represent the citizens. And, of course, we would have to include the citizens themselves in what has been said. For, whatever the degree of attention professionals of law give these reasons of an ethical nature, it is probably reasons of this sort that make most mortals believe that certain of their requirements — such as those touching on their dignity, liberty, and equality — will with good reason sustain the expectation that they be recognized in the legal statutes, nationally and internationally, as human rights.

Now we come to the problem of the *ethical foundation* of these rights. But before proceeding, we ought to ask ourselves if this is a problem that still deserves our attention, for there may be some who feel that perhaps this problem has been overcome. No less an authority than Norberto Bobbio maintained this thesis in his already classical text, "Presente e avvenire dei diritti dell'uomo" (1967), in which he assures us that the principal problem of our time regarding human rights is no longer their grounding but their protection, that is, they are a problem that has ceased to be philosophical and has become a juridical and, in a wider sense, a politi-

---

[31] [A recent case in the course of which two presiding Madrid magistrates — there is no jury system in Spain — were discovered to have accepted bribes in exchange for releasing a famous Italian Mafia soldier from jail.]

[32] Dworkin, *Taking Rights Seriously*.

cal one.[33] This led Bobbio solemnly to pronounce that "we do not consider the problem of grounding to be nonexistent but rather, in a certain sense, as solved, so that there is no further need to concern ourselves with its solution." To which he added: "Indeed, now we can say that the problem of founding human rights was solved by the Universal Declaration of Human Rights that the General Assembly of the United Nations approved on December 10, 1948." [34] Which is to say that this Declaration would be the best possible proof that a system of values is deemed to have a grounding and thus be recognized as, in short, "the proof of the general consensus as to its validity." In Bobbio's view there are three primary ways of founding such values. One way consists in deducing them from some invariable objective datum such as, for example, human nature (which is what jusnaturalism has always done and what in one way or another will have to continue to do in order to avoid debasing itself to the point where it admits to any interpretation we wish to make of it; but the truth is that human nature can be imagined in many different ways and an appeal to it can serve to justify extremely divergent and even contradictory value systems, so that the "right to dignity, liberty and equality" would be just as natural as the "right of the strongest"). A second way considers the values in question to be self-evident truths (but an appeal to evidence is no more promising than the appeal to human nature, since what at one moment in time is considered evident may not be at another moment: in the eighteenth century property was considered "sacred and inviolable," a view which is certainly not held today, whereas the "evidence" today that "torture is intolerable" was no impediment to its being considered a normal legal procedure in the past, nor does it keep

[33] N. Bobbio, "Presente e avvenire dei diritti dell'uomo," *La Comunità Internationale* 23 (1968): 3–18. I have quoted from the Spanish translation of this text, delivered the previous year at the Royaumont Colloquia, by A. Ruiz Miguel, "Presente y porvenir de los derechos humanos," *Anuario de Derechos Humanos* 1 (1982): 7–28.

[34] Bobbio, "Presente e avvenire," 10.

it from being practiced today extralegally). A third way is the one held by Bobbio when he tries to justify values by demonstrating that the latter are supported by consensus and that therefore a value will have a stronger grounding the more widely it is shared (in the argument from consensus,[35] the proof of the "objectivity" of values — held to be impossible or, at least, extremely uncertain — has been replaced by that of "intersubjectivity," a proof that only provides a "historical" and "nonabsolute" grounding, which nevertheless is the only one capable of being "factually" proven). So the declaration of 1948 — together with all the legislation it engendered, whether at the international or at the various national levels — constitutes the strongest historical proof ever of a *consensus omnium gentium*, that is, of a real universal consensus as to a given value system: that is, the system of human rights.

But perhaps things are not as clear as Bobbio thinks, and in truth his proclamation can be objected to on several fronts. At least, and within the same *factual point of view* in which he sites his argument, one could object that the "universal consensus" on human rights is not as universal as it seems, besides the fact that — as Bobbio himself would admit — the process of recognition, and even of creation, of these rights is "a process that is under way" and nothing and no one guarantees the perpetuation of the corresponding consensus, especially when some of these rights — such as the so-called "economic and social rights" — become a bone of contention between conceptions of human rights as different as the liberals' and socialists' conceptions. It has also been argued from a *juridical point of view* whether or not the declaration of 1948 is a "juridically consistent document," a condition which Kelsen would deny — however positively he might evaluate it from other perspectives — but which many lawyers concede, albeit to varying degrees and on the basis of quite different suppositions. But, naturally, the objections that interest us the most

---

[35] Ibid., 11ff.

are those made from a *philosophical point of view*. And so we will examine one such possible objection, which, in view of our interest, is of decisive importance.

During the decade of the sixties, when Bobbio wrote the text we have been discussing, his thought passed from a preferably "coactivist" conception of the law — the view of the legal statute as an apparatus whose functioning is ultimately guaranteed by the possible use of force — to a preferably "consensualist" view of the same.[36] And *consensualism*, in the history of ideas, is indissolubly linked to contractualism, that is, to the different versions — at least to the different classical versions — of the theory of the social contract. Bobbio and his disciples have dedicated subtle, penetrating historiographical studies to this theory, but their accounts often stress too much, in my view, the resemblance between the classical theories of the contract and contemporary or immediately prior theories of natural law.[37] In contrast, and for reasons we will soon see, I am especially concerned to emphasize the counterexample of Jean-Jacques Rousseau, the Rousseau of *On the Social Contract*. As I already remarked in connection with Kant, in Rousseau too there is unquestionably a clear trace of jusnaturalism—studied with authority and care by Robert Derathé— but the Rousseau theorist of the contract is in no way a jusnaturalist.[38] On the contrary, faithful in this to the remote origins of contractualism, Rousseau takes *conventionalism*, which is just the opposite of jusnaturalism, as his position. For, as everyone knows,

[36] See Alfonso Ruiz Miguel, *Filosofía y derecho en Norberto Bobbio* (Madrid, 1983), 297ff.

[37] See, for example, Norberto Bobbio and Michelangelo Bovero, *Società e stato nella filosofia politica moderna* (Milan, 1979); see also N. Bobbio and M. Bovero, *Origen y fundamentos del poder político*, selection and translation of texts by both authors by José Fernández Santillán (Mexico City, 1985).

[38] R. Derathé, *Jean-Jacques Rousseau et la science politique de son temps*, 2d ed. (Paris, 1970).

the tie between "conventionalism" and "contractualism" dates from many centuries ago.[39]

However, in our case we have no need to go back to the distinction of the Greek Sophists between "nature" (*physis*) and "convention" (*nomos*), a distinction whose applicability in the domain of politics Aristotle rejected when he defined man as "by nature a political animal." To Rousseau, without going any further back, it was quite obvious that the grounding of the social order represented by the contract was not to be sought in nature — "nature," he wrote, "produces no law" — but instead was the product of a convention.[40] Quite another matter is Rousseau's establishing at once a distinction between "legitimate" and "illegitimate" conventions — according to his thesis, no agreement could ever legitimize the voluntary submission of one man to another or of a whole people to a despot — but this involves the distinct question of *legitimacy*, to which we will return at the proper time.

Regarding our present interest, and if we interpret the United Nations declaration of 1948 in contractualist terms, the consensus of which Bobbio speaks is no more than what is called a "factual consensus" or merely contingent agreement, that is, what we called a "convention," for such a consensus — to which Bobbio entrusted the definitive de facto solution of the problem of grounding human rights, but which he himself offered as no more than a simple historical fact — might express no more than a strategic compromise of the interested parties instead of being the result of a *rational discussion* between them (remember Maritain's anecdote of which we spoke at the beginning: the delegates of the countries represented on the commission were "in agreement" as to the list

[39] See J. W. Gough, *The Social Contract: A Critical Study of Its Development*, 2d ed. (Oxford, 1957).

[40] J.-J. Rousseau, *Du contrat social*, Oeuvres complètes, Bibliothèque de la Pléiade, vol. 3 (Paris, 1964), 353ff.

of human rights to be approved, but on condition they not be asked Why? that is, For what "reason"?).

In which case, Bobbio's trust might well be betrayed, and he would risk the charge — a charge that contemporary ethics of discourse, or "communicative ethics," levels at any conventionalist position more or less inspired in the tradition of the social contract — that no factual collective agreement, not even a true *consensus omnium gentium*, can contain its own rational grounding, since the factuality of such agreements would never by itself be a guarantee of their rationality. As is well known, the cultivators of this communicative ethics tend to believe that a *factual consensus* of this sort can be considered "rational" only to the extent that the means of obtaining it approximate those that the members of an ideal assembly — presumably less subject to spurious considerations than the United Nations General Assembly — would have to follow to obtain, in uninhibited communication and by no other means than "discourse" or cooperative discussion, a similarly ideal and even *counterfactual consensus*, one whose rationality would be above suspicion. For — as is also well known — discourse or communicative ethics is extremely sensitive to the "theory of rationality," and with good reason, since it attempts to offer itself as a *theory of practical reason*, which is what ethics amounts to for many of us.

If we wish to put it this way, the "theory of consensus" that this sort of ethics of discourse or *communicative ethics* defends, tries in some sense to go "beyond the social contract," [41] as these extracts from the chef d'oeuvre of one of its representatives show:

> The free acceptance undertaken by human beings only constitutes a *necessary*, but not a *sufficient*, condition of the moral validity of norms. Immoral norms can also be accepted by men as obligatory, out of error or on the assumption that only

---

[41] I refer the reader to my paper "Más allá del contrato social (Venturas y desventuras de la ética comunicativa)," chap. 7 of *Desde la perplejidad* (Madrid, in press).

others (only the weakest!) will have to obey them: as, for example, the presumed duty to offer human sacrifice to the gods, or the legal norm that subordinates all social considerations to the free play of economic competition — or to the biological selection of the fittest. It is true that to be binding every *contract* presupposes the free acceptance of authentic, that is, moral, norms by both parties, but the moral validity of the presupposed norms cannot be grounded in the fact of their acceptance, that is, following the model of the setting up of a contract.[42]

To which question he returns later:

The sense of moral argument might be adequately expressed with a principle that is by no means new: that is, that all man's *necessities* that can be accommodated to the necessities of others through discussion ... must be the concern of the "ideal community of communication." With this I believe I have outlined the grounding principle of an *ethics of communication* which, at the same time, also constitutes the grounding ... of an ethics of the democratic formation of the will, achieved by means of agreement or "convention." The basic norm outlined here does not derive its obligatory character from its *factual acceptance* by those who arrive at an agreement based on the "contractual model," but rather it obliges those who have achieved communicative competency through the process of socialization to reach an understanding with the object of arriving at a solidary formation of the will on every affair that affects the *interests* of others.[43]

Regarding the two texts just quoted, both from a justly famous essay by Karl-Otto Apel, one can be as ironic as one likes about their aprioristic "community of communication" that sets up shop in the One-Way Castle of philosophical transcendentalism, to

[42] Karl-Otto Apel, *Tranformation der Philosophie*, 2 vols. (Frankfurt am Main, 1973), 2: chap. 7, "Das Apriori der Kommunikationsgemeinschaft und die Grundlagen der Ethik," 415–16.

[43] Apel, *Transformation*, 425–26.

which there are certainly as many access roads as there have been transcendental philosophers throughout history, but not one return road, because none of these philosophers has ever returned. Or it might be compared, as I once did, to the "communion of saints," beyond the reach of any mortals except those Tibetan monks to whom Kant attributed a certain familiarity with the *Versammlung aller Heiligen.*[44] Or, finally, one might allege the unlikelihood of discovering the grounding we seek for human rights in that sort of angelic community, where it is by no means clear that we are likely to find anything truly human. But Apel's allegation against conventionalism *must be taken seriously,* which really means "taking ethics seriously," inasmuch as it is no less deserving of seriousness than rights or the law. For, all irony aside, the moral of his texts is conclusive. If our conventions will serve equally to support just and unjust norms, they will also serve to ground human and inhuman rights, from which it follows that such conventions will not serve our purposes.[45] And, as for the accusation of idealism, it should not be forgotten that in those texts Apel also speaks of quite realistic and even material things, such as "interests" and "needs," even though he reminds us that both require linguistic expression in order to be shared in communication.

But this last is something that even so prominent a theoretician of needs as Agnes Heller makes no bones about recognizing, in dialog, furthermore, with an equally prominent theoretician of the ethics of discourse, or communicative ethics, Jürgen Habermas, when she writes that even though the Habermasian theory cannot speak to people with any more authority than its rivals about what their "interests and needs" are, at least "it can tell one that — whatever their interests and needs — people must argue com-

---

[44] Kant, *Zum ewigen Frieden*, Werke, 8:359–60n.

[45] For a more detailed evaluation of Apel's critique of conventionalism, see my contribution, "El aposteriori de la comunidad de comunicación y la ética sin fundamentos," to *Estudios sobre la filosofía de Karl-Otto Apel*, ed. Adela Cortina (in preparation).

municatively in favor of them," that is, "must relate them to values by means of rational arguments." [46]

Nor is the advent of Habermas and his *ethics of discourse* at all fortuitous at this point.[47] His position, as everyone knows, is close to Apel's, albeit with certain important differences of nuance (for example, a considerable reduction in degree of transcendentalism). And, like Dworkin, he is interested in bringing ethics closer to law (Habermas's ethics is clearly influenced by Kant, but it also contains certain Hegelian features that are worth keeping in mind). As to the first, Habermas holds that the criterion for grounding a norm can only be a consensus obtained through rational discourse, a consensus, then, that is a *rational consensus*, the obtaining of which depends on a series of hypothetical conditions — the well-known hypothesis of the "ideal speech situation" — such as that all those involved in the dialog enjoy a symmetrical distribution of the opportunities to intervene, and that the dialog proceed with no more coercion than that imposed by the quality of the arguments (conditions which obviously ought to be called "counterfactual," that is, contrary to fact, rather than hypothetical, for in reality they never arise — with the probable exception of the discussion sessions that will follow the reading of this lecture). As to the second — that is, the *liaison*, I would not want to say at this point whether *hereuse* or *dangereuse*, between ethics and law — perhaps it would be better to let Habermas himself speak. We are told that "the counterposition between the areas regulated respectively by morality and politics would be relativized, and the validity of all norms would then depend on the *communicative formation of the will of those potentially interested*," given that "(even if) this does not alter the need to

---

[46] A. Heller, "Habermas and Marxism," in *Habermas: Critical Debates*, ed. J. B. Thompson and D. Held (Cambridge, Mass., 1982), 21–41, 32.

[47] For the most complete exposition of his ethics of discourse, see J. Habermas, "Diskursethik: Notizen su einem Begründungsprogram," in *Moralbewusstsein und kommunikatives Handeln* (Frankfurt am Main, 1983), 53–124.

establish coactive norms, because no one can know — at least not
at present — to what degree it is possible to reduce aggression and
achieve a voluntary recognition of the 'principle of discourse,' . . .
only in this latter case, which for the moment is no more than a
construct, would morality become strictly universal, in which case
it would also cease to be 'mere morality' in the sense of the usual
distinction between law and morality." [48] (There is no need to
insist on the Hegelian overtones of these paragraphs, where —
rather than bringing ethics closer to law — it would be more
proper to speak of their mixture, with politics included, once the
aforementioned *mere morality* had been overcome.)

Habermas has reiterated his viewpoint in a recent essay —
"Wie ist Legitimität durch Legalität möglich?" (1987) — where,
in the course of attempting to answer the question "how can legitimacy be achieved through legality?" the general sense of his position on the problems of grounding that we have been discussing
is considerably clarified.[49]

Habermas takes them up in the process of defending the thesis
that the autonomization of law — effected in modern times with
the help of rational law (the Kantian *Vernunftrecht*), which
rendered possible the introduction of differences into the previously solid block of morality, law, and politics — cannot mean
a complete divorce between law and morality, on the one hand,
or politics, on the other, since law that has become positive cannot
do without its inner relationship with either of the two. Habermas,
then, considers Austin's or Kelsen's concept of juridical autonomy
(to which we referred a short while ago) indefensible, and he
then asks how the aforementioned autonomization of law was
effected. The turning point comes with modern rational law,
which — in connection with the theory of the social contract

---

[48] J. Habermas, *Legitimationsprobleme in Spätkapitalismus* (Frankfurt am Main,
1973), 87.

[49] Habermas, "Wie ist Legitimität durch Legalität möglich?" *Kritische Justiz* 20
(1987): 1–16.

(Kant's, but before him, Rousseau's) — reflected the articulation of a new posttraditional state of moral conscience, which in turn would eventually serve as a model of *procedural rationality* for law. As Habermas writes elsewhere:

> In modern times we have learned to distinguish with greater clarity between theoretical and practical arguments. With regard to questions of a practical nature, which concern the justification of norms and actions, Rousseau introduces *the formal principle of Reason*, which takes the role formerly played by material principles such as Nature or God. . . . Now, since ultimate reasons are no longer theoretically plausible, the *formal conditions of justification* end by taking on a legitimizing force of their own, that is, the procedures and the premises of the rational agreement acquire the status of principles. . . . [That is], the formal conditions for the possible reaching of a rational consensus replace the ultimate reasons in their capacity as *legitimizing force.*" [50]

Of course, there can be theories of contracts of very different stripe, and obviously Hobbes's is very different from Kant's. Whereas for Hobbes, for example, in the last analysis law becomes an instrument at the service of political domination, law for Kant — including positive law — retains its essentially moral character, which leads Habermas to assert that law (and the same could be said of politics) "is reduced by Kant to the condition of a deficient kind of morality [*Recht wird zu einem defizienten Modus der Moral herabgestuft*]." [51] According to Habermas, the reason for this is the tendency of Kantian rational law to occupy the place vacated by the old natural law. In Kantian terms, as interpreted by Habermas at least, the positivation of law would amount to the realization in the empirical or phenomenal political world (*res publica phaenomenon*) of rational juridical principles — which

---

[50] J. Habermas, *Zur Rekonstruktion des historischen Materialismus* (Frankfurt am Main, 1976), 250.

[51] Habermas, "Wie ist Legitimität," 7.

supposedly would correspond to a moral or noumenal political world *(res publica noumenon)* — principles derived from, and dependent upon, imperatives (moral imperatives) of reason (practical reason). But according to this metaphysical doctrine of the two worlds or "two kingdoms [*Zwei-Reiche-Lehre*]," both law and politics would in fact lose their positivity, thereby threatening, still according to Habermas, to destroy the very viability of the distinction we spoke of before between legality (of a positive law within an also positive conception of politics) and morality.

Be that as it may, the dynamics of modern social life seems to flow through quite different channels from those foreseen, or dreamed of, in Kantian ethics. And the dogmatics of private law, as well as of public law, would contradict Kant's juridical construct, according to which positive politics and positive law would have to be subordinate to the moral imperatives of rational law. Now, if on the one hand, the moral foundations of positive law could no longer be modeled on a Kantian subordination to rational law, on the other hand it is also clearly impossible to deal with, or avoid either, without first having found a substitute for rational law itself. Habermas quotes the dictum of the German jurist G. F. Puchta, who in the last century proclaimed that the creation of law could not be exclusively the work of political legislators, since in that case the state could not be founded on law, that is, not be a state of law, where "state of law" is offered precisely as a substitute for rational law.[52] But, in addition to the question of strict legality, the idea of a state of law poses the problem of "legitimacy," unless one wants to interpret in strictly positivistic terms a no less famous dictum, which another jurist, H. Heller, quoted during the Weimar Republic: "In a state of law the laws are the totality of the juridical norms promulgated by the Parlia-

[52] Ibid., 8ff.

ment." [53] Therefore, the definition of legality neither resolves the problem of legitimacy nor allows us to dismiss it. And, according to Habermas, the *plus* required by the demands of legitimacy would have to be supplied by the introduction "in the interior of positive law itself [*im inneren des positiven Rechts selbst*]," and not by subordination to something exterior, "of the moral point of view of an impartial formation of the will [*der moralische Gesichtpunkt einer unparteilichen Willensbildung*]," so that "the morality nested in law would have . . . the transcendent capacity of a self-regulating procedure charged with controlling its own rationality [*die ins positive Recht eingebaute Moralität hat . . . die transzendierende Kraft eines sich selbst regulierenden Verfahrens, das seine eigene Vernünftigkeit kontrolliert*]." [54]

Let us try to clear a path through Habermas's dense prose in order to see what he means. The rationality Habermas speaks of is nothing but the "procedural rationality" that was already presaged in the eighteenth century, when Kant, basing himself on Rousseau, liked to repeat that the ultimate proof of the legality of any judicial norm lay in asking oneself "if it could have arisen as a result of the joint will of a whole people." [55] Now then, what are we to understand, when this sort of criterion is proposed, by "the joint will of a whole people"? Obviously, for Kant, that will had much more to do with Rousseau's "general will" than with the plain and unadorned "will of all," which is the only will that plain and unadorned conventionalism takes into account.[56] And this would also appear to be the choice of the "rational will" to which Habermas refers — a will produced by "an impartial formation of the will," that is, of the collective will — a will that,

[53] Ibid., 9.

[54] Ibid.

[55] Ibid., 10; see Kant, *Rechtslehre*, part 2, and *Über den Gemeinspruch: Das mag in der Theorie richtig sein, taugt aber nicht für die Praxis*, Werke, 8:273–313.

[56] See Howard Williams, *Kant's Political Philosophy* (Oxford, 1983), 161ff.

like the general will, would not be content with a consensus that merely reflected the total of a series of individual interests but one that shed light on the general interest of the community, that is, the "generalizable interests" of its members, by means, as we saw, of a rational consensus. Naturally, the Habermasian version of consensualism — an heir of Rousseau's general will — faces no fewer problems than conventionalism, some of which we will mention presently. But, for the moment, let us deal with Habermas's insistence on procedural rationality.

According to Habermas, procedural rationality gains consideration "with the proof of its capacity for generalization of interests [*durch die Prüfung der Verallgemeinerungsfähigkeit von Interessen*]."[57] This would provide a critical standard for the analysis and evaluation of the political reality of a state of law, a state, in other words, "that derives its legitimacy from a rationality of the procedures for the promulgation of laws and the administration of justice designed to guarantee impartiality [*der seine Legitimität aus einer Unparteilichkeit verbürgenden Rationalität von Gesetzgebungs- und Rechtsprechungsverfahren zieht*]."[58] As a matter of fact, the procedural rationality that presides over Habermas's ethics of discourse is naturally no stranger to law, to positive law. We must look, therefore, to the "rationality of law" for an answer to the question of how legitimacy is achieved through legality. Now, Habermas does not agree with Max Weber's belief that the rationality inherent in the law as such provides — aside from all kinds of moral presuppositions and implications — the ground for the legitimizing force of legality: in Habermas's opinion, the legitimizing force would correspond rather to the procedures charged with institutionalizing the foundational demands of the current legality, as well as to the argumentative resources available to achieve those demands.[59] The

[57] Habermas, "Wie ist Legitimität," 11.
[58] Ibid.
[59] Ibid., 12.

"source of legitimation," therefore, should not be sought uni-
laterally in such places as political legislation or the administration
of justice. For example, the grounding of norms — no less than
their application — presupposes the idea of impartiality. And
this "idea of impartiality," which in turn is strictly dependent on
the idea of the "moral point of view," [60] constitutes, Habermas
recalls, the very root of practical reason, forming part of communicative ethics and of any other ethical theories (Habermas
mentions those of John Rawls and Lawrence Kohlberg) that consist of providing a *procedure* with which to meet practical problems from the moral point of view.[61] In Habermas's communicative ethics, it is already quite clear just what that procedure is:
"Whoever takes part in the praxis of argumentation," Habermas
concludes, "must assume pragmatically that, as a matter of principle, all of the potentially interested parties can and may participate freely and equally in a cooperative search for truth, where the
only coercion is in advancing a better argument [*Jeder Teilnehmer
an einer Argumentationspraxis muss nämlich pragmatisch voraus-
setzen, dass im Prinzip alle möglicherweise Betroffen als Freie
und Gleiche an einer kooperativen Wahrheitssuche teilnehmen
könnten, bei der einzig der Zwang des besseren Argumentes zum
Zuge kommen darf*]." [62]

Personally I would object, in such a characterization, to the
blatant cognitivism of the allusion to the "cooperative search for
truth." In practical discourse, as a matter of fact, "truths" are not

[60] [The words "moral point of view" were in English in the original.]

[61] Habermas, "Wie ist Legitimität," 12. According to José Luis L. Aranguren,
"Sobre la ética de Kant," in *Kant después de Kant (En el segundo centenario de la
Crítica de la Razón Práctica)*, ed. J. Muguerza and R. Rodriguez Aramayo (Madrid,
in press), "proceduralism" — that is, the reduction of practical reason to procedural
reasoning — is a "neokantian" characteristic of those trends in contemporary ethics,
and is the result, among other things, of an extreme assimilation of ethics by law
(this assimilation is, in fact, more neokantian than Kantian, since it is scarcely in
line with the spirit of Kant's distinction between legality and morality). For my
part, I have already pointed out that in Habermas's case the same assimilation also
includes a good bit of "neohegelianism."

[62] Habermas, "Wie ist Legitimität," 13.

sought (even "truths by consensus") and the best refutation of a cognitivist position such as this is the one developed by Paul Lorenzen, who encapsulates it in the precept "You ought to seek only the truth," where the "ought" removes us from the cognitivist perspective and places us in a normative and, finally, an ethical one.[63] But, in fact, there would be no problem — that is, no new problem — if, for the phrase "cooperative search for truth," we simply substituted "search for a consensus." With the characterization understood this way, we can also understand better why Habermas wants to consider "juridical proceduralism" as *continuous* with ethical proceduralism. "It is not a question," he tells us, "of confusing law and ethics [*Freilich dürfen die Grenzen zwischen Recht und Moral nicht vermischt werden*]." [64] As institutionalized procedures, the juridical ones may aspire to a "completeness" that would not be attainable for ethical procedures, whose rationality is always an "incomplete rationality" that depends on the perspectives of the interested parties. Not to mention the greater degree of "publicity" of juridical procedures, compared with the "privacy" of an internalized and autonomous morality; or the instrumental condition of law when used to achieve this or that political goal, which locates law "between ethics and politics." But, be that as it may, there is also, he warns us, an "ethics of political responsibility," and law and ethics "not only complement each other but one can even speak of their mutual coupling," such that "procedural law and proceduralized morality could control one another." [65] But what is the ultimate meaning of this "control one another"?

As he himself says, Habermas does not confuse ethics and law, but he does mix them when he speaks not only of their "complementarity" (*Ergänzung*) but also of their "mutual cou-

[63] P. Lorenzen, *Normative Logic and Ethics* (Mannheim, 1969), 74.

[64] Habermas, "Wie ist Legitimität," 13.

[65] Ibid., 14–15.

pling" (*Verschränkung*). And I am not at all certain if we can expect much from this mixture to which I previously referred. For Habermas ends up not so much with "the *moralization* of Law" or "the *juridicalization* of Ethics" as with the *politicization* of both elements.

In what is thus far the canonical version of his ethics of discourse,[66] Habermas has been able to encapsulate it as the proposal of a communicative transformation of the Kantian "principle of universalization," that is, one of the formulations of Kant's categorical imperative. Where the former prescribed, "Act only according to that maxim by which you can at the same time will that it should become a universal law," Habermas's version prescribes instead, "Rather than ascribing as valid for all others any maxim that I can will to be a universal law, I must submit my maxim to all others for the purpose of communicatively testing its claim to universality," where "communicatively" simply means "democratically." [67] In the essay we have been commenting on, Habermas closes with this affirmation: "No autonomous law without real democracy [*Kein autonomes Recht ohne verwirkliche Demokratie*]." [68] He might have said the same about ethics, for, in the end, we not only find law between ethics and politics, but also ethics between politics and law (for a graphic idea of their mutual relations, one has only to conceive of ethics, law, and politics as the three sides of a triangle). Habermas does not tell us what kind of "democracy" this would be, in keeping with his reservations elsewhere which led him to write, "it is a question of finding mechanisms that will serve to ground the supposition

66 Ibid., 14–15 n. 45.

67 Habermas, "Diskursethik," 77. As Habermas acknowledges, the reformulation of the principle of universalization, within the ethics of discourse, was inspired by a version of his own thought by Thomas McCarthy, *The Critical Theory of Jürgen Habermas* (Cambridge, Mass., 1978; 2d ed., London, 1981), 326.

68 Habermas, "Wie ist Legitimität," 16. See, in connection with this point, the paper by María Herrera, "Etica, derecho y democracia en J. Habermas," in the collective volume *Teorías de la democracia* (Mexico City, in press).

that the basic institutions of society and the fundamental political decisions would be willingly approved by all those affected by them if the latter were able to participate — freely and equally — in the processes of the communicative formation of the will, [but] democratization cannot mean an a priori preference for a specific type of organization." [69] But whether we are dealing with a participatory or a representative democracy, or with a combination of the two, the collective decisions that are made there will have to recognize in some way or other the prevalence of some version of the "rule of the majority," something that, with good reason, Professor Elías Díaz never tires of reminding us of in our country.[70]

Still, as Díaz is the first to recognize, the rule of the majority is far from guaranteeing the justice of the decisions it enables. In truth, nothing excludes the possibility that the decision of a given majority may be unjust, and the fact that decisions that are not majority ones may also be unjust — and, very likely, or certainly, even more unjust — does not provide us with any ethical solace, especially if what we hope to do is use Habermas's imperative (or the Habermasian version of the Kantian principle of universalization) to ground human rights. When it comes to putting it into practice, the sophisticated consensualism of Habermas, or of Apel, unfortunately does not seem much more useful than conventionalism, or, if one prefers, Bobbio's consensualism.

Take, for example, those human rights having to do with the requirements of liberty and equality of which I spoke at the beginning of this lecture. Habermas seemed to take them for granted when he affirmed that in argumentative praxis we would have to consider the possibility, even the necessity, that all those potentially interested participate (precisely as free and equal and in no other way) in the cooperative search for consensus. In which case,

[69] Habermas, *Zur Rekonstruktion*, 252.

[70] E. Díaz, *Da la maldad estatal y la soberania popular* (Madrid, 1984), 57ff.

freedom and equality would be something like transcendental, or quasi-transcendental, conditions of possibility for discourse itself. And, when we descended from this transcendental or quasi-transcendental plane to the miserable sublunary world of daily political realities, those conditions would not be sufficient to exclude the possibility that a majority decision might infringe on the freedom and/or equality of a number of people, such as those forming an oppressed and/or exploited minority (for our purposes it would be too much if it infringed on the freedom and/or equality of even one individual). Just as it could happen that this decision might infringe on the dignity of those people if, for instance, to their oppression and/or exploitation, humiliation and even the denial of their condition as human beings were added.

The preceding observations — I hasten to add in order to reassure Díaz — are by no means intended to disqualify democracy, which undoubtedly is made legitimate to an acceptable degree with Habermas's procedural rationality, in addition to a series of complementary elements (respect and protection of minorities, safeguards for the rights of the individual, guarantees as to the extension of the concept of democracy beyond the mechanical functioning of the rule of the majority, etc.), elements that would be important to Habermas and that are included in the notion of legitimacy that Díaz suggests we call "critical legitimacy." [71]

But the question that we are concerned to clarify here is whether this procedural rationality, with as many complementary elements as we wish to add, completely exhausts the domain of practical reason, which is to say the domain of ethics: the answer, I believe, would be in the negative, since thus far ("thus far," of course, simply means "until this moment in my lecture") practical

---

[71] See ibid., 21ff., 127–48, as well as his postscript, "La justificación de la democracia," *Sistema* 66 (1985): 3–23. For Habermas's view, see also "Die Schrecken der Autonomie," on the disqualification of democracy by Carl Schmitt and his present curious revival, in *Eine Art Schadensabwicklung* (Frankfurt am Main, 1987), 101–14.

reason still has not managed to provide us with the desired foundation of human rights that we seek.

In order to explore a different strategy, I want to turn to a
different formulation of Kant's categorical imperative, one whose
ethical importance — for our purposes undoubtedly superior to
that of the *principle of universalization* — has been pointed out
by several contemporary philosophers, by Ernst Tugendhat for
instance.[72] Although my approach to this formulation is not the
same as his, I too have had recourse more than once to the prescription "Act in such a way that you always treat humanity,
whether in your own person or in that of any other, never simply
as a means but always at the same time as an end." And on one
such occasion I called that imperative *the imperative of dissidence*,[73] with the understanding that — unlike the principle of
universalization, which was meant to promote subscription to
values such as dignity, liberty, and equality — what this imperative
would really have to do was to ground the possibility of saying
no to situations where indignity and a lack of liberty or equality
prevailed.

To put it succinctly, we ought to ask ourselves if — after so
much insistence on factual or counterfactual consensus with regard to human rights — it would not be more advantageous to
attempt a "grounding" on the basis of *dissensus*, that is, a "negative" foundation for human rights, which I will term "the alternative of dissent."

---

[72] See E. Tugendhat, *Probleme der Ethik* (Stuttgart, 1984). See Tugendhat's
"Retraktationen" (1983), included in this book (132–76) and written in reaction to
the criticism Ursula Wolf (*Das Problem des moralisches Sollens*, Berlin, 1984)
leveled at his earlier "Drei Vorlesungen über Probleme der Ethik" (1981), 57–131.
For other views of this question, see P. Haezrahi, "The Concept of Man as End-
in-Himself," in *Kant: A Collection of Critical Essays*, ed. R. P. Wolff (London,
1968), 291–313; T. E. Hill, "Humanity as an End in Itself," *Ethics* 91 (1980):
84–99; and, especially, Albrecht Wellmer, *Ethik und Dialog: Elemente des mora-
lischen Urteils bei Kant und in der Diskursethik* (Frankfurt am Main, 1986).

[73] For instance, in my paper "La obediencia al Derecho y el imperativo de la
disidencia (Una intrusión en un debate)," *Sistema* 70 (1986): 27–40.

In fact, the idea here of recourse to "dissensus" instead of consensus hardly seems wrongheaded if we notice that the historical phenomenology of the political struggle for the conquest of human rights, of whatever variety, has always had to do with the dissent of individuals or groups of individuals with respect to a prior consensus — usually written into the current legislation — that in one way or another denied them their intended condition of subjects of those rights. Although historical accounts of human rights often go back to the beginnings of time, if we located the start of this struggle in modern times, it would not be hard to find — behind each and every one of the documents that serves as a precedent for the Universal Declaration of Human Rights of 1948 (from the English Bill of Rights of 1689, or that of the Good People of Virginia of 1776, or the Déclaration des droits de l'homme et du citoyen of the French National Assembly of 1789, by way of our own Constitution of Cádiz of 1812, to the Mexican Constitution of 1917, or the Declaration of Rights of the Working People of the Soviet Union of 1919) — either the vindications that accompanied the rise of the bourgeoisie in the sixteenth, seventeenth, and eighteenth centuries, or the workers' movements in the nineteenth and twentieth centuries, just as the anticolonialist struggles of our own era are to be found behind this declaration of 1948. Nor would it be hard to identify the contemporary social movements directly or indirectly responsible for the International Pact on Civil and Political Rights, and the International Pact on Economic, Social, and Cultural Rights, both dating from 1966, which are an outgrowth of the UN declaration and together with it, in the context of the United Nations' efforts to coordinate legislation, make up what is known as the Human Rights Act.[74] Today, indeed, we will have to look to the so-called "new social movements" — pacifist, ecologist, feminist, and so on — for any future

[74] See *Derecho positivo de los Derechos Humanos*, ed. Gregorio Peces-Barba (Madrid, 1987), and *Historia de los Derechos Humanos*, ed. E. Fernández, G. Peces-Barba, A. E. Pérez Luño, and L. Prieto (in preparation).

advances in the struggle for those rights, which, as we hope and presume, will one day be added to the appropriate legislation, however indifferent to them the present legislation now is.

In this perspective, the social and political history of mankind — with its perpetual, one could almost say Sisyphean, construction and destruction of prior consensuses broken by dissent and later restored on different bases, only to be struck down by other dissents in an infinite succession — is rather like the description of the history of science that we owe to Thomas Kuhn, with its characteristic alternating periods of "normal science" under the hegemony of a given scientific paradigm, and its periods of "scientific revolution." As Michael Walzer remarked somewhat acidly, the application of Kuhn's schemata to the history of human mores "is more melodrama than realistic history." [75] But perhaps human history is somewhat melodramatic, if not something worse — as Shakespeare well knew — since it is normally, or revolutionarily (in the Kuhnian as well as the usual sense), written in blood. And if there is any doubt that the history of mores involves discovery and invention just as the history of science and technology does, the invention of human rights ought to serve to dispel this misapprehension, inasmuch as human rights constitute "one of the greatest inventions of our civilization," in exactly the same sense that scientific discoveries or technological inventions do, according to Carlos Santiago Nino. [76] But as to my remark that the historical phenomenology of the struggle for these rights has involved at least as much dissent as it has consensus — if not more — the truth is that I am unable to develop this line further. I am neither a historian nor a sociologist of conflict, nor do I have any other professional qualifications in this respect, and I do not wish to burden the thesis I will be defending with the inevitable accusa-

[75] M. Walzer, *Interpretation and Social Criticism* (Cambridge, Mass., 1987), 26.

[76] C. S. Nino, "Introducción," *Etica y derechos humanos* (Buenos Aires, 1984), 13–17.

tion that I am guilty of some version of the "genetic fallacy," of a historicist or sociologistic variety, because I attempted to derive philosophical conclusions from the historical development of events or from this or that circumstance of social reality.

On the other hand, one would indeed have to keep in mind that, when viewed in a strictly philosophical perspective, the imperative I called one of dissidence — from which Kant drew his idea of "a kingdom of ends" (*ein Reich der Zwecke*), tending to be promoted by the establishing of "perpetual peace" on the face of the earth—demands to be connected not only with Kantian ethics but also with Kant's much less sublime political thought and, especially, with his disturbing idea of mankind's "unsociable sociability" (*ungesellige Geselligkeit*), which barely disguises a considerably conflictual vision of history and society.[77]

Nevertheless, in the remainder of this lecture I will concentrate on the ethical aspects of this question and pass over its political-philosophical ones with the sole observation that the imperative of dissidence might allow us to ponder the importance, together with the *critical legitimacy* of which we spoke before, of the *critique of legitimacy*, that is, of any legitimacy that tries to ignore the condition of ends in themselves which that imperative assigns to human beings.[78]

Now, moving on to the final point, this second imperative of the *Foundation of the Metaphysics of Morals* rested, according to Kant, on the conviction, which he solemnly affirmed in this work, that "man exists as an end in himself" and, as he added in the *Critique of Practical Reason*, that "he can never be used by anyone (not even God) only as a means, without at the same time being

[77] Kant, *Grundlegung der Metaphysik der Sitten*, Werke, 4:433ff.; *Zum ewigen Frieden*; *Idee zu einer allgemeinen Geschichte in weltebürgerliche Absicht*, Werke, 8:20ff. On this point see my paper "Habermas en el *reino de los fines*: Variaciones sobre un tema kantiano," in *Esplendor y miseria de la ética kantiana*, ed. Esperanza Guisán (Barcelona, 1988), 97–139.

[78] Here see my paper "¿Legitimidad crítica o crítica de la legitimidad?" in *Elogio del disenso* (in preparation).

an end." [79] As I suggested before, our imperative has in some sense a *negative character*, since — behind its apparent grammatical affirmation — it does not actually tell us "just what" we ought to do but instead what we "ought not to do," that is, not treat ourselves, or anyone, solely as an instrument. Kant is definite on this point when he affirms that the end that man is, is not one of those specific ends that we can decide to achieve with our actions and that are generally means to achieve other ends, as, for example, well-being or happiness. Man is *not* an end to be effected. As far as man as an end is concerned, Kant warns, "end is not to be thought of here as an end to be effected, but as an independent end and therefore in a purely negative way, that is, as something that should never be acted against." [80] "Ends to be effected," as specific ends, are, according to Kant, "only relative ends." And for this reason they cannot give rise to "practical laws" or moral laws, but at most serve as a basis for "hypothetical imperatives," such as those dictated by prudent consideration when we say, "if we want to remain healthy, we shall have to follow this or that medical advice." But, according to him, the only specifically moral end or "independent end" we have — that is, human being invested with "absolute value" — requires no less than a "categorical imperative" such as ours.[81] In this sense, and while the relative ends amount to no more than "subjective ends" such as any of us might attempt to realize, men as ends, that is, "persons," Kant calls "objective ends," as in a famous passage from the *Foundation of the Metaphysics of Morals* that I cannot help but quote:

> Those beings whose existence does not depend on our will, but on nature, have, in the case of irrational beings, a merely relative value, as ends, and for that reason are called *things*;

[79] Kant, *Grundlegung*, 428; Kant, *Kritik der praktischen Vernunft*, Werke, 5:132.

[80] Kant, *Grundlegung*, 437.

[81] Ibid., 439ff.

by contrast, rational beings are called *persons* because their
nature already distinguishes them as ends in themselves, that
is, as something that cannot be used merely as a means and
which, thereby, checks any caprice (and is an object of respect). The latter are not, therefore, mere subjective ends,
whose existence, as an effect of our action, has a value *for us*,
but are *objective ends*, that is, things whose existence is in
itself an end." [82]

This is why, Kant adds in another equally famous passage from
the same work, man has "dignity" instead of a "price": "What
constitutes the condition that makes something an end in itself,
has not merely a relative value or *price*, but instead an intrinsic
value, that is, *dignity*." [83] These are indeed moving words, but
why should everyone accept Kant's proclaiming that man exists as
an end in himself?

That this is not self-evident is proven, to give a single counterexample, by the difficulty of arguing in favor of Kant's assertion—
or even understanding it — that those would have who hold that
rationality can only be *instrumental reason*, that is, a reason
capable of concerning itself only with making the "means" adequate to the "ends" pursued by human action, and incapable of
concerning itself with "ultimate ends" that do not serve as means
for achieving other ends. This, of course, renders such reason incapable of assuring *that man be an end in himself*, a point that
must never have bothered Heinrich Himmler, inasmuch as in his
bulletins to the SS he emphatically insisted — according to Hannah
Arendt — on "the futility of posing questions about ends in themselves." [84] Theoreticians of instrumental rationality, on the other
hand, would consequently deny that one can speak of a *practical*

[82] Ibid., 428.

[83] Ibid., 434–35.

[84] Quoted by H. Arendt in *The Origins of Totalitarianism* (New York, 1968).
I have quoted from the Spanish translation by G. Solana (*Los orígenes del totali-
tarismo*), 3 vols., Madrid, 1982, 3:440, n. 33.

reason, but — if we refuse to accept, as we are free to do, that the "rationality" of human "praxis" can be reduced to "instrumental rationality" — we would at least be authorized to examine the possibility of arguing in favor of the Kantian assertion that man is an end in himself.

In my opinion, the author who has most convincingly advanced the possibility of this sort of argument is Tugendhat, when he considers it an "empirical fact" — the recognition of which is aided by the study of the process of socialization — that regarding our lives and those of others we enjoy relations of mutual esteem (and its opposite), which make us feel that each of us is "one among many" and subject in this way to a common morality (unless, that is, we suffer a *lack of moral sense,*[85] a state that Tugendhat is inclined to consider "pathological").[86] Upon such a fact one could go on to build a "morality of mutual respect," a morality Tugendhat feels, in my opinion correctly, to be the "basic nucleus" of all other morality. This does not mean that every morality must needs be restricted to this nucleus, since even Kant's own ethics — especially in connection with his idea of the "supreme good" — could be derived from sources other than "respect."[87] But it certainly would be significant if the *morality of mutual respect* — according to which the members of a moral community would treat one another as ends — were discovered as a matter of fact at the base of every morality, which would render it truly universal.[88] And, of course, Tugendhat's position represents an advance over all those — this writer included — who have ever felt like conceding that the Kantian affirmation that man is an end in himself is no more than a "humanitarian

[85] [The words *"lack of moral sense"* were in English in the original; J.M.'s italics.]

[86] Tugendhat, *Probleme der Ethik*, 150ff., esp. 154–55, 156ff.

[87] See José Gómez Caffarena, "Respeto y Utopía: ¿Dos fuentes de la moral kantiana?" *Pensamiento* 34 (1978): 259–76.

[88] Tugendhat, *Probleme der Ethik*, 163–64.

superstition," albeit a fundamental one if we are to go on speaking of ethics.[89]

Still, has Tugendhat really managed to convince us? However convincing his thesis, and it does have considerable force, he himself would say it was doubtful that it could convince anyone who lacked moral sensibility, since with such a person, he confesses, "discussion would be impossible." [90] But if, as indeed is the case, it is a question of discussing or arguing, this is precisely the case where discussion ought to be most relevant.

In my view, Tugendhat's reasoning unfolds in such a way that the imperative of dissidence would have to presuppose the principle of universalization, since this lies at the root of his conception of the morality of mutual respect, valid at the same time for *one* and *all*. But perhaps this presupposition is not indispensable, since the imperative of dissidence could in principle hold *only* for one person, that is, *for the dissenter* who upheld the morality of mutual respect, understood as a resolution never to tolerate being treated, nor consequently ever treat anyone, merely as a means, that is, as a mere instrument (where the resolve "never to tolerate being treated merely as a means" would in some way claim a prius over the consequent resolve "not ever to treat anyone merely as a means," that is, it would be prior to the reciprocity and not only the principle of universalization). Naturally, from what I have said it is clear that *ethical individualism* is not the same as an impossible ethical solipsism and is obligated to entertain the question of what happens to the other individuals.

But before returning to this point, and to clarify what I mean to understand by "individual," I will indulge in a brief detour through John Rawls's "Justice as Fairness: Political Not Meta-

---

[89] Muguerza, "Habermas en el *reino, de los fines*," 126–28.

[90] Tugendhat, *Probleme der Ethik*, 155: "Wenn *das Individuum*, . . . die Moral, und das heisst die moralische Sanktion überhaupt, in dem Sinn in Zweifel stellt, dass es für diese Sanktion kein Sensorium hat, *lässt sich nicht argumentieren*" (italics mine).

physical" (1985), where — in explaining the ultimate sense of his "theory of justice" — Rawls specifies, in passing, the ultimate, or near ultimate, sense of his own individualism.[91] With a great deal more clarity than in the essay by Habermas that I quoted from earlier, Rawls begins by pointing out that his procedural construction refers only to our present democratic societies and in this light we are to interpret the condition of the contractual partners (that is, "free and equal subjects") in his mental experiment concerning the *original position*. (With or without the "veil of ignorance," they are the citizens whom we daily meet and who take part in our day-to-day political life, in addition, of course, to personifying the "liberal political doctrine.")[92] And this is why Rawls's conception of the individual or the person needs no more than the *overlapping consensus*[93] which, in a society that is pluralistic as to religious beliefs and ideology in general, allows the citizens to agree on certain "basic principles of justice." Moreover he is saved from having to contemplate — as Rawls himself explicitly admits — any "stronger" conceptions of the "subject," such as the Kantian one.[94]

As Rawls himself acknowledges, "when [in his theory of justice] we simulate being in the original position, our reasoning no more commits us to a metaphysical doctrine about the nature of the self than our playing a game like *Monopoly* commits us to think that we are landlords engaged in a desperate rivalry, winner take all."[95]

We may be, then, the same in real life as in the original Rawlsian position, just as Saul of Tarsus remained in some sense

---

[91] J. Rawls, "Justice as Fairness: Political Not Metaphysical," *Philosophy and Public Affairs* 14 (1985): 223–51.

[92] Rawls, "Justice as Fairness," 231ff.

[93] [The words *"overlapping consensus"* were in English in the original; J.M.'s italics.]

[94] Ibid., 245ff.

[95] Ibid., 239.

"the same" when he became the apostle Paul on the road to Damascus. But it is more likely that in real life one feels less equal and less free than in Rawls's mental experiment. And, be that as it may, it still seems reasonable to say that, after all, a little daily "metaphysics" keeps the doctor away.

Of course, I have no intention here of reviving the Kantian doctrine of the *two kingdoms,* the empirical or phenomenal and the moral or noumenal ones. But one could still maintain that the "moral subject" and the "empirical subject" are not completely coextensive. Of course, with this we are not saying that the moral subject and the empirical subject are actually distinct, but rather that the first one is the integral subject, but a subject that is far from being reducible to just its empirical manifestations. For example, even the most hardened criminal could never be reduced to his observable conduct, since the latter does not allow us to scrutinize his most secret motivations and intentions, and this fact is a powerful reason never to cease treating him as a moral subject, which is like saying, as "an end in himself." Another example: as empirical subjects we humans are different as to talent, strength, beauty, and so on, but none of that keeps us from considering ourselves "equals" as moral subjects. Just as, to give a final example, the fact that we, as empirical subjects, may have to suffer a whole set of natural or sociohistorical conditions does not allow us to say that we are thus kept from being "free," unless at the same time we renounce our status as moral subjects. Our self-consciousness and our self-determination as an indissoluble unit are derived from that moral subjectivity which seems to be the seat of "human dignity," that is, what makes us "subjects" and not "objects." [96]

[96] The thesis of the indissolubility of "self-consciousness" and "self-determination" has been brilliantly defended by Tugendhat in his study *Selbstbewusstsein und Selbstbestimmung* (Frankfurt am Main, 1979). As Tugendhat points out, Andreas Wildt — in *Autonomie und Anerkennung* (Stuttgart, 1982) — was the first to give his considerations an explicitly moral-theoretical meaning, an interpretation Ursula Wolf also stresses (*Das Probleme das moralisches Sollens*), and in his turn, he has developed this point in his *Probleme der Ethik,* 137ff., discussing the thesis of

Perhaps today it is difficult to accept the idea that the *moral subject* and the *empirical subject* do not entirely coincide, but the impossibility of reducing the subject to its manifest properties was at least part of what the Greeks meant when they termed the subject *hypokeimenon*.[97] The moral subject exemplifies par excellence the subject understood in this way, and this is also the reason for the distance separating the moral subject from the so-called "subject of rights" (*sujeto de derechos*), which is, among others, a variety of the empirical subject. For the rest, not all subjects of rights are moral subjects, since a moral subject is always an individual, while the subjects of rights might well be "impersonal subjects," such as collective bodies or institutions, from a business all the way to the state itself. And even when, by analogy with moral subjects, we allow one of these impersonal subjects such as a social class or a nation the capacity for "self-consciousness" and for "self-determination," we must not forget that in any case both depend on the self-consciousness and self-determination of the corresponding individuals. Now then, moral subjects can, and in fact do, aspire to recognition as subjects of rights. And of those aspirations one of the most fundamental is the aspiration to recognition as "subjects of human rights." In a certain sense, this would be the first human right and even the quintessence of any other human right; in other words, *the right to be a subject of rights*.

But to the question of who or what would concede them this right, prior to any possible recognition of rights, I would answer that nothing and no one has to concede it to a moral subject in full command of his faculties but that it must be the subject him-

---

"morality" as a necessary condition for the "(practical) identity of the self." For such an interpretation of Kant's idea of man as "an end in himself," see my "Habermas en el *reino, de los fines*," 123ff.

[97] In a somewhat similar vein, Tugendhat speaks of a person's "being oneself" (*Selbstsein*), which he identifies with one's "existence" (*Existenz*), as a "quasi-property" (*Quasi-Eigenschaft*), which according to him has to do — rather than with a substantial property that is different from the accidental ones — with the Kantian notion of "end in itself."

self who appropriates it by affirming his condition as human being. "I am a man," said the signs carried by the followers of Martin Luther King. And how could one deny the human condition to someone who asserts that he has it, even if for the present it is not recognized in law.

The denial of this condition, that is, the reduction of a *subject* to an *object*, was what Marx, the critic of the ideology of human rights, called "alienation," and the struggle for human rights — be it said in his honor — is, ironically, nothing but the struggle against the multiple forms of *alienation* that man has known and suffered.

To this end, the subject must begin by being consciously a subject, that is, by unalienating itself. Or, in the words of the later Foucault, by freeing itself of the "subjection" that keeps one from being a subject or imposes on one an unwanted subjectivity.[98] No subject can aspire to be recognized as a subject of rights unless he or she is first of all a subject plain and simple — which means, among other things, being a moral subject. For this reason Rousseau correctly saw that the prior theory of the social contract was contradictory, in allowing for the possibility of a *pactum subjectionis*, since no subject could rightfully renounce being a subject through any kind of legal agreement.[99] But, in addition, there are many other "states" of subjection, very different from those characterized by Jellinek with that technical expression.[100] And in the grip of all of them, subjects, just as they find occasions to struggle against alienation, will also find occasions to exercise dissent.

[98] Michel Foucault, "Why Study Power: The Question of the Subject," in his afterword, "The Subject and Power," to Hubert L. Dreyfus and Paul Rabinow, *Michel Foucault: Beyond Structuralism and Hermeneutics* (Chicago, 1982), 208–26.

[99] Rousseau, *Du contrat social*, 359, 432–33.

[100] Georg Jellinek, *System der subjektiven öffentlichen Rechte*, 2d ed. (1919; repr., Aalen, 1964); for his four-part classification of the *status* of Public Law — *status subiectionis* or *pasivus*, *status libertatis* or *negativus*, *status civitatis* or *positivus*, *status activae civitatis* or *activus* — see 81ff.

And what is even more important, they will discover occasions
to exercise this dissent, not only by and for themselves, but by and
for other moral subjects, inasmuch as the imperative of dissidence — which did not need to presuppose the principle of universalization — is capable, in contrast, of incorporating it into
itself. Sartre's version of this last principle read, "when I choose,
I choose for all mankind," since individual acts already carry
within them a potential universality (*l'act individuel engage toute
l'humanité*).[101] But equally when I dissent I can dissent for all
mankind, even for *those who cannot dissent*, either because they
are biologically or psychologically unable to do so (as with children or mental patients, for example), or because they are unable
to do so for sociopolitical reasons (that is, because they suffer a
state of subjection that at the moment cannot be removed).[102]
And, of course, when I dissent I can, by the same token, *dissent
with others* (but without such dissension causing us to lose sight
of the fact that, although often exercised by "*groups* of individuals," it is still exercised by "groups of *individuals*").[103] The
dissenter is always an individual subject and — no matter how
much solidarity there is in his decision to dissent — his dissidence
is ultimately solitary, that is to say, the result of a decision taken
in the solitude of an individual conscience.

If we now correlate the categories of moral and empirical subjects with those of ends and means, considered before, we could

---

[101] Jean-Paul Sartre, *L'existencialisme est un humanisme* (Paris, 1946), 17ff.

[102] Despite the "negativeness" of dissent, we must not forget that it too may be
threatened by the shadow of "paternalism" and no one ought "to be forced to
dissent" anymore than they should be forced to consent (for an examination of
paternalism, see *Paternalism*, ed. Rolf Sartorius (Minneapolis, 1983) and Ernesto
Garzón Valdés, "¿Es éticamente justificable el paternalismo?" in *Actas del II
Encuentro Hispano-Mexicano de Filosofía (Filosofía Moral y Política)*, ed. J. A.
Gimbernat and J. M. González García (Madrid, in press).

[103] In any case, ethical individualism, not to be confused with the so-called
"methodological individualism," vindicates only the *autonomy* of the moral subject
and not its *autarchy* (for the difference, see Domingo Blanco, "Autonomía y
autarquía," in *Kant después de Kant*, and also my paper "¿Qué es el individualismo
ético?" in *Elogio del disenso*).

say that — unlike a means, which in a certain sense is of measurable magnitude (for example, in terms of "instrumental efficiency") — an end in itself, that is, a moral subject, admits no such "comparative measurability." Like Aristotle's substance — with which, nevertheless, it must not be confused, since for the moral subject perpetually *in fieri* one would have to say that "the subject is not substance" — *subjectivity does not admit of degrees* and one could perfectly well say that all subjects have the same import as to their moral demands of dignity, liberty, and equality and, in general, as to their aspirations to be subjects of rights. In this way, any human right could be accessible to any subject, with the proviso that in being accessible to one subject it would be no less so for all the others. For, as far as those rights are concerned, there is a sort of *principle of U-tubes* that, so to say, levels the legal *status* of the subjects — at least potentially. The popular saying "No one is any more a person than anyone else" has sometimes been presented as the fruit of an objectionable attitude of resentment that rejects all excellence, but the meaning of that saying could perhaps be made clearer by saying, "No one is any less a person than anyone else," if human beings are taken as ends in themselves.

By way of concluding, it might be well to recall that for Bentham speculation about the foundation of human rights was nothing but a string of *anarchical fallacies*.[104] As far as my speculations are concerned, I would like to think that they cannot be refuted as "fallacious," but I realize they are somewhat "anarchic," at least in the etymological sense of this second adjective. For, in truth, to entrust the grounding of those rights to the individual is in a way to bet on behalf of *an-archy*, at least to the degree that

---

[104] In Bentham's favor, it must be said that he was more careful in his disqualification of such speculations as "fallacies" than, in our own day, was Alasdair MacIntyre, *After Virtue* (Notre Dame, 1984), when he maintains that human rights "do not exist and to believe in them is like believing in witches and unicorns," a statement that will disturb only those who insist on defending these rights from a position akin to ethical cognitivism.

ethical individualism lies at the opposite pole from any ethical *fundamentalism*.[105]

In consequence, I do not believe any jusnaturalist will be prepared to assume a position such as this, which I would like to see go by the name of "ethical individualism." But, just in case anyone should try to lay it on that sort of Procrustean bed, I will simply offer one argument or, better still, counterargument. I have been asked on occasion if, for example, what I call the "imperative of dissidence" would not, in the end, be similar to the traditional *right of resistance*.[106] My answer is a categorical no. As has been pointed out more than once, and in a magisterial way by Professor Felipe González Vicén,[107] the so-called "right of resistance" is a fairy tale created by jusnaturalism. To be precise, it was invented by the latter as the sole recourse, the sole natural right, capable of opposing the natural right to oppress that jusnaturalism itself awarded to those in power. As such, González Vicén has quite correctly termed it "a juridical monster" and has called attention to Kant's perspicacity in rejecting it as though it were a *contradictio in adiecto*.[108] But one should add that for

---

[105] On the late Foucaultian "subject," Reiner Schürmann, "Se constituer soi-même comme sujet anarchique," *Etudes philosophiques*, October–December 1986, 451–71, speaks of an "an-archic" subject in a sense of "anarchy" similar to the one we have used, since the former would have to be the builder of the different "forms of subjectivity" (or "subject situations") that in each case constitute it.

[106] See Eusebio Fernández, *La obediencia al Derecho* (Madrid: Ed. Civitas, 1987), 109–15, as well as my paper "Sobre el exceso de obediencia y otros excesos," in *Actas de las X Jornadas de Filosofía Jurídica y Social*.

[107] See F. González Vicén, "Kant y el derecho de resistencia," in *Kant después de Kant*, where his approach to the problem of the right of resistance — with which he also dealt in chapter 5 of his early *Teoría de la revolución* (Valladolid, 1932) — echoes the views from his monograph *La filosofía del estado en Kant* (La Laguna, 1952), included as part of his *De Kant a Marx* (Valencia, 1984). In my opinion, González Vicén's interpretation competes to its advantage with other interpretations of Kant's attitude to this supposed right. See, to give only three examples of different approaches, Robert Spaemann, "Kants Kritik des Widerstandsrechts," and Dieter Heinrich, "Kant über die Revolution," both in Batscha, *Materialien zu Kants Rechtsphilosophie*, 347–58, 359–65, as well as Hans Reiss, "Kant and the Right of Rebellion," *Journal of the History of Ideas* 17 (1956).

[108] González Vicén, *La filosofía del estado en Kant*, 92ff.

Kant the rejection of the right to resistance was perfectly compatible with the positive, even enthusiastic, value he placed on the political revolutions of his day, from the American Revolution to the French Revolution or the Irish Rebellion. From my point of view, which I would not dare attribute either to Kant or to González Vicén, what the dissenter ought to do when faced with a legally unjust situation, with "unjust law," is not to invoke some right to resist but simply to resist.

The renaissance of jusnaturalism following the Second World War was due largely to the *argumentum ad hominem* — or to the *reductio ad Hitlerum*, as it has also been called — used by partisans of the former against juspositivism, an argument according to which the monstrous outrage against human rights of the Nazi regime was the fault of legal positivism.[109]

But as Ernesto Garzón Valdés has recently reminded us, jusnaturalism — take the by no means unusual case of Hans Helmuth Dietze's *Naturrecht der Gegenwart* — was not far behind juspositivism in serving as a legitimizing ideological cover for Nazism.[110] And, of what use, in the face of so much abject submission to the established order, would it have been to invoke any right of resistance? In contrast to such empty invocations, an authentic resister like the Protestant theologian Dietrich Bonhoeffer — imprisoned and finally hanged for participating in the conspiracy leading to the attempt on Hitler's life on July 20, 1944 — simply invoked, as we read in his *Ethics*, "the voice of conscience," that

[109] See in this regard the book by E. Garzón Valdés, *Derecho y "naturaleza de las cosas" (Análisis de una nueva versión del derecho natural en el pensamiento jurídico alemán contemporáneo)*, 2 vols. (Córdoba [Argentina], 1970–71).

[110] See the previous work and his response to the poll by *Doxa* 1 (1985), "Problemas abiertos en la Filosofía del Derecho," 95–97, where he writes: "Because of my Kelsenian formation, I was not a little disturbed by the severe accusations that were leveled at legal positivism (in the post-War era), . . . which was virtually held responsible for the establishment of National Socialism. . . . The discovery of H. H. Dietze's book (Bonn, 1936) . . . put an end to that turn of events, since it was clear proof of the ideological importance of jusnaturalism in the justification of the regime in power in Germany from 1933 to 1945."

is, "a voice that, originating at a depth well beyond one's own will and one's own reason, calls human existence to a unity with itself." [111]

Unfortunately for me — although, given the proportions this lecture is assuming, I am not sure I may include the reader here — I have time to mention only a few points that might be developed as corollary paths leading off from what we have seen thus far. The first is connected with the curious fact that the distinction — conceptual, not real, but more or less metaphysical (in the sense, at least, of a "moral metaphysics") — between moral and empirical subjects demands rather than excludes an empirical investigation (to be undertaken, for example, by the social sciences) into how dissidence in fact arises and how it might serve to reduce the distance between the two subjects and, especially, the moral subject and the subject of rights. The sociologist Barrington Moore has suggested a direction this investigation might take, in a book — written at the same time as Rawls's *Theory of Justice*, which the author declined to read in manuscript so as to avoid "contaminating" the writing of his own text — titled, significantly, *Injustice: The Social Basis of Obedience and Revolt*.[112] What is decisive in explaining the origin and the effects of dissidence (quite a different matter from its justification, which would be the job of ethics) is not, according to Moore, the Rawlsian "sense of justice,"

---

[111] D. Bonhoeffer, *Ethik* (Munich, 1949), 257. To be fair to Bonhoeffer, one should point out that, as a good theologian, he further takes into account "the great transformation [that] takes place at the moment when the unity of human conscience no longer consists in its autonomy, but rather, thanks to the miracle of faith, is discovered beyond the Self and its law, in Jesus Christ" (see Tiemo Rainer Peters, *Die Präsenz des Politischen in der Theologie Dietrich Bonhoeffers* [Munich, 1976], 61ff.). But, he adds, for just that reason (Bonhoeffer, *Ethik*, 258–59): "When National Socialism says that the Führer is my conscience, it is an attempt to ground the unity of the Self beyond itself. This has as consequence a loss of autonomy in favor of an absolute heteronomy, which in turn is only possible if the other man in whom I seek the unity of my life serves as my redeemer. This would be the closest secular parallel as well as the most blatant contradiction with Christian truth."

[112] B. Moore, Jr., *Injustice* (New York, 1978).

but a "sense of injustice," which undoubtedly corresponds to another constellation in the phenomenology of moral life. The second point has to do with the problem of "civil disobedience," which ought perhaps to be treated as a section or chapter of dissidence in general. As Jorge Malem maintains in his excellent study, *Concept and Justification of Civil Disobedience*, it has been normal from Hugo Adam Bedau forward (as in the case, for example, of Peter Singer's *Democracy and Disobedience*) to consider civil disobedience as a group of conscious, public, nonviolent, and illegal acts carried out with the intention of frustrating the laws, programs, or decisions of a government, while accepting (at least within the context of a representative democratic society) the current constitutional order.[113] The drawback of this kind of characterization of civil disobedience is that it leaves somewhat in the dark the relation between this and other forms of disobedience — from "ethical disobedience of the law" to "revolutionary disobedience" — not forgetting that what we call "democracy" in our present democratic societies has not always existed nor can it be said to exist today in countries like South Africa where civil disobedience is practiced. And, what is even more serious, we cannot even be certain that this democracy will survive in a "totally administered world," to use Horkheimer's terrifying expression, toward which we are most probably headed and in which disobedience will be — in any of its now known, or future, guises — more necessary than ever. But, as I said, we cannot treat these themes, which belong in their own right to an ethics of resistance that has still to be written for our times.

I cannot help but pause, however briefly, over a third and final corollary, with which I would like to close. The main moral, if one may speak of a moral, that might perhaps be derived from

---

[113] In addition to the text by J. Malem (Barcelona: in press), see those of H. A. Bedau, *Civil Disobedience: Theory and Practice* (New York, 1969) and P. Singer (Oxford, 1973), as well as the study by J. A. Estévez Araujo, "El sentido de la desobediencia civil," in *Filosofía Política*, ed. J. M. González García and F. Quesada, a special issue of *Arbor* 503–4 (1987): 129–38.

these hasty reflections on the imperative of dissidence — the imperative, please remember, that prescribes that we say *no* to the unjust law (or at least authorizes us to do so), no matter how much consensus lies behind it — would have to be that we are all the protagonists of the life of the law or at least *should* be. To parody a very famous thesis, one might say that the jusphilosophers have thus far only theorized about human rights (which, by the way, is the only thing they could do and should keep on doing). But it is the task of *every human being* as human being (and not only of jurists, whether jusphilosophers or not) to fight for the juridical realization of those demands of dignity, liberty, and equality that make each human being a human being. Just as it is the task of everyone to fight to preserve and protect those demands that are already satisfied as rights, keeping them from being emptied of meaning, and avoiding their degeneration to mere rhetoric once they have been incorporated into the corresponding legal texts.

What remains to be said is only that this struggle to effect what Bloch once called "justice from beneath" forms an extremely important part of the dissent from the not infrequent inhumanity of the law, which is no less unfortunate and dangerous in its consequences than the absence of any law. (The above-mentioned "justice from beneath" would be a justice, to borrow from Dworkin's mythology, that ought to be left to the pygmies that we mortals are — the children, like Antaeus, of Mother Earth — and not to an exceptional judge like Hercules, endowed, as his name suggests, with uncommon faculties.)[114]

But perhaps it would be best in this regard to let Bloch have the last word: "Justice, whether retributive or distributive, answers

[114] Dworkin, *Taking Rights Seriously*, chap. 4, §§ 5–6 (I confess that my antipathy for Hercules the judge, always able to come up with the "right answer," is due in no small measure to his kinship with that old friend the Rational Chooser [*Preferidor Racional*], with whom I was obliged to deal in my book *La razón sin esperanza*, 2d ed. [Madrid: Ed. Taurus, 1986], 69–100, 227ff.).

to the formula of the *suum cuique*, that is, it presupposes the head
of the family, the father of his country, who dispenses to all *from
above* their share of punishment or of social well-being, earnings
and position. . . . The scale that, even in the Zodiac sign of Libra,
rises all the way up so as to perform from there, is quite in accord
with this ideal of justice seated on thrones. . . . [But] *real justice*,
inasmuch as it is justice *from below*, usually rebels against such
justice, against the essential injustice that reserves exclusively for
itself the role of justice." [115]

[115] Bloch, *Naturrecht und menschliche Würde*, 228–29.

The Trouble with Confucianism

WM. THEODORE DE BARY

THE TANNER LECTURES ON HUMAN VALUES

Delivered at
The University of California at Berkeley

May 4 and 5, 1988

For Fanny — to celebrate the fiftieth anniversary
of our meeting.

On recent visits to mainland China I have been asked, most often by young people, a question that would have seemed almost unthinkable twenty years ago: What is the significance of Confucianism today? Though for me it is not a question easy to answer, I can sympathize with the curiosity and concerns of my questioners. Their eagerness to learn about Confucianism comes after decades in which it was virtually off-limits to any kind of serious study or discussion in Mao's China. Indeed so neglected had Confucius become by the time of the Cultural Revolution, and so shadowy a figure was he in most people's minds that the Gang of Four at the start of their anti-Confucian campaign found him a poor target of attack. Confucius had first to be resurrected before he could be pilloried and crucified. Yet, ever since, he has continued to haunt the scene. Like Harry in Alfred Hitchcock's film *The Trouble with Harry* Confucius has refused to stay buried.

Today too, despite the new, more considered attention given to Confucius, his place is still unsettled and his status unclear. For some younger people, the bitter disillusionment that followed the Cultural Revolution and the eclipse of Mao has left them looking everywhere, abroad and at home, for something to replace the god that failed. For others, heirs of the May Fourth movement and steeped in the anti-Confucian satires of Lu Hsun as they never were in the Confucian classics, Confucianism still lurks as the specter of a reactionary and repressive past, surviving in antidemocratic, "feudal" features of the current regime. The suspicion, among those who, forty years after "liberation," still seek to be liberated, is that the new pragmatic policy in Beijing gives tacit support to the revival of a conservative ideology that would dampen dissent and buttress the status quo. Even the West's newfound interest in Confucianism is, from this point of view, apt to be dismissed as hopelessly anachronistic. Indeed, for those still disposed to consider religions (perhaps now along with Marxism) as the opiate of the people, any sympathetic approach to Confucianism in the West seems to be a romantic illusion, a wishful idealization of China's past on a par with other pipe dreams of Westerners seeking some escape into Oriental mysticism, Zen Buddhism, or transcendental meditation.

Nor are such divergent views found only in post-Mao China. Similar questions are asked and the same doubts expressed in much of "post-Confucian" East Asia. In Singapore Lee Kuan-yew, the aging leader of probably the most spectacular effort at rapid industrialization in Asia, now fears the corrupting effects of secular liberalism on the traditional Confucian values and social discipline he considers essential ingredients of Singapore's success. Young Singaporeans, however, express deep reservations about Lee's authoritarian ways and fear any revival of Confucianism as a prelude to further political repression.

Likewise in Korea, regimes widely viewed as no less authoritarian than Lee's have seemed to promote Confucianism as a conservative force, while students and many intellectuals remain distrustful of it (to such an extent that even an official publication of the Korean Academy of Sciences, *An Introduction to Korean Studies*, reflects a critical view of Confucianism among many modern scholars and discounts its contributions to Korea's historical development). In Taiwan, even though more serious attention is paid to Confucianism as integral to China's cultural heritage, young people do not always share the same loyalty to it and seek reassurance that there is no essential conflict between it and modern life. Meanwhile in Japan Confucianism is widely believed to have played a profound, though subtle, role in Japan's rise to a dominant position in the world economy, yet in Ronald Dore's new book, *Taking Japan Seriously: A Confucian Perspective on Leading Economic Issues*,[1] readers so far unpersuaded of it will have difficulty identifying in traditional terms what is specifically Confucian in the attitudes Dore describes among the Japanese.

In these circumstances it is probably a healthy thing that the official line in the People's Republic today speaks of "seeking truth through facts," by looking into what is both "good and bad" in Confucianism. Indeed, only a broad and open-minded approach to the subject will do. Yet if I still have difficulty with the questions, so often put to me, What do you think of Confucianism? or What are the strong and weak points of Confucianism? my reaction is not just the typical disinclination of the academician, or supposedly "disinterested scholar," to commit himself. Without objuring all value judgments I still feel obliged to ask: Whose Confucianism are we talking about? If it is the teachings of Confucius in the *Analects*, then almost nothing in Ronald Dore's book speaks to that, and the same, as a matter of fact, was already true of the anti-Confucian diatribes earlier in this century, which rarely spoke to Confucius's own views but only to later distortions of them. If it is the teaching of Confucius, plus those of the other classic thinkers (say, Mencius and Hsün-Tzu) that is meant, then even assuming one can identify the common denominator among those classical Confucians, on what ground do we stop there, disallowing the testimony of still later Confucians, like Chu Hsi and Wang Yang-ming, who have contributed to the development and amplification of the teaching? What purpose is served by freezing the definition at some moment far in the past, when what we want to know is something about the role of Confucianism just yesterday or today? Again, since the question, as we have it, is one raised all over East and Southeast Asia, the answer can take many forms: Korean, Japanese, and Vietnamese as well as Chinese. Strictly speaking, we would have to consider in each such case how

[1] Stanford University Press, 1987.

Confucianism was understood and practiced — how it came to be transmitted, interpreted, accepted, and acted upon in this time and that place.

If in the face of such complications, I am still willing to attempt an answer to these questions, it is with the proviso that you indulge my choice of title, "The Trouble with Confucianism," and accept its intended ambiguity with respect to the word "Trouble," which is meant to include the different kinds of trouble Confucianism either fell into, made for itself, or created for others. In my view Confucianism was a problematical enterprise from its inception, and, as it responded to the challenges of each age, addressing some perhaps but not others, it had both its successes and its failures. Looked at in this way, the "good and bad points of Confucianism" actually tend to go together. We get nowhere by conceiving of them as fixed points in a static system. They are to be recognized, if at all, as mirroring each other in a convoluted historical process, as constants and continuities in the midst of discontinuities and difficulties.

Further, if we think of "trouble" as what was wrong or went wrong with Confucianism, our first consideration must be to ask ourselves, By whose standards? My answer is that any failure should, in the first instance, be judged by the standards and goals Confucians put before themselves. Simply to establish those criteria will be more of a task than most of us have so far realized, but it takes priority over any other historical judgment we might hope to render.

Finally, I should mention that among the topics to which Confucianism gave priority or special attention, one would have to include rulership and leadership, scholarship and the school, the family and human relations, rites and religion. I shall focus on the first, with lesser reference to the second. This, as it happened, was the order in which Confucius first addressed them.

I. SAGE-KINGS AND NOBLE MEN

The trouble with Confucianism was there from the start, to become both a perennial challenge and a dilemma that would dog it through history — there in the founding myths of the tradition as the ideal of humane governance, and thereafter, even in Confucianism's movements of apparent worldly success, as the ungovernable reality of imperial rule. We encounter it first in the "Canon of Yao" in the classic *Book of Documents*, with this idealization of the sage-king:

> Examining into antiquity, we find that the Emperor Yao was named Fang-hsun. He was reverent, intelligent, accomplished, sincere and mild. He was genuinely respectful and capable of all modesty. His light spread over the four extremities of the world, extending to Heaven above and Earth below. He was able to make bright his great virtue and bring affection to the nine branches of the family. When the nine branches of the family had become harmonious, he distinguished and honored the great clans. When the hundred clans had become illustrious, he harmonized the myriad states. Thus the numerous peoples were amply nourished, prospered, and became harmonious.[2]

No depth of insight is required to see embodied here in Yao all the civilized virtues of a good Confucian ruler; his reverent and respectful manner, his intelligence, his disciplined attainments, his self-restraint and modesty, his concern for others — all having a marvelous efficacy in the moral transformation of his people, all manifest in the beneficent power of his paternal care, radiating from the luminous center of his personal virtue, outward through successive degrees of kinship to distant states and the very ends of the world, harmonizing all mankind in one loving family and bringing them into a cosmic unity with Heaven and Earth.

---

[2] *Shu Ching,* Yao tien; translation modified from *The Shoo King,* trans. James Legge, Chinese Classics 3 (London, 1865), pp. 15–16.

Note, however, what is simply given, what is so naturally
assumed in the presentation of this heroic ideal: its setting is altogether a human world, a familial order, with its patriarchal leader
already in place and, what is more, already in place at the center.
There is no creation myth here, no Genesis. Even as a founding
myth, the Canon of Yao projects neither conquest nor struggle;
neither antagonist nor rival to overcome nor any countervailing
power to be met. The sage-king stands alone, unchallenged and
unchecked except by self-imposed restraints. And in the sequel
to this account of Yao's commanding virtue, the question is simply
one of finding a worthy successor. There is nothing contested,
nothing problematical except how to find another paragon of
humble virtue to whom rulership may be entrusted.

All this, as I have said, may well be taken as a founding myth
of the Confucians, emblematic of a school which thought of itself
as the prime bearer and upholder of civilized tradition. Yet, the
myth and the tradition were more than just Confucian. Before
Confucius put his own stamp and seal on them, they were waiting
for him in the record of China's primordial age. Much of the
classic canon itself antedates Confucius, and others of the pre-
Confucian texts celebrate the ideal of the sage-king, as does this
passage from the *Book of Odes* eulogizing King Wen, a founder-
father of the Chou dynasty, as bearer of Heaven's mandate:

> King Wen is on high;
> Oh, he shines in Heaven
>
> . . . . .
>
> August was King Wen
> Continuously bright and reverent.
> Great indeed was his mandate from Heaven.[3]

In Confucius's passing down of the *Odes* and other classics to
later generations there is reason to credit what he says of himself

[3] *Shih ching*, Ta Ya, Wen Wang; translation modified from *The She King*,
trans. James Legge, Chinese Classics 4 (London, 1871), pp. 427–29.

in the *Analects* — that he was a transmitter of tradition — even if
we cannot accept at face value, but only as typical of his appealing
modesty, the Master's further disclaimer that he was making any
original contribution of his own to that tradition. In this case, the
idea of the sage-king was Chinese before it became Confucian.
Archaeological evidence confirms the suspicion that centralized
rule and the dominance of a single ruler, combining religious and
political authority, were already facts of historical life before
Confucius came on the scene. That this centralized rule was
already rationalized and bureaucratized to a high degree, as David
Keightley's recent studies confirm, warrants the view that late-
Shang-dynasty China already prefigured the characteristic imperial
order of the Ch'in and Han in this important respect: a symmetrical structure of power, with varying degrees of control or autonomy at the outer reaches, but converging on a center of increasing
density, though not always of heightened power, in terms of
bureaucratic administration, economic control, and cultural afflu-
ence.[4] Though it is no doubt also true that this process of cen-
tralization emerged as a developing trend, was intensified, and
became further rationalized in the late Chou period, such increasing concentration of power implies no radical discontinuity from
the past. Even the so-called feudal order, or enfeoffment system,
looked, at least in theory, to such a commissioning, if not commanding, center. As Hsü Cho-yün has characterized this "feudal
order": "Kingship was at the center of a vast kinship organization, . . . coupled with a strong state structure." [5]

Testimony from the non-Confucian schools of the middle and
late Chou period supports this conclusion. Different though they
are among themselves in other respects, Mohists, Taoists, and
Legalists (or for that matter even the different wings of the Con-

[4] David N. Keightley, "The Religious Commitment: Shang Theology and the
Genesis of Chinese Political Culture," in *History of Religions* 17 (1978): 211–25.

[5] Hsü Cho-yün, *The Western Chou Civilization* (New Haven: Yale University
Press, 1988), chapter 4.

fucian school) all alike assume that the original, natural, and normal order of things is a unified realm, with one ruler presiding over a single structure of authority, looser or tighter perhaps in one case or another but never multicentered. Even the political pluralism and cultural particularism cherished by the Taoists was something to be fostered by a sage-ruler rather than protected by a system of checks and balances or countervailing powers.

That this represents, even more than a Confucian attitude, a persistent proclivity of the larger Chinese tradition, is suggested too by its recrudescence even in the post-Confucian modern era. True, the worship of the great leader, the "cult of personality," was no Chinese invention, nor should we look on the benign countenance of Mao Tse-tung, ubiquitously displayed in public to brighten the world with his genial visage, solely as an avatar of the Chinese sage-king. Yet by whom, even in the Soviet Union, was Mao's mentor Stalin more apotheosized than by the unofficial poet laureate of Communist China, Kuo Mo-jo, when he celebrated Stalin's seventieth birthday in 1949? Where else was the great leader so ecstatically acclaimed, not only as the fulfillment of all human aspiration, but even as playing a role of cosmic proportions:

> The Great Stalin, our beloved "Steel," our everlasting sun!
>
> Only because there is you among mankind,
>   Marx-Leninism can reach its present heights!
>
> Only because there is you, the Proletariat can have
>   its present growth and strength!
>
> Only because there is you, the task of liberation
>   can be as glorious as it is!
>
> It is you who are leading us to merge into the stream
>   flowing into the ocean of utopia.
>
> It is you who are instructing us that the West
>   will never neglect the East.

It is you who are uniting us into a force
    never before seen in history. . . .

    . . . . .

The history of mankind is opening a new chapter.

The orders of nature will also follow the direction
    of revolution.

The name of Stalin will forever be the sun of mankind.[6]

A writer, historian, and activist before 1949, Kuo became a supposedly "nonpartisan" representative in the People's Political Consultative Conference and later vice-president of the Standing Committee of the People's Congress. In this congratulatory hymn presumably he speaks for the Chinese people and celebrates their age-old undying faith in sage-rulers.

At any rate, to return to the earlier case, such evidence as we now have indicates that unified, centralized rule by a single, preponderant figure had become the established pattern very early in ancient China, and that for Confucius the king at the center was already a given, not something he originated or would propose to establish except on the classic model. What he did suggest was how the exercise of such power might be guided and restrained in a humane way, through the moralization of politics. So too it would be with later Confucians who, for the most part, made no attempt to seize power through the mobilization of armies or parties, or to found and organize a new regime. Rather they kept their peace and bided their time, waiting for the conqueror to come to them, meanwhile preparing themselves to deal with the same historical givens, the same recalcitrant facts of political life, through their study of the lessons of the past. When, then, opportunity arose, they would pursue through the same process of persuasion and moral transformation the taming of power and modi-

---

[6] As translated by Fang Chao-ying and privately circulated, 1949.

fication of existing structures. In such situations, this connate pairing — this ideal of sagely rule cohabiting with the actuality of autocratic power — remained both a supreme challenge for the Confucians and a source of endless trouble.

THE NOBLE MAN AS COUNTERPOINT TO THE SAGE-KING

In the ode to King Wen, part of which I quoted earlier, there is another stanza, addressed to the scions of the Chou house, which refers to the Shang dynasty's loss of Heaven's mandate to the Chou:

> The charge is not easy to keep
> May it not end in your persons.
> Display and make bright your good fame
> And consider what Yin [the Shang] had received
>   from Heaven [and then lost].
> The moral burden of high Heaven
> Is unwritten, unspoken.
> Take King Wen as your model
> And the people will trust in you.[7]

Here the power of the ruling house is subject to the intangible moral restraint which Heaven imposes as the unstated condition of the Chou's exercise of sovereignty. While King Wen stands as the model of such restraint, the moral burden falls on his house, his descendants, as a public and collective responsibility.

When, in the *Analects*, we encounter the same charge, it assumes a new form. The idea of power held in public trust is still there, but when Confucius talks about Heaven's mandate he does not address a ruling house, urging fidelity to the example of its founder as a condition of its longevity and tenure. Rather

[7] *Shih ching*, Ta Ya, Wen Wang; translation modified from Legge, *She King*, pp. 429–31.

the mandate has been reconceived as an individual mission and personal commitment to the service of humankind in the broadest sense. Confucius speaks of this to his students and companions as members of an educated elite with a high calling to leadership and public service, even when they hold no power. For them Heaven's imperative (*t'ien ming*) is no dynastic commission but a claim on their individual political and moral conscience.

By the same token or tally the sage-king as model for a dynasty has little direct relevance for Confucius and his followers, who, with the decline of the old aristocracy, are hardly in a position to emulate it. More pertinent is the example of the noble man (*chün-tzu*), who may now hold no office at all.[8] This is not for want of a vocation to public service but because, unlike the scions of the Chou in former times, the noble man may be politically displaced or unrecognized. Heaven may not have destined him for office or disposed of his personal circumstances so as to give him direct access to power or political influence.

Several passages in the *Analects* illustrate this conception of the noble man fulfilling his personal moral mission even in political adversity, simply by preserving his own self-respect and remaining true to his interior sense of what it is right and proper for him to do. In the opening lines he asks the question whether truly being a noble man does not mean remaining unsoured even if one is unknown or unrecognized (*Analects* 1). The normal expectation for the *chün-tzu* would be that he receive some recognition (i.e., position) from the ruler, yet Confucius pointedly subordinates the outward status (the political or social standing of the nobleman) to the inner nobility and peace of mind of the noble man. The one-time aristocrat, now "unknown" and politi-

[8] The Chinese term for "noble man" is not specific as to gender, and in later times *chün* could be applied to women as well. Thus a reading like "noble person" is not impossible. But I think in patriarchal times "noble man" is closer to the actual meaning, and "person" should be reserved for *shen*, "one's own person," and the respect it is entitled to.

cally a nobody, could make something of himself by becoming a
truly noble man.

Confucius stresses the point again by speaking of the noble
man as one who stands by his professed principles, his dedication
to the True Way, no matter what the ignominious fate he may
suffer. "He is never so harried, never so endangered, but that he
cleaves to this" (*Analects* 4:5). This requires more than the
courteous behavior of the gentleman. Uncompromising adherence
to principle cannot be served simply by a nice diffidence or polite
disengagement from human affairs. A life of continuing struggle
may be called for. When it is suggested that Confucius abandon
his efforts to reform rulers, he counters by asserting the need to
persist even against the indifference of those in power. "If the
Way prevailed in the world [i.e., simply of itself, without the
need for conscientious effort on man's part], I would not be trying
to change things" (*Analects* 18:6).

Confucius had already been derided for "fleeing from this
man and that" (i.e., avoiding service to one ruler or another),
when, as he was advised, he would do better "to flee from this
whole generation of men" (i.e., to give up on political reform
altogether). His response was neither to give up nor to give in,
neither to retire from the scene in order fastidiously to preserve
his inner integrity, nor on the other hand, to accept whatever office
might be available simply for the sake of keeping himself politically occupied and comfortably provided for. Rather, peripateti-
cally on the political circuit of ancient China, Confucius traveled
the twisting road that lay between easy accommodation and total
withdrawal.

Given this example of Confucius and his portrayal of the
noble man, one understands how later Confucians would have had
to stray rather far from the Master's precepts if they were to fit
Max Weber's characterization of the Confucian as a gentleman
politely accommodating himself to the status quo or rationally

adjusting to the world in which he found himself.[9] True, the modest, respectful manner and careful prudential conduct expected of the Confucian *chün-tzu*, lend some plausibility to Weber's view. But if the Confucian is worldly and urbane in this respect, he, like Confucius, must heed the imperatives of Heaven as the supreme moral order in the universe, and answer to it in his conscience. "He who offends against Heaven has none to whom he can pray" (*Analects* 3:3). In Confucius's account of his own life-experience, the ultimate meaning and value of his mission in life is bound up with "recognizing the imperatives of Heaven" and "learning to follow them" (*Analects* 2:4). "There are," he says, "three things of which the noble man stands in awe: the imperatives of Heaven, great men, and the words of the sages" (*Analects* 15:8). And finally, in the last lines of the *Analects*, Confucius says, "Unless one recognizes the imperatives of Heaven one cannot be a noble man (20:3).

It is this compelling voice of conscience and ideal standard represented by the imperatives of Heaven which serves as the ultimate criterion and court of judgment in assessing human affairs. If, according to the Confucian conception of humanity or humaneness (*jen*), man can indeed be the measure of man, it is only because this high moral sense and cosmic dimension of the human mind-and-heart give it the capacity for self-transcendence. Likewise if the Confucian, even while accepting the world, still hopes to gain the leverage on it necessary for its transformation, Heaven's imperative in the minds of men serves as the fulcrum. So it is too with the stance of the noble man, standing on the same moral ground at court, hoping to transform the ruler.

Recognizing this potential transformative power in Confucian thought, the neo-Weberian sociologist Shmuel Eisenstadt has amended Weber's characterization of Confucianism, calling it now, quite seriously though paradoxically, a "this-worldly tran-

---

[9] Max Weber, *The Religion of China* (New York: Macmillan, 1965), pp. 227, 235.

scendentalism."[10] Thus Eisenstadt acknowledges the tension between the given world and Heaven's imperative, a tension expressed by Confucius when, ridiculed for his unrealism and still
unwilling either to accommodate or abandon the ruler of his day,
he insisted on the need both for himself and for them to make the
Way prevail in the world.

In earlier work I have drawn attention to what I call the
"prophetic voice" in the later Confucian tradition — in the Neo-
Confucianism of the Sung dynasty and after — which challenged
and judged severely the politics of the late imperial dynasties in
China. Without intending any exact or entire equation of the Confucian noble voice with prophetic utterance in the more theistic
traditions, wherein the prophet has often renounced the world and
"gone out into the desert," I wished to show that even a world-
affirming Confucian could render severe judgments on the established order, asserting absolute claims on behalf of inner conscience. As I said of this distinction:

> "Prophetic" I use here to indicate an extraordinary access to
> and revelation of truth not vouchsafed to everyone, which by
> some process of inner inspiration or solitary perception affords
> an insight beyond what is received in scripture, and by appeal
> to some higher order of truth gives new meaning, significance,
> and urgency to certain cultural values or scriptural texts. Con-
> fucian tradition does not customarily speak of such a revela-
> tion as "supernatural," but it has an unpredictable, wondrous
> quality manifesting the divine creativity of Heaven. By con-
> trast I use "scholastic" to represent an appeal to received au-
> thority by continuous transmission, with stress on external or
> public acceptance of it as the basis of its validity.[11]

---

[10] S. N. Eisenstadt, *This Worldly Transcendentalism and the Structuring of the
World — Weber's Religion of China and the Format of Chinese History and Civilization* (Jerusalem: Hebrew University of Jerusalem, 1983).

[11] W. T. de Bary, *Neo-Confucian Orthodoxy and the Learning of the Mind-
and-Heart* (New York: Columbia University Press, 1981), p. 9.

Confucius is no Moses or Mohammed, conveying the direct words of a very personal God, but his critique appeals to the authority of high Heaven and invokes the ideal order of the sage-kings. Time does not allow for a full discussion of the classical antecedents of this prophetic function in Confucianism. The Neo-Confucians, however, drew particularly on the teachings of Mencius, and I should like briefly to point out his special contribution in asserting this prophetic role. Mencius, of course, is not simply a carbon copy — or perhaps I should say a rubbing from the graven tablets — of Confucius. He does, however, echo strongly the latter's views on Heaven, the ideal order of the sage-kings, and the role of the noble man in challenging the rulers of his day. Indeed Mencius heightened considerably the tension between the Confucian ideals of humanity (*jen*) and rightness (*i*), and, by contrast, the brutal politics of his time. Notwithstanding his affirmation of the essential goodness of human nature, he was quick to expose the faults of contemporary rulers — their callousness, selfishness, pretentiousness, and even their minor failings. Nothing short of a scrupulous adherence to the Way was demanded. Even the sacrifice of one's life itself was not too much to ask of those who would live up to the full measure of their humanity (*Mencius* 6A:10). For himself, Mencius insisted that even the gaining of power over the whole world would not justify killing one man or committing a single act of unrighteousness to accomplish it (*Mencius* 2A:2). And of the noble man he said that among his three greatest pleasures in life to rule the world would not be one of them (the three are that his parents still be alive and his brothers well, that he feel no shame over his own conduct, and that he have able students; *Mencius* 7A:20).

By no means the last Confucian to speak in these idealistic terms, Mencius was probably the first to express realistically what would be required of ministers who sought to convey the Confucian message to rulers. No one has exposed more forthrightly than he the danger of co-optation that lay in the ruler-minister relation or the seductive ease with which officials could fall into the obsequiousness of servitors or slaves, awed by autocratic power. Like Confucius, he distinguished between true nobility, identified with moral and intellectual worth, and the superficialities of worldly rank. The former he called the "nobility of Heaven" (*t'ien-chüeh*), again identifying high moral standards with Heaven. Worldly rank he termed the "nobility of men," empty and ephemeral unless grounded in man's inborn moral sense and reflective of a hierarchy of true values (*Mencius* 6A:16). No one inveighed so fearlessly as Mencius against the pretensions of power and prestige (though admittedly this could be seen as more the fearlessness of the teacher in a classroom than that of the minister at court or the soldier in battle).

> Those who counsel the great should view them with contempt and not have regard for their pomp and display. Lofty halls with great beams — these, even if successful, I would not have. Quantities of food, hundreds of girls in attendance — these, even if successful, I would not have. . . . What they [princes] have, is nothing I would have. What I would have is the restraints and regulations of the ancients. Why should I stand in awe of princes? (*Mencius* 7B:34)

And of the ruler's treatment of the *chün-tzu* at court, Mencius said:

> To feed him and not love him is to treat him as a pig. To love him and not respect him is to treat him as a domesticated animal. Respect must come before gifts. Respect not substantiated in action can only be taken by the noble man as an empty gesture. (*Mencius* 7A:37)

In this way Mencius attempted to invest the Confucian noble man as minister and official with the privileged position necessary for him to serve as independent counsel, and thus provide a counterpoint to the dictates of the ruler. His vision was of a regime no less unitary than that attributed to the sage-kings, whose ideal order he too evoked, but Mencius could conceive of a center that did not arrogate all power to itself, balanced by an autonomous feudal nobility and ministered to by truly noble men, exercising this independent prophetic function as a counterweight to the concentration of power and wealth in the ruler.

After Mencius had so asserted the dignity and independence of the minister, Chinese rulers who still claimed the authority, omniscience, and omnicompetence of the sage could not expect that claim to go undisputed by the Confucians. Though officially unrecognized and politically powerless against the highly organized and efficient Legalists, who succeeded in conquering, unifying, and reorganizing China in the third century B.C., the Confucians' influence was nonetheless acknowledged by the Legalist prime minister of the Ch'in empire, Li Ssu, who called for the burning of the Confucian books and directed those seeking an education to get their instruction from official sources, not from impractically bookish and yet ideologically troublesome Confucians who "harp on the past to injure the present." In a memorial to the throne, Li accused the Confucians of promoting open criticism and expressing views contrary to the ruler's. He recommended that "Those who dare to talk to each other about the *Book of Odes* and *Book of Documents* should be executed and their bodies exposed in the market place. Anyone referring to the past to criticize the present should, with all the members of his family, be put to death." [12]

Even allowing for the alacrity and frequency with which Legalists of Li Ssu's stripe resorted to extreme punishments, one may infer from the drastic measures he proposed that, to his mind, the Confucians represented a veritable threat. Despite their antiquarian and pedantic ways, Li speaks of them as having influence with the multitudes and stirring up opposition. This, in his eyes, cannot but jeopardize the authority of the emperor, who, Li says,

[12] *Shih Chi* PNP 6:23b; *Sources of Chinese Tradition* (New York: Columbia University Press, 1960), 1:141.

has reunified the empire after its earlier disintegration, brought all thought and activity under his own direction and dictation, and "established for himself a position of sole supremacy." [13]

Apparently these Confucian traditionalists, punctilious pedants though they appeared to be, were more than just gentlemen scholars and courtly ritualists in the Weberian mold, but noble men of the type Mencius called for: critics whose protest could be quite telling. Plainly, if self-proclaimed sage-rulers meant trouble for the Confucians, the trouble with Confucianism for the ruler could be found in the noble man.

THE TROUBLE WITH CONFUCIAN SCHOLARSHIP

When Confucianism finally emerged as a state-sanctioned teaching, with official status at court, it was in the reign of the great Emperor Wu of the Han Dynasty. Tung Chung-shu (179?–104? B.C.), a leading scholarly authority on the *Spring and Autumn Annals* who might best be described as a philosopher of history, was also a leading figure at court, recognized as such by the Confucian scholars of his time and especially respected for his character and integrity. Tung had definite views about political and economic reform, and in advocating them recalled both the ideal order of the sage-kings and the principles of Mencius. Arguably as a proponent of such ideals and critic of the Ch'in-Han system he could be considered a political prophet, but that may be going too far. Though he believed in the equalization of landholding and hoped for a return to the ancient well-fields system advocated by Mencius, in the end Tung felt the need to compromise with the established order, settling in his own mind for a moderate limitation on landholding rather than insisting on radical redistribution. By Mencius's criteria, as conscientious statesman and reformer Tung might well merit the title "noble man,"

[13] Ibid.

but as the embodiment equally of Confucian courage and prudence, and as quintessential classicist and philosopher, he was unlikely to press his case with the shrill or stern voice of the prophet.

Officially Tung and his Han Confucian colleagues were honored at court as erudite scholars and professors of the classics, but as the Emperor Wu turned increasingly to professional bureaucrats — technicians and fiscal experts identified with Legalist methods — for the management of his finances and imposition of expanded state controls over the economy, the Confucians arose in opposition. Things came to a head in 81 B.C. with the historic Debate on Salt and Iron (so-called because it centered on the issue of state monopolies over these essential resources).

Significantly, however, the debate departed from the familiar Confucian-Legalist contest over the primacy of state power. Rather than assuming state supremacy as the highest value (as had Li Ssu earlier), here the supposedly "Legalist" types argued that their policies primarily served the people's interest, that is, promoted the public development, fair distribution, or conservation of limited resources, instead of allowing uncontrolled private exploitation. Confucian spokesmen, basing themselves on Mencius, contended that this economic function was better left in the hands of the "people" themselves, that is, better in private hands (what today might be called free-enterprise) than those of the state bureaucracy.

Which party, then, could really speak for the "people's" interest? We may not be in a position to arrive at a definitive judgment, but two points are worth noting. The first is that in the debate itself, the government experts belittled the Confucians as poor, threadbare, impractical scholars, incompetent to handle their own affairs, let alone those of the state. The imperial secretary is recorded as saying of the Confucians: "See them now present with nothing and consider it substance, with emptiness and call it plenty! In their coarse gowns and cheap sandals they walk gravely along sunk in meditation as though they had lost something. These are not men who can do great deeds and win fame. They do not even rise above the vulgar masses!" [14]

This diatribe perpetuates the long-standing reputation of the Confucians as straitlaced but impecunious scholars, not at all men of the world or well adjusted to it but almost misfits. Here we need a word for them that conveys their sense of mission and disciplined, even if arcane, lifestyle. "Academician" (especially when thought of in cap and gown) might do and is certainly closer to it than "preacher" or "prophet," yet Confucians professed a greater dedication to defined moral values than we customarily associate with the "value-free" academics of today. In any case the distinguishing characteristic of the Confucians, in the eyes of their contemporaries, is their cultural commitment, self-denying dedication, and shared values as a company of scholars, rather than any economic class interest, proprietary power, party organization, or entrenched social position.

The second point worth noting is that the great debate was won ostensibly by the Confucians but practically by elements in the inner court surrounding the imperial family, who exploited the rhetoric of the Confucians to advance their own interests in a power struggle with the dominant faction in the regular state (i.e., civil) administration. Once in power themselves, the latter largely dispensed with the Confucians and made their own compromise with the established revenue-raising agencies, which, though somewhat curbed, remained essentially intact.[15]

The actual weakness of the Confucians then, seems not to have lain in a failure of advocacy, but in their indisposition or inability to establish any power base of their own. They could serve important functions for the bureaucratic state, by virtue of their literacy, their knowledge of history and ritual, and their high-minded ethos, but except on rare, momentary occasions, they faced

[14] *Yen t'ieh lun*, sec. 19, 4:10b; *Sources of Chinese Tradition*, 1:223.

[15] Nishijima Sadao, "Butei no shi: Entetsuron no haikei," in *Kodaishi kōza* (Tokyo: Gakuseisha, 1965).

the state, and whoever controlled it, as individual scholars un-supported by any organized party or active constituency. It is this institutional weakness, highly dependent condition, and extreme insecurity in their tenure of office (correctly diagnosed by Weber), and not any failure to uphold transcendent values (since they were hard enough on, demanding enough of, themselves), that marked the Confucians as *ju* ("softies") in the politics of imperial China.

In the mature dynasties, with the rise of Neo-Confucianism in the Sung dynasty and after, the literati acquired an even stronger identity as bearers of high culture and transcendental values but did not succeed in overcoming this crucial handicap. Even when Neo-Confucianism became firmly established as official doctrine, with a key role in both education and the civil service examination system, Confucian scholar/officials remained exposed to the vicissi-tudes of a system that took advantage of their disciplined talents while keeping them in a condition of extreme dependency and insecurity — though whether in servitude or not is another matter.

The pathos of this situation for the conscientious Confucian — mindful of Confucius's own persistent sense of mission, and refus-ing, in the face of extreme difficulties, either to give up or give in — had been touchingly expressed by the great T'ang poet Tu Fu (712–70), as he struggled to carry on his own political vocation when out of office and almost had to go begging for help from friends in different parts of the country. Here are two poems writ-ten in his last years:

EARLY SAILING

Every quest is preceded by a hundred scruples; Confucianism is indeed one of my troubles! And yet, because of it, I have many friends. And despite my age, I have continued to travel. . . .

Wise men of ancient times would not expose themselves to any chance of danger; Why should we hurry now at the risk of our lives? . . .

Having come a long and hard way to be a guest; One can make few appeals without injuring one's self-respect. Among the ancients, there were good men who refused to compromise and starved to death; There were able men who humored the world and received rich gifts. These are mutually exclusive examples; The trouble with me is that I want to follow them both![16]

ON THE RIVER

On the river, every day these heavy rains —
bleak, bleak, autumn in Ching-ch'u!
High winds strip the leaves from the trees;
through the long night I hug my fur robe.
I recall my official record, keep looking in the mirror,
recall my comings and goings, leaning alone in an upper room.
In these perilous times I long to serve my sovereign —
old and feeble as I am, I can't stop thinking of it![17]

So much for the noble man in T'ang China. Can we call him a failure? Politically yes, Tu Fu was a failure, but humanly speaking?

In the later period let me cite two early Ming emperors as typical of the relationship between Confucianism and the dynastic system. The founder Ming T'ai-tsu (1368–99) confirmed the important role of Confucian scholars in the civil bureaucracy by resuming the civil service examinations, based on the Neo-Confucian curriculum of Chu Hsi, which the Yüan dynasty had first adopted in 1313–15. Indeed T'ai-tsu strengthened the system by allowing almost no access to office except through this merito-cratic route. On the other hand, as a man of humble origins and largely self-educated, he showed considerable distaste for Neo-

[16] William Hung, *Tu Fu: China's Greatest Poet* (Cambridge: Harvard University Press, 1952), p. 266.

[17] Burton Watson, *The Columbia Book of Chinese Poetry* (New York: Columbia University Press, 1984), p. 234.

Confucian scholarship and philosophy as such, making plain his preference for men who combined literacy with practical learning, in contrast to Neo-Confucians, distinguished by their literary refinements and philosophical sophistication.

A ruthless despot in dealing with ministers he came to distrust, his megalomania led T'ai-tsu to abolish the prime ministership in order to centralize and concentrate all executive power in his own hands, while also, through a series of imperial pronouncements and directives, he exercised supreme ideological authority in matters of moral, social, and political doctrine.[18] It will not surprise my readers to learn that, even while giving the Four Books their greatest prominence in education and the examination system, T'ai-tsu saw to it that the text of Mencius was expurgated so as to remove from it passages considered contumaceous or subversive of the ruler's supreme authority.

The third Ming emperor, Cheng-tsu (r. 1402–25), a usurper of the throne, was no less assertive of imperial authority and ruthless in dealing with his ministers. To enhance his legitimacy, he made a great show of patronizing Neo-Confucianism, even though outspoken ministers (loyal in the Confucian sense of giving the ruler honest advice) were subjected by him to terror, imprisonment, torture, and death. At Ch'eng-tsu's direction a massive compilation of Neo-Confucian texts was printed and officially promulgated in 1415, to become the authoritative canon of Neo-Confucian teaching for centuries — in Ming China, in Yi dynasty Korea and Tokugawa Japan. Ch'eng-tsu also compiled and had published in his own name a guide to self-cultivation and mind control identified as the "learning of the sages." This latter work had far less influence, no doubt because Ch'eng-tsu's presumptuousness in claiming to speak as a sage did not impress later generations. On the contrary the Ch'ing dynasty editors of the Imperial Manuscript Library Catalogue later castigated Ch'eng-tsu for this pre-

[18] See my *Neo-Confucian Orthodoxy*, p. 158.

sumption, when more properly he should, as the ruling authority, simply have authorized and given his imprimatur to what more competent scholarly authorities had been asked to prepare. As I have summarized this scholarly judgment elsewhere, the editors said of Ch'eng-tsu that "he showed no sense of modesty or shame." They note the blood spilled in his rise to power, the harshness of his rule, the many who suffered unjustly from his arbitrary decrees and excessive punishments, all in contrast to the benevolent professions of the work in question. They conclude: "Men of later generations would not be taken in by this hypocrisy." [19]

There is great irony in the Ming situation considering that it was in a real sense *the* first full "Neo-Confucian" period — the first in which nearly all educated men, from the beginning, received their intellectual and moral formation through Neo-Confucian teachers and a Neo-Confucian curriculum. Neo-Confucian texts served as the basis for state examinations, and even Ming emperors, whether as crown princes or after, were constantly lectured to by Neo-Confucian mentors. Yet by the almost unanimous verdict of historians, Ming rule has been adjudged the ultimate extreme in Chinese despotism. Lest one dismiss this as just a Western judgment, prejudiced perhaps by ignorance, cultural preconceptions, or a predisposition to denigrate the Chinese, it must be said that Chinese scholars themselves, by the end of the Ming, had already arrived at this condemnation.

Modern writers have sometimes explained this ironic outcome as an indication that Neo-Confucianism itself was to blame, that it bore the seeds of such despotism in its own "dogmatism" and authoritarian ways. Still others who find Neo-Confucians to blame do so for almost opposite reasons, citing their impractical idealism, naive optimism, and simple moralistic approach to politics that was altogether incapable of coping with the economic complica-

---

[19] De Bary, *Neo-Confucian Orthodoxy*, p. 164.

tions and Byzantine complexities of imperial politics.[20] This latter
explanation may be closer to the truth than the former, in that
Neo-Confucian self-cultivation — the heart of its educational doctrine — put such heavy emphasis on the power of the individual
moral will to master any situation. When, then, his ministers
and mentors, with all the best intentions, seemed to lodge in the
emperor ultimate responsibility for whatever went wrong in the
world as the very necessary implication and consequence of imperial claims to absolute authority, it was an unbearable moral
burden for the man at the top — "the one man" — to bear. There
are signs that Ming rulers developed deep psychological resistance
to this unequal situation, resenting being lectured to in such terms,
and in some cases refused even to meet with their Neo-Confucian
ministers for long periods of time — even years on end.[21] A strik-
ingly similar syndrome appeared in Yi dynasty Korea, where the
same system of Neo-Confucian instruction for the ruler was
adopted, sometimes with incongruous results.[22]

Thomas Metzger's theory that Neo-Confucian doctrine inevitably placed its adherents in a kind of ultimate "predicament"
is particularly applicable here,[23] yet more applicable to the ruler
than to the minister, since the latter could ease his Confucian
conscience and extricate himself from this psychological dilemma
by noting the disjointed times and likening himself to Confucius's
noble man, who "remains unsoured even though unrecognized."
Though he might take the ritual blame at court, the scholar/

[20] This is a recurring theme in Ray Huang's *1587 — A Year of No Significance*
(New Haven: Yale University Press, 1981).

[21] See Charles O. Hucker, *The Censorial System of Ming China* (Stanford:
Stanford University Press, 1966), pp. 42–45; L. C. Goodrich and C. Y. Fang, eds.,
Dictionary of Ming Biography (New York: Columbia University Press, 1976),
pp. 308–11.

[22] See Ja-Hyun Kim Haboush, "The Education of the Yi Crown Prince: A
Study in Korean Pedagogy," in de Bary and Haboush, eds., *The Rise of Neo-
Confucianism in Korea* (New York: Columbia University Press, 1985).

[23] Thomas A. Metzger, *Escape from Predicament, Neo-Confucianism, and
China's Evolving Political Culture* (New York: Columbia University Press, 1977).

minister could reassure himself that even the Sage, Confucius, had had to struggle on in adverse circumstances, and political frustration was not necessarily a sign of moral failure. The ruler, however, had no one to blame but himself. Though the historical situations are not quite parallel, his "predicament" bears some resemblance to that of the emperor of Japan at the end of World War II, when he was glad to renounce any claims to "divinity," since he found it a rather "uncomfortable" position to be in, as well as an impossible role to fulfill.[24]

Neo-Confucian historians, though, saw more in this situation than simply a test of individual moral wills. Huang Tsung-hsi (1610–95) and Ku Yen-wu (1613–82) wrote searching critiques of the dynastic institutions which placed so many conscientious Confucians in seemingly hopeless predicaments — situations wherein even the most extraordinary heroism and self-sacrifice could do little to overcome the inherent defects in such a flawed system, or cope, as I said at the outset, with the "ungovernability of imperial rule" by supposed sage-rulers. Reassessing the prime Neo-Confucian political dictum that self-cultivation (self-discipline) was the key to the governance of men (*hsiu-chi chih-jen*), Huang, as I pointed out in *The Liberal Tradition in China*, insisted that without the right laws and institutions it was almost impossible for the individual to do right.[25] Only with a proper governmental system could men be properly governed (*Yu chih fa erh hou yu chih jen*). Nor were these wholly exceptional views, expressed only by a few nonconformists. There is much evidence, increasingly being brought to light in recent studies, that such views were indeed shared among seventeenth-century scholars, deeply shaken

[24] As recorded in 1945 by Maeda Tamon, minister of education, who played an important role in drafting the rescript of January 1, 1946, whereby the Showa emperor renounced his divinity.

[25] W. T. de Bary, *The Liberal Tradition in China* (Hong Kong: Chinese University Press, 1983), p. 84.

by the catastrophic consequences of Ming despotism in both its violent excesses and dire deficiencies.[26]

As I conclude this portion of my discussion, we still face in seventeenth-century China the same tension we started with between Confucian ideals and Chinese imperial rule. This may well leave one with the strong impression of a standoff between the two. Without trying to reverse that impression, I would at this point only caution against viewing the "standoff" as a complete stalemate. Western history exhibits more motion, development, and seeming progress than does Chinese, but if we are truly concerned to get a new perspective on human value issues, on a global scale and in their full depth and complexity, we must also learn to look at them with Chinese eyes, and with something of the patience and longanimity of the Chinese. It is with this thought that I propose to extend the discussion into the nineteenth century, when the seemingly static tensions we have observed so far are forced into direct and explosive confrontation with the expansive drives of the West.

II. AUTOCRACY AND THE PROPHETIC ROLE IN ORTHODOX NEO-CONFUCIANISM

In *The Liberal Tradition in China* I chose to start, not deductively from a preconceived Western definition of liberalism, but inductively from examples in Sung and Ming Neo-Confucianism that might reasonably be thought "liberal" by ordinary understandings of the term. Together, for me they represented a distinctive Chinese phenomenon, expressed in Chinese terms and to be understood in a Chinese context — by no means the exact equivalent of modern Western "liberalism." On this basis various forms of "liberal" criticism or protest in China might be defined positively, in terms of the ideal standards they tried to uphold,

---

[26] Lynn Struve, "Huang Zongxi in Context," *Journal of Asian Studies* 47, no. 3 (August 1988).

but also negatively, by what they opposed. Thus Chinese liberalism was conditioned significantly by Chinese despotism, as it was also delimited by it. Acts of heroic protest, such as, for instance, Fang Hsiao-ju's self-sacrifice in resisting the usurpation and oppression of Ming Ch'eng-tsu (the Yung-lo emperor, 1403–24) or Hai Jui's excoriation of Ming Shih-tsung's incompetence and corruption in the Chia-ching (1522–66) period, would not have been evoked had not the consciences of these Confucian ministers first been aroused and then put to the ultimate test by their rulers. For Confucius, self-sacrifice was nothing to be sought after; endurance and survival were preferable to martyrdom (*Analects* 15:7). Thus, had it not been for Chinese despots, who first called forth the noble man and then tried to silence him, there would have been few Confucian martyrs.

But if autocracy in China both bred and stunted its own kind of liberal protest, it is noteworthy that these critics, prophets, and martyrs mostly came from among the Confucians — and in the cases just cited, specifically from the ranks of orthodox Neo-Confucians — not from among Buddhists or Taoists. The latter were, as we say, out of it, not engaged in the kind of struggle religion waged against Caesar in the West. In this respect Confucianism — not a teaching usually considered "religious" — performed the critical function Max Weber assigned to religion as the effective bearer of commanding, transcendental values in vital tension with the world, while Buddhism and Taoism, normally considered "religions," rarely did so.

Robert Bellah once said, "Every religion tries to remake the world in its own image, but is always to some extent remade in the image of the world." [27] This is true of Confucianism, Taoism, and Buddhism as well, but how they are remade reflects also the extent to which, and the manner in which, they themselves actually

[27] Robert Bellah, *Tokugawa Religion: The Values of Pre-Industrial Japan* (Glencoe, Ill.: Free Press, 1957), pp. 196–97.

try to remake the world. In the case we have here it is a question whether they even *tried* in the way Confucianism did.

No doubt some readers, recalling certain messianic movements and peasant rebellions in China, often of Buddhist or Taoist inspiration, will ask if these religions did not represent some revolutionary potential. Professor Eisenstadt, for his part, would explain these movements as failing in political effectiveness or transformative power mainly on account of extrinsic factors — the ability of the state to deny them any purchase on central ground, to hold them off and contain them at the periphery of power. Thus marginalized, they could exert no leverage on the political world.[28]

However this may be, it is also true that the state rarely had to contend with more than an ephemeral challenge from these religions, inasmuch as they failed to generate any systematic political doctrine, ideology of power, or set of principles on which to ground an organizational ethos. For them the failure to mount a serious challenge at the center was more a matter of default than of actual defeat or containment. In the West Stalin is said to have dismissed Roman Catholicism as a force to be reckoned with by asking, "How many divisions has the Pope?" In China, Buddhist and Taoist messianism, even though capable of rousing rebellions, could be discounted as viable political forces by asking the opposite question, Where is their alternative to the civil service?

If, then, we see both the imperial bureaucratic tradition and its liberal critics in Ming China as somehow joined in association with Neo-Confucianism, what later became of this uneasy combination and troubled union? Did Confucian scholars cease to offer a challenge to the state in the succeeding Manchu dynasty? Did the prophetic function lapse with the rise of a new and more efficient autocracy? Was Neo-Confucian orthodoxy, as reaffirmed by the Ch'ing, somehow decontaminated, rendered sterile of such self-criticism and protest? And if this vital challenge were miss-

[28] Eisenstadt, *This Worldly Transcendentalism*, pp. 55–57, 66–70.

ing, without it did Chinese civilization find its further growth stalemated, lacking the stimulus of prophecy and the goad of criticism? Did China, for want of such, develop an inertia or fall into a torpor from which it could only be roused by the more dynamic, transformative power of the West?

In at least partial answer to these questions, I should like here to offer two examples, drawn from the heart of Neo-Confucian orthodoxy, which demonstrate that the essential tension between ideal and reality was sustained, and that, at least in the realm of ideas, there remained the possibility of a radical critique of the established order being generated from within the tradition, drawing on the same concepts, transcendent values, and prophetic utterances as in the past. Moreover both of the scholars I shall cite, though largely neglected in histories of Ch'ing thought, were recognized in their own time as leading spokesmen for Neo-Confucian orthodoxy, not just minor exceptions or dissidents without real influence. The failure of recent scholarship to take them into account when theorizing about Neo-Confucianism shows how the modern mentality can wear blinders at least as narrowing as those of the supposedly blind orthodoxies of the past.

Lü Liu-liang as an Orthodox Neo-Confucian Radical

In the early years of this century Lü Liu-liang (1629–83) was known primarily as a Ming loyalist who refused to serve the Manchus and yet was also a leader in the revival of Chu Hsi's teachings in the early Ch'ing period. There was nothing implausible about this combination of Neo-Confucian orthodoxy and dynastic loyalty, but in the revolutionary ferment at the end of the Ch'ing period it is understandable that Lü's anti-Manchu sentiments would have attracted more attention than his Neo-Confucian convictions. The latter, however, included radical political ideas akin to those of his better-known contemporary Huang Tsung-hsi (1610–95).

Lü's views, parallel to Huang's at many points, are embedded
in his recorded dialogues and commentaries on the Four Books,
widely circulated in his own day on account of their usefulness to
examination candidates, but later suppressed by the Yung-cheng
emperor as a consequence of the Tseng Ching case (1728). What
is particularly intriguing about Lü is that he had resigned as an
official stipendiary, refusing to serve under the Manchus, but made
a living writing, printing, and selling model examination essays,
along with his commentaries. In this way Lü took advantage of
the very system he repudiated in order to reach an audience whose
political ambitions and utilitarian motives would lead them to
study him. There, embedded in his commentaries on the Four
Books (the *Great Learning*, *Mean*, the *Analects*, and *Mencius*),
one finds his radical political views.

Like many of his Sung predecessors, Lü was a "restorationist"
who tended to reject existing dynastic institutions as flawed and
corrupt in comparison to those of high antiquity. Hence not only
was his stance far from conservative of the status quo, it was no
less than radical in its attack on the established order: for example, on the dynastic system, hereditary monarchy, the state
bureaucracy, the corruption of ministership, the land and tax system, the lack of a universal school system, laws that violate basic
principles rooted in human nature, and a failure to encourage the
people's participation in government.

Time does not suffice for me to elaborate on this summation
of Lü's critique of dynastic rule, but as a historical postscript I
should like to note that about midway through the Yung-cheng
reign, in 1728–29, a revolt broke out against the dynasty. Though
the rebellion was quickly put down, its leader, the aforementioned
Tseng Ching, confessed to having been inspired by the antidynastic
views of Lü Liu-liang. The fact that Lü had been a major influence
on Lu Lung-ch'i (1630–93), himself revered as a beacon of strict
Chu Hsi orthodoxy in the early Ch'ing, did not mitigate the
offense. At this juncture the emperor had Lü Liu-liang punished

posthumously and with a vindictive thoroughness. His remains were dug up and exposed to desecration, his family survivors punished, his writings proscribed, and numerous favorable references to him in the works of Lu Lung-ch'i expurgated.[29]

FANG TUNG-SHU, A PROPHETIC VOICE IN THE EARLY MODERN AGE

During the early Ch'ing period, thanks to the efforts of Lü Liu-liang and Lu Lung-ch'i, the Ch'eng-Chu teaching emerged as something more than just an examination orthodoxy; it grew into an active intellectual force both in and out of court. Meanwhile alongside it a new movement developed, the so-called Han learning, or school of evidential research, which rode the same wave of conservative reaction against alleged Ming subjectivism and libertarianism, but also drew from both Ch'eng-Chu and Wang Yangming schools new developments in critical historical and textual scholarship. These enabled the Han learning increasingly to assert its own independence, at which point, as the new learning came to stand side by side with the established orthodoxy, an uneasy coexistence ensued. The latter remained well established in education and the examination system, while the influence of the new criticism was exerted mainly in the field of advanced scholarly research. In both of these spheres the developing contest between them cut across official and nonofficial lines.

Intellectually speaking, the influence of the school of evidential research had, by the eighteenth century, become so dominant that Liang Ch'i-ch'ao, in his *Intellectual Trends in the Ch'ing Period* (*Ch'ing-tai hsüeh-shu kai-lun*), would later describe this Han learning, which "carried on empirical research for the sake of empirical research and studied classics for the sake of classics,"

[29] Wm. Theodore de Bary, *East Asian Civilizations: A Dialogue in Five Stages* (Cambridge: Harvard University Press, 1988), pp. 65–66.

as the "orthodox school." [30] This may be too simple a characterization of the evidential learning, but Liang's reference to it as the
"orthodox school" is symptomatic. That there could be such a
new intellectual "orthodoxy" coexisting with an older Ch'eng-Chu
orthodoxy in education, as if in some symbiotic relationship, tells
us that even the mature Confucian tradition was far from simple
and fixed but generated contending forces on more than one level
at a time.

Toward the end of the Ch'ing period, however, the Han learning had long been entrenched in scholarly circles, as well as among
their patrons in high Ch'ing officialdom, and in the early nineteenth century a powerful challenge came from the rear guard of
Ch'eng-Chu orthodoxy in the writings of Fang Tung-shu (1772–
1851). A sharp controversialist himself, Fang has also been seen
as a highly controversial figure by intellectual historians, recognized as perhaps the most articulate spokesman for the Ch'eng-
Chu school in his time. Liang Ch'i-ch'ao said of Fang's treatise
Reckoning with the Han Learning (*Han-hsüeh shang-tui*) (1824)
that "its courage in opposing [the 'orthodox' school] made it a
kind of revolutionary work." [31] Other modern writers like Hu
Shih, by contrast, have seen Fang as leading a last reactionary out-
burst against the Han learning on behalf of the decadent remnants
of Neo-Confucianism, defending their sacred textual ground
against the higher criticism.[32]

Fang came from a family of scholars identified with the T'ung-
ch'eng school, which had attempted to revive the prose style and
thought of the neoclassical movement in the Sung dynasty, represented in literature by Ou-yang Hsiu (1007–72) and in philosophy
by Chu Hsi. Fang had little success in rising through the examination system and spent most of his life as an impecunious tutor in

[30] Trans. Immanuel Hsü (Cambridge: Harvard University Press, 1959), p. 23.
[31] Liang, *Intellectual Trends*, p. 78.
[32] Hu Shih, *Tai Tung-yuan ti che-hsüeh* (Peking: Jen-jen wen-k'u 1926),
p. 175.

private homes, lecturer in local academies, and scholarly aide to high officials. If this suggests an insecure, marginal existence on the edge of the literocratic elite, such a dependent condition, economically speaking, in no way inhibited Fang's independence as a scholar and thinker. His outspoken views commanded attention, if not always assent. Fearless in challenging eminent scholars and high officials alike, he faulted the former for their scholarly errors and philosophical bankruptcy, the latter for the inadequacies of China's foreign policy and national defense.

One of the most frequent targets of Fang's criticism, Juan Yüan (1764–1849), was a highly respected scholar of the Han learning, senior official, and governor-general of Kuangtung and Kwangsi, whose policies Fang openly censured even while his livelihood as a scholar depended on Juan's patronage of a major scholarly project in 1821–22. That Fang could speak so boldly, despite his low status, is an indication of the high regard in which his scholarship and opinions were held. Indeed the breadth and depth of his scholarship were most impressive. Contrary to the view of earlier twentieth-century scholars that the T'ung-ch'eng school was characterized by a "bigotry . . . which limited [the school] to the study of Chu Hsi's commentaries and to the prose-writing of a few men, branding other types of literature as harmful to the mind," [33] Fang's learning actually stands as testimony to the Chu Hsi school's pursuit of "broad learning." This extended to the in-depth study of all the major schools of Chinese thought, including Buddhism, Taoism, and — even more rare — some ventures into Japanese *kangaku* scholarship. While the same might equally be said of an eclectic scholar-dilettante, Fang's

---

[33] So characterized in Fang Chao-ying's biography of Fang Pao in A. W. Hummel, ed., *Eminent Chinese of the Ch'ing Period* (Washington, D.C.: Library of Congress, 1943), 1:237. Fang Chao-ying was himself an excellent historian, and it was no particular prejudice of his but rather the common assumption of his "emancipated" generation that he gave vent to in such an opinion.

seriousness as a scholar is attested by the notably analytic and penetrating critiques he made of other thinkers and schools.[34]

Fang is best known, however, for his *Reckoning with the Han Learning*,[35] which features a detailed list of charges against scholars of the evidential research movement, giving point-by-point rebuttals.

A major theme of the *Reckoning* is the continuing debate over the Han learning's primary concern with evidential research in historical linguistics and text criticism, on the one hand, and the primacy of moral principles among orthodox Neo-Confucians, on the other.[36] Fang's objection to the former is on grounds of priority, not principle. Philology and phonology have for him a genuine instrumental value but, however sophisticated in technique, still no more than that. They are among the language skills which, according to the classical definition, had been treated as "elementary learning" (*hsiao-hsüeh*) preparatory to the higher studies discussed in the *Great Learning*. Indeed, by Fang's time *hsiao-hsüeh* had come to have the secondary meaning of "philology." Yet from his point of view the top priority given to philology by the Han learning has stood things on their head. Scholarly specialization has taken to the solving of philological puzzles and antiquarian conundrums rather than to dealing with the larger human issues of self-cultivation, order in the family, disorder in the state, and peace in the world — all involving moral principles and thus, for Fang, the moral mind.[37] Fang pays special tribute

[34] As shown, for instance, in Fang's extensive critique of Huang Tsung-hsi's *Nan-lei wen-ting* (*T'ung-ch'eng Fang Chih-chih hsien-sheng ch'üan-chi*, Kuang-hsü ed., fasc. 42) or his discussion of Buddhism in *Hsiang-kuo wei-yen* (fasc. 34, 35, 36), as well as in the *Han hsüeh shang-tui* itself.

[35] Fang Tung-shu, *Han-hsüeh shang-tui*, Che-chiang shu-chu ed., 1840 (hereafter abbreviated *Shang-tui*).

[36] Fang underscores this in his preface to the *Shang-tui*, 1b. As a major issue in Ch'ing thought, the subject is more fully dealt with in Benjamin Elman, *From Philosophy to Philology: Intellectual and Social Aspects of Change in Late Imperial China* (Cambridge: Harvard University Press, 1984).

[37] As excerpted in *Shushigaku taikei* (Tokyo: Meitoku shuppansha, 1974), 11:427a (291).

to his forebear Fang Pao (1668–1749), an early leader of the T'ung-ch'eng school, who had evoked the reformist spirit of the northern Sung scholars with their primary concern for the larger meaning (*ta-i*) or general sense of the classics.[38] In this there is a notable resemblance also to Lü Liu-liang.

Fang too has his own prophetic warning and message to convey. This involves an aspect of his thought much discussed in the final chapter of his *Reckoning*, but rarely noted if at all by modern writers: the importance to him of human discourse and open discussion (*chiang-hsüeh*) as means of advancing the Way. *Chiang-hsüeh* had often been translated as "lecturing," and it may be that in later times *chiang-hsüeh* had become so routine as to approximate mere lecturing. But there is another term *chiang-i* (*kōgi* in Japanese) more often used for formal lectures in both Chu Hsi's time and Fang's, and Chu himself made some distinction between the two. As it was understood among Neo-Confucians and by early historians of Neo-Confucianism, *chiang-hsüeh* had the clear implication of dialogue, group discussion, and even something approximating our "public discussion."[39] "Public" might be misleading if it conjured up a picture of modern publicists at work, a substantial Fourth Estate, or the availability of media for wide communication that would contribute to the formation of "public opinion" in the current idiom. Such agencies did not exist in Sung and Ming China. The implicit original context is one of discussion among scholars, or in any case among a comparatively limited, literate social stratum, as well as one of debates largely carried on in schools and academies.

Especially significant in the Ch'ing context, and against the background of the Ch'ing scholarly establishment, is Fang's insistence on the role of schools and academies as centers of discussion

---

[38] *Ch'üan-chi, K'ao-p'an chi*, 4:32b–33b, "Fang Wang-chi hsien-sheng nien-p'u hsü."

[39] So noted in the original editions of standard dictionaries such as *Tz'u-hai* and *Tz'u-yüan*.

and debate. Earlier, Huang Tsung-hsi, in his *Plan for the Prince*
(*Ming-i tai-fang lu*) had made the same point, only to have it
largely ignored through the long Ch'ing dominance — and also,
we may be reminded, the dominance of the Ch'ing "orthodoxy"
which Liang Ch'i-ch'ao had identified with the school of evidential research.

Fang, however, had his own experience of this kind of academic research as a scholar attached to major scholarly projects
at leading academies in the Canton area, including the Hsüeh-hai
t'ang Academy, center for the production of the monumental com-
pendium of Ch'ing commentaries and treatises on the classics, the
Huang Ch'ing ching-chieh in 1,400 *chüan* and 366 volumes, under
the patronage and direction of the governor-general Juan Yüan.
Whether Fang was aware of it or not, support for this academy
and its projects more than likely came in part from profits of the
opium trade and official collusion in it.[40] Nor was this something
Fang needed to know in order to feel keenly, as he did, that the
kind of classical scholarship conducted there, though respectable
enough in its own way, fell far short of meeting the academies'
responsibility for speaking out against dire evils like the opium
trade and the threat of encroaching foreign military power.[41] To
do this they would have to concern themselves with principles, not
just facts.

THE PROPHET AND THE PEOPLE

From this brief exposition of Fang's views it should be clear
that, as of the mid-nineteenth century, the Confucian tradition
of criticism and protest had not lapsed, even though some of its
sharpest and most cogent expressions had been effectively suppressed or contained, as was the case with Huang Tsung-hsi's

---

[40] See Hamaguchi Fujio, "Hō Tō-shu, no kangaku hihan ni tsuite," in *Nihon
Chūgoku gakkaihō* 30 (1978): 175a, citing the studies of Ōkubo Hideko in *Min-
shin jidai shoin no kenkyū* (Tokyo: Kokusho kankō kai, 1976), p. 337.

[41] The point is discussed in Hamaguchi, "Hō Tō-shu," pp. 170a–72b and
Elman, *From Philosophy*, pp. 242–45.

Ming-i tai-fang lu and most of the writings of Lü Liu-liang. It is significant too that this line of protest, rather than emerging from the supposedly heterodox teachings of Buddhism and Taoism, peripheral to the power structure, came out of the core of the "Great Tradition," from scholars known as prime spokesmen for Confucian orthodoxy, or from the main line of Confucian scholarship.

But if indeed this represents a still vital, self-critical Confucian tradition, one naturally asks why its capacity for self-renewal did not operate to greater effect, or show more transformative power, in enabling China to meet the challenges of the nineteenth and twentieth centuries? A full answer to these questions obviously lies beyond the reach of these lectures, but having ventured earlier to *compare* examples of such Confucian protest to the prophets of the West, I should like at this juncture to suggest a contrast with the West in how the prophet relates to "the people," as distinct from "a people." This applies also to "public" service, in the sense of meeting a common need or shared interest, in contradistinction to serving "a public," understood as a body of people actively engaged or effectively represented in public affairs. The point here is whether the question of transformative power can be understood solely in relation to the ideas and ideals propounded by prophets and carried by traditional elites, or in terms of the tension between the transcendent and the mundane, without also considering how "prophets" relate to "people" or "a public."

If I make such a distinction more particularly in respect to the "troubles" Confucianism got itself into, I reiterate that "trouble" here implies no general judgment of a kind so easily and widely reached, both in East and West, concerning the "modern failure" of either China or Confucianism. My intention is simply to address the critical questions Confucians have asked themselves, or would acknowledge as fair and relevant in view of their own avowed aims and historical projects.

The most central of these questions, I would say, pertains to the Confucians' roles as officials, scholars, and teachers. While Confucius had said that learning should be for the sake of one's true self-understanding and self-development, rather than to gain others' approval, it was still the social dimension of this self and its engagement in public life that most distinguished the Confucian's conception of self from that of other traditions. From the beginning, Confucians had accepted a responsibility for the counseling of rulers and the training of men for social and political leadership, as expressed in the ideal of the noble man. From the start too they considered learning and scholarship to be indispensable to the performance of these functions.

It is no less true that their view of learning underwent change over time, as the Confucians responded to new challenges. Expansive periods of intellectual and philosophical growth alternated with phases of retrenchment in which fundamentalist instincts demanded a regrounding of the tradition, as if to keep scholarly inquiry from straying too far from its moral and social base, or, at the opposite extreme, moral zeal from blinding itself to facts. Thus the greatest Confucian minds have managed something of a balance between loyalty to core values and the continued pursuit of "broad learning" through scholarly investigation. Nathan Sivin reminds me that the intensely orthodox Lü Liu-liang had a strong interest in Western science and contributed significantly to medical learning. Likewise, Fang Tung-shu, while complaining of a philology pursued at the expense of moral philosophy, accepted philology and text criticism as necessary branches of learning and himself spoke of "pursuing truth through facts."

One can of course ask whether this pursuit of truth, as conceived in Confucian humanistic terms, would ever lead to the kinds of speculation being advanced in the West during the eighteenth and nineteenth centuries. Jerome Grieder, in his review of Benjamin Elman's *From Philosophy to Philology*, asked why Ch'ing evidential scholarship, though methodologically innovative, remained "epistemologically sterile." " 'Why no Newton in China?' " he says, "has become almost a dismissive cliché. Should we not be asking instead (or as well) 'Why no Kant?' " [42]

That kind of question, if fairly and fully explored, would lead us off into the kinds of trouble the West got into, while I must stick here to the troubles Confucians faced — questions such as Fang Tung-shu left us with at the end of his *Reckoning with the Han Learning.* The trouble with China, as he saw it, in the mid-nineteenth century, was its failure to sustain the kind of discussion and consultation he considered vital to the promotion of the common welfare. If then, as he claims, the sage-kings, Confucius, Mencius, and all the great Confucians had urged the indispensability of such learning by discussion (or discussion of learning) to the political process; if, moreover, it had already been a distinguishing mark of the Confucians, according to Li Ssu in the third century B.C., that they "talked together about the Odes and Documents" as a way of invoking the past to criticize the present; and if, further, generations of Neo-Confucians, following the Ch'eng brothers and Chu Hsi, had insisted on self-criticism and open discussion of political means and ends, then how is it that, in Fang's own estimation, so little had come of this by the late Ch'ing period?

In the early and middle twentieth century this question went unaddressed by most modern scholars, no doubt on the widespread but mistaken assumption that the fault lay with the Confucians for their elitism — their unwillingness to share literacy and learning with the masses, and their alleged tendency to reserve education to the upper classes. This, the prevalent theory went, prevented the great majority of Chinese from any significant participation in public affairs. There is some truth in this idea but it fails to credit the actual intention of the Confucians to do quite otherwise — to share learning as widely as possible with the

[42] *Journal of Asian Studies* 46, no. 2 (May 1987): 390.

people. I have touched on this problem in my Ch'ien Mu Lectures at the Chinese University of Hong Kong, again in my Reischauer Lectures at Harvard University, and yet again in a book entitled *Neo-Confucian Education* now in the process of publication by the University of California Press. If I reopen it here, it is in recognition of the Confucians' own sense that, ironically considering the great value they attached to education, the results had to be seen as a real disappointment.

Nowhere is this more evident than in the Confucians' lack of success in public education. Neo-Confucians regularly bewailed the failure to achieve the universal school system advocated by Chu Hsi, following other proponents of this idea earlier in the Sung dynasty. Yet if everyone endorsed this proposal, still the repeated exhortations of scholars and recurrent edicts of rulers accomplished little. Even in the schools that did get built, as Chang Po-hsing, champion of Chu Hsi orthodoxy in the high Ch'ing, complained, education was too much oriented to the civil service examination and failed to achieve Chu Hsi's liberal, humanistic aim that education should serve the moral renewal and cultural uplift of the people as a whole, that is, that it should serve broader, more fundamental, purposes than simply bureaucratic recruitment.[43]

One could explain this to a degree by pointing to certain basic facts of life in China. As an agrarian society, with a dense population depending upon intensive agriculture, its farming families felt strong economic pressures to keep the young and able-bodied laboring in the fields rather than release them from work for study in school. Throughout the land, even the poorest peasants may have prayed for their offspring to be so well endowed with scholarly talents that they might succeed in the examinations, but as a practical matter few would be able to fulfill such an ambition. Moreover, the imperial bureaucracy, though dominating most

---

[43] Chang Po-hsing, *Cheng-i t'ang ch'üan-shu*, Fu-chou cheng-i hsüeh-yüan ed., 1868, 1:1, personal preface to the *Ch'eng-shih jih-ch'eng*.

areas of national life, was not sizable enough and possessed of enough offices to absorb large numbers of candidates, however eager and promising they might appear to be. Lacking too was any substantial middle class that could provide alternative careers or could support, with their surplus wealth and leisure, cultural pursuits or institutions substantially independent of the literocracy and the official establishment (or at least sufficiently so as to constitute attractive, alternative paths of educational advancement).

A similar situation existed with respect to what in the West would be called the church. Religious organizations in China were fragmented and offered no institutional base for schools, colleges, or universities such as the church supported in the West. Religious vocations there were, but these led in radically different directions from secular education. Training for the religious life was commonly understood to demand disengagement from established society and culture, though not of course from the people's worldly sufferings or their persistent religious aspirations.

The resulting pattern then, was marked by ironies and paradox, with a dominant Confucian tradition that exalted learning and insisted on its wide diffusion as the sine qua non of a viable political and social order, yet found itself incapable of realizing its educational aims except on the basic level of the family or in the higher but much more restricted sphere of the ruling elite. In contrast to this stood a welter of clan cults and native or hybrid popular faiths, answering to the religious needs of the common people but participating hardly at all in government, secular learning, or practical education. Thus, among the peasant masses religion remained as out of touch with the higher learning and with rational discourse on public issues as the Confucians were removed from the dynamics of religious faith in the "hearts and minds of the people."

In this situation the Confucians could be seen as constituting a political and cultural elite, not by any intention of theirs, but rather by virtue of their heavy involvement in the mandarinate as well as their engagement in a high level of scholarly erudition, distinguished for its critical rationality and literary sophistication but mostly beyond the reach of minimally educated masses. Confucius had wanted all men to be brothers; Mencius had taught that any government would fail if it did not see to the education of its people; and Chu Hsi had insisted on the renewal of the people through education as fundamental to all governance, yet in the end, in the final days of late imperial China, this noble ambition proved impossible for Confucius to achieve.

In *East Asian Civilizations* I have pointed to the growing realization on the part of late-nineteenth-century reformers like K'ang Yu-wei and Liang Ch'i-ch'ao that the failure in education had been a crucial factor in China's inability to mobilize its human resources against the challenge of the West and Japan. Some of these same reformers, as well as conservative critics of reform, agreed that the obvious lack of a unified national consciousness betrayed a failure of leadership to reach the "hearts and minds" of the people. Some contrasted this perceived weakness of China to the power of nationalism in Japan and the West, and some saw the latters' power to mobilize peoples' energies as further linked to the religious dynamism of Shinto and Christianity — whence K'ang Yu-wei's belated and futile attempt to recast Confucianism as a state religion, in the erroneous belief (of a kind to which mandarins were so prone) that a state religion could serve just as well as a popular or mass religion.

It is perhaps significant too that many of these reformers, in both Japan and China in the nineteenth century, saw this crisis as prefigured, philosophically speaking, by the split in Neo-Confucian ranks between Wang Yang-ming and the Chu Hsi school — between Wang's emphasis on the moral and spiritual springs of human action, on the one hand, and the careful balance Chu Hsi had maintained between the moral and rational, affective and intellective, faculties. One could perhaps argue that such a reconciliation was not inherently implausible, as witness the successful blending of Confucian scholarship, feudal loyalties, and Shinto religious beliefs in later Tokugawa and early Meiji Japan. In the conditions of Ch'ing China, however, this was not so practicable or so easily accomplished. Whether one sees Confucianism as represented by the mandarinate and its civil service mentality or by the alternative scholarly "orthodoxy" Liang Ch'i-ch'ao identified with the evidential research (*k'ao-cheng*) movement in classical studies, one can see that in the given circumstances it had proven difficult for Confucians to fulfill all that their own legacy demanded of them.

In classical, humanistic learning Ch'ing scholars, arguably, lived up to Chu Hsi's high standards of critical scholarship. Even in terms of human governance one might allow(notwithstanding the severe negative judgments of a Huang Tsung-hsi, Lü Liu-lang, or Fang Tung-shu), that the Ch'ing record up to 1800 in managing the affairs of so large a country and so massive a population was probably unmatched by any other regime in history. Yet for all this the Confucians fell well short of fulfilling their primitive and perennial vision of achieving Heaven on earth through the rule of sage-kings guided by noble men.

This was, of course, a vision of the noble man as prophet, and the failure of the Confucians to achieve it, while no greater than that of any other major world tradition fully to realize its ideals, reminds us again of the original limitations and qualifications of the prophetic office as exercised by the noble man. These had to do with his specific and distinctive commitment to public service (government and education) in ways not typically associated with prophets in the Semitic religions. But it also involved a significant difference between the Confucian concept of Heaven and its mandate and the more intensely theistic conception in the Judeo-Christian tradition of a personal god dealing with his human creation both as persons and as a "people." For the Confucians "the people" were indeed Heaven's creation, and Heaven presided over their fate and fortune in a way expressed by the mandate of

Heaven, with the ruler as the crucial intermediary or surrogate — the "Son of Heaven," who alone offered sacrifice at the temple of Heaven. As our Neo-Confucians Lü Liu-liang and Fang Tung-shu interpreted this, it was the people who spoke for Heaven and the noble man who spoke to the ruler, but still not Heaven which spoke directly to its people in the way God spoke through Moses, Isaiah, and Jeremiah to *"His* people," the people with whom He had made a personal contract and covenant. In the language of Jeremiah (31:31):

> The days are coming, says the Lord, when I will make a new covenant with the house of Israel and the house of Judah. It will not be like the covenant I made with their fathers the day I took them by the hand to lead them forth from the land of Egypt; for they broke my covenant and I had to show myself their master, says the Lord. But this is the covenant I will make with the house of Israel in those days, says the Lord. I will place the law within them and write it upon their hearts. I will be their God and they shall be my people.

In Confucianism, though Heaven's imperative (or decree) is, as human nature,[44] likewise "placed within them and written upon their hearts," the people remain subject to the ruler by Heaven's mandate. It is, then, the ruler who leads the people (not God leading them "by his own hand"), while the "people" are seen as commoners *(min)* — the vast undifferentiated mass who serve the ruler and in turn are meant to be served by him. For his part the noble man, in his prophetic role, could be a warner to the ruler, reminding him of his obligation to provide for the public welfare, but as one committed to public service, as a member of the ruling class, the noble man ministered to the ruler and, ideally, acted as his colleague and mentor. His function was to warn the emperor but not, it seems, like Moses and Jeremiah, ever to warn or scold the people, as if they too were active and responsible par-

---

[44] See the *Mean*, chap. 1, or Chu Hsi, *Chung-yung chang-chü* 1, for Heaven's imperative as manifested in human nature.

ticipants in the fulfilling of a covenant. When and how, in China
were the people to become involved, as if they too were answerable to God for their part in fulfilling the covenant? When and
how, as "his people" carrying out his commandments, were the
Chinese people to come together in organized congregations,
assemblies, and churches, with their own leaders, priests and ministers, to do the will of God? No, the Confucians were ministers
to the ruler, not to a "people," themselves answerable to Heaven.

What could be at issue here is the sense in which we understand the word "public" in these different contexts, and how this
understanding conditions or qualifies the role of the prophet. In
classical Confucianism, Mencius, the spokesman par excellence
for the noble man, underscored the fundamental importance of
the "people" (*min*) in politics, but the people seen primarily as
deserving of leadership responsive to their needs, and only in the
extreme case with rulers responsible to them by virtue of the
people's reserved "right of revolution." Mencius also distinguished between an educated ruling class serving the interests
of the "people," and the larger mass of those who worked with
their hands and lacked the education and training needed for them
to take an active part in government, except when things got bad
enough for the people to revolt (*Mencius* 3A:4). In making this
distinction Mencius foreswore none of his meritocratic, egalitarian
principles in favor of a social or political elitism, but only reflected
a functional differentiation between leaders and commoners already well established by his time and not even to be effectively
overturned by modern Maoists, with all their commitment to a
classless society.[45]

---

[45] Even the social leveler Mo Tzu affirmed the need for such a functional
dichotomy: "[Heaven] desires that among men those who have strength will work
for others, those who understand the Way will teach others, and those who possess
wealth will share it with others. . . . It also desires that those above will diligently
attend to matters of government, and those below will diligently carry out their
tasks" (*Basic Works of Mo Tzu*, trans. Burton Watson [New York: Columbia University Press, 1963]), p. 85.

For their part the Neo-Confucians, advocates of universal education in furtherance of the peoples' welfare, promoted popular education primarily through self-cultivation and disciplined self-governance (*hsiu-chi chih jen*) in the context of family life and the local community, leaving a considerable gulf between learning on this level and the higher forms of scholarship or of the expertise required in the civil servant. In the absence then of any significant infrastructure between family and local community on the lower level, and the political and cultural organizations of the educated elite on the higher level, there were few channels that could serve as organs of "public opinion" to communicate between the two or support the noble man at court in his service of the public interest.

No doubt this oversimplified model of China's political structure and process will invite challenge from those who can think readily of the infrastructure represented by local and regional organizations of an economic, social, and religious character, which at times played a significant part in Chinese life. The question is, however, whether these were able to perform any role in the political process — that is, address themselves to and carry on a sustained discourse concerning issues of the larger, public interest — to such an extent that either mandarins or scholars would think of the "people" as in any sense an active, corporate body, able effectively to support a sustained political program. More especially it would be a question whether such a program was reformist or radical enough to achieve the transformation of the established order (presumably, in the view of Max Weber and Karl Jaspers, the mission of prophets).

To me it is striking that our Neo-Confucian scholars, handicapped in performing their "prophetic" office by the lack of organized support among an articulate citizenry or from organs of public opinion, all too often stood alone in facing the power concentrated in the ruler, or in coping with the Byzantine workings or factional infighting of the imperial bureaucracy. The more con-

scientious of them could easily become martyrs, or more often
political dreamers, but rarely successful statesmen achieving noble
goals. Thus, for Confucians as scholars in the late Ch'ing, it was
natural enough to look to the schools and academies (the way
Fang Tung-shu did) as the only likely sources of informed support
and for nineteenth-century reformers to turn to scholarly circles
when, moved perhaps by Fang Tung-shu's line of argument, they
wished to mobilize public opinion through what was called *ching-i*
(disinterested discussion). Yet the term "public" discussion could
be applied to this advocacy only in the sense of what was in the
common interest, conforming to Heaven's universal principles, not
in the Western sense of a "public" as a "people."

Still, as Fang Tung-shu himself complained, the schools and
academies had long since ceased to serve as centers of public discussion, as they had formerly in the middle and late years of the
Ming dynasty. And if, among religious or fraternal organizations,
one still might think to turn to secret societies, their very secret
or esoteric character ensured their ineffectuality as organs of public
advocacy.

Thus reform movements at the end of the dynasty lacked any
effective political base. Out of touch with the masses, unsupported
by any party that could claim to be "popular" (i.e., more than a
faction), reformers were prophets without a people. Sun Yat-sen
recognized this when he spoke of the Chinese as a "heap of loose
sand" and sought, in the first of his "People's Principles," to make
of them a people or nation in the Western sense. To the left of
Sun, socialists and anarchists faced the same problem. Though
their doctrines were predicated on a claim to represent the people
or the proletariat, in fact, as Bertrand Russell noted in 1921, this
remained, in the absence of any organization of people or workers,
purely theoretical.[46] The collapse of the monarchy in 1911 had
not altered this age-old condition.

[46] Bertrand Russell, *The Problem of China* (London: Allen & Unwin, 1922),
pp. 169–70.

Thus, it was left to Mao Tse-tung to "go to the people," mobilize them politically and organize them militarily in pursuit of revolutionary goals. Unfortunately, having learned little from the long and conflicted Confucian experience, and understanding poorly the true depths and persistence of the troubles Confucians had run into, Mao underestimated the magnitude of the problem and made the historically unprecedented attempt, as revolutionary leader, of trying to combine in himself the roles of both prophet and sage-king. In the end, though Mencius's "people" exercised no right of revolution, they turned their backs on Mao and his retinue, leaving him too, like so many of his predecessors, a prophet without a people.

It takes no great expertise or political insight to discern the persistence of the same problem in China today. The current leadership may be somewhat more enlightened and collegial in character than it was under Mao, but the political process has not yet been significantly broadened. Rule by a political elite, justifying itself as a party dictatorship ruling *for* the people, still tends to inhibit and repress the expression of popular opinion. Especially by coming down hard on political activism in the universities, the Communist party has tended to insulate itself from such "public opinion" as might be found there, in the absence of any other forum for open discussion and debate.

Before concluding, since my assignment has been to discuss "some problem in human values," it would not be enough if I showed that the trouble with Confucianism was only a problem for China but not for us, or if I seemed to contrast historical conditions in China to those in the West without acknowledging that we too face many of the same troubles today. True, in the West we do not lack for political advocacy or legal institutions to protect it, but can we say, in the schools and universities of the West today, that they sustain serious political dialogue and rational discussion of major public issues? The University of California at Berkeley and Columbia University, in 1968, became great symbols of political activism, but in my experience, all too often this activism was of a kind that resorted to political pressure — striking, marching, chanting, and sloganizing — and not of a kind that encouraged rational discussion or mutual dialogue. Often, dissenting voices could not be heard because of the threat of disruption or intimidation, while many faculty and students preferred, like the great Ch'ing scholars of evidential research, to go about their own specialized studies, rather than run the political gauntlet awaiting those who would try to participate in civil dialogue on public issues.

On another level, however, these may well be only superficial manifestations of a more deep-seated problem: the difficulty the Confucians had of sustaining their humanism in the midst of an increasingly complex society and culture, which necessitated new technologies if not new sciences, and, as it has turned out in our own day no less than in Ch'ing times, even new and highly refined technologies in the so-called "humanities." Whatever judgment one might make about Confucianism and China's success or failure in science and technology, it will, now and in the future, imply a similar question for us — how do we sustain the core values of a humanistic tradition in the midst of rapid social and technological change? If the Confucians paid a price for their stubborn adherence to a classical tradition, and to a canon enshrined in a difficult classical language, can we not see ourselves facing a similar dilemma in American education as to how such core values — and a core curriculum to communicate them — are to be maintained? Television and modern means of almost instant electronic communication may seem to facilitate mass education, but if we are talking about active learning and participation, can we say that the modern audience is any less passive and inert a "public" than China's peasant masses were, or that even our TV debates do substantially more than register certain personalities on the popular mind, without engendering much serious, substantial, and rational discourse?

No doubt these questions themselves allow of no simple yes or no answer, but they may help to make us aware that the "trouble" with Confucianism, like the trouble with Harry, has not gone away, but remains there — in fact, all over the place — for us and the Chinese to reckon with.

The Varieties of Value

ANTHONY QUINTON

THE TANNER LECTURES ON HUMAN VALUES

Delivered at
The University of Warsaw

May 19, 1988

ANTHONY QUINTON (LORD QUINTON) was born in Kent in 1925. He studied history before serving as a navigator in the Royal Air Force during World War II, and after the war studied philosophy, politics, and economics at Christ Church, Oxford. He became a fellow of All Souls College in 1949 and was a fellow and tutor in philosophy at New College from 1955 to 1978. From 1978 until 1987 he was president of Trinity College, and since 1985 he has been chairman of the British Library. He is a fellow of the British Academy and received an honorary degree from New York University in 1987. His main publications are *The Nature of Things* (1973), *Utilitarian Ethics* (1973), *The Politics of Imperfection* (1978), *Francis Bacon* (1980), and *Thoughts and Thinkers* (1982).

I

My starting point is a strange and remarkable disproportion in the way in which philosophers distribute their attention between the two main parts of their subject. The two parts I have in mind are theoretical philosophy and practical philosophy: the critical study of thought as bearing on knowledge or justified belief and the critical study of thought as bearing upon action. I believe that what I am saying is definitely true, with very few exceptions, of the philosophers of the English-speaking world, and I am inclined to think that it is largely correct as regards European philosophers in general.

The disproportion in question is that, while theoretical philosophy concerns itself with the whole range of thinking that is oriented toward knowledge and belief, practical philosophy concentrates almost exclusively on moral action, action, that is to say, considered from a moral point of view. Individual theoretical philosophers may specialize, but, as a group, they attend with comparable degrees of closeness and thoroughness to perception, memory, our awareness of our own mental states, our beliefs about the mental states of others, and to inference, whether deductive or inductive, including the principles of logic, mathematics, and methodology, whose truth is implied by belief in the validity of inferences.

But, while every kind of thinking that leads to belief not directly related to conduct has had, and continues to receive, serious attention from philosophers, only moral thinking, among the whole broad range of our styles of thinking about action, is positively investigated. All the other kinds of thinking that determine choice and action tend to get lumped indiscriminately together, in a kind of common grave, as if worthy of consideration only for purposes of contrast, as in service to self-interest, inclination, or desire.

Theoretical philosophy takes serious account of all the main institutionally organized interests of the intellect: natural science — physical, biological, and psychological; history; theology; linguistics; social science. Practical philosophy gives detailed, sharply focused attention only to morality.

There are, admittedly, blind spots in theoretical philosophy. But they occupy so small a part of the total possible field that the extremity of the opposite situation in practical philosophy is brought into higher relief by acknowledging them. The most important case is that of the very fitful attention given to the place of testimony or authority in the domain of knowledge or justified belief. Works of theoretical philosophy that aim to be comprehensive so as to serve as textbooks more often than not make no mention of the matter. But most of what each of us claims to believe with justification has been accepted on the authority of someone else, whether in person, as parent or teacher, or in the pages of a book.

It could be argued, however, that this is not too serious an omission, since testimony is inevitably a secondary, derivative source of knowledge. The authority, or his ultimate source, is worth believing only if he established the belief he is communicating for himself, and his clients can, and sometimes should, check his reliability.[1]

But what is left out of the effective scope of practical philosophy, by its preoccupation with morality and its undiscriminating amalgamation of all nonmoral aspects of thinking about action, is the greater part of the total field. Matthew Arnold once made the puzzling remark "conduct is three-fourths of life." I shall not pause to interpret it or to question its confident numerical precision. But, in something of the same spirit, I want to say:

---

[1] Throughout this lecture "he" is to be interpreted as "he or she" and "his" as "his or her" wherever no reference to a specific individual is made.

the greater part of conduct is nonmoral. The great majority of everybody's practical thinking includes no moral considerations whatever. Shall I clean my teeth before or after I have my bath? Shall I choose an apple or a banana from the fruit bowl that is being passed around? Shall I wear my white shirt or the one with the green stripes? Shall I work in the garden or tidy up my desk? When practical problems like these confront us we ordinarily do not consider the question from a moral point of view and that is reasonable, for there is ordinarily nothing in the situation of choice to which moral considerations apply and to which they can attach themselves.

That is not to say that such choices never have a moral aspect. Consistent neglect of personal hygiene is morally objectionable as showing a lack of consideration for others. If the choice at table had been between animal meat and a salad, a vegetarian would see it as a moral issue. Somebody may just have given me a green shirt as a present and will think I do not like it if I do not wear it as soon as an opportunity arises. Perhaps the state of my desk is weighing more heavily on my wife's mind than the leaves lying about the garden. But these are special cases.

Another thing that needs to be acknowledged is that our actions are, in a way, much more systematically interrelated than our beliefs. Much of our action is carried out as a part of some fairly complex program, into which morality may enter. A man hurries to catch a train. Why? To get to work on time. What is the point of that? To avoid sour looks from his immediate superior at his place of work; to avoid prejudicing his chances of promotion; not to leave his two colleagues without help in the grim task of bringing up today's deliveries from the basement. Our beliefs, on the other hand, are comparatively atomic or autonomous. Many of them are worth having even if they are not part of some organized system.

Later on I shall consider whether some explanation can be found for this asymmetry in philosophical investigation of theory and practice. But first I shall go on to illustrate it by looking at some strange views philosophers have been led to adopt; after that I shall distinguish nonmoral values, together with the motives that inspire action directed toward them, and inquire what the significant differences are between them and how they are related to each other; and I shall also argue that their neglectful amalgamation has had bad consequences for the philosophical understanding of morality.

II

The basis of the ordinary, and in my view mistaken, way in which moral and nonmoral values are contrasted is an ancient and, surprisingly, persistent theory about the springs of action. That is, of course, the Platonic doctrine which derives the conclusion that human beings are induced to act either by reason or by desire from the conception of human beings, in their life on earth, at least, as compounds of an immortal mental thing, a soul, and a transient physical thing, a body.

Roughly speaking, the soul is the seat of reason, and the body is the seat of appetite or desire. It is the function of reason to control desire. At a kind of ascetic extremity the demands of the body are wholly transcended, that is, when a human being is engaged in the ideal form of life, completely absorbed in theoretical contemplation. In Plato's version (of which what I have just presented is an exceedingly summary abridgment) this ideal of life is not conspicuously moral in any sense that we should recognize in the modern world. But the incorporation of the fundamental ideas of Platonism into Christian theology led to an identification of reason with the moral aspect of human nature, that is, as a combination of intellect with the will to act in accordance with its dictates, conceived as altogether opposed in character to desire or appetite.

The most influential expression of this point of view in post-medieval philosophy is that of Kant. The human agent, according to him, is the scene of a constant battle between duty and inclination, and duty is something discovered by the only kind of reason which he sees as equipped to arrive at truth, the practical reason.

A familiar difficulty for the doctrine that human action is the outcome of a persistent competition between reason and desire is that it does not account for the power which it assumes that reason has to move us to action. Kant is insistent that the moral motive, which he takes to be the will to do duty for the sake of duty, is not part of the natural, body-bound equipment of human beings. It is purely rational in character. How, then, can it move us to act more than the knowledge that twenty-seven is three to the power of three?

Another difficulty for his kind of dualistic theory of human agency he deals with rather more persuasively. After all, reason, broadly understood as the intellectual or cognitive aspect of human nature, plays an important part in nonmoral activity, and as well, in immoral activity. A great deal of intellectual skill may be exercised in such seemingly morally indifferent activities as playing chess or proving a theorem in mathematics and also in activities that would conventionally be regarded as immoral, such as planning and executing a complex bank fraud or robbery.

For Kant such things are the work of understanding, not reason, *Verstand*, not *Vernunft*. In allowing this he does at least acknowledge that the domain of desire, inclination, or appetite is internally variegated in more ways than by simply being directed onto different objects. Some desires are immediate and more or less instinctive, such as those for food, drink, and sexual partners. Others, for more remote objects, like an elevated position in the world, call for a great deal of planning and calculation and require a lot of knowledge of causal relationships. Besides the imperatives of morality he recognizes that there are counsels of prudence and rules of technical skill. But he maintains an absolute distinction between these as hypothetical imperatives, leading us to act only upon the prompting of desire, from what he sees as the categorical imperatives of moral obligation. When we follow our inclinations, then, our intellects, here called understanding, are in the role of servants to desire. When we do our duty, intellect, here called practical reason, is master.

An earlier eighteenth-century account of the springs of action, that of Bishop Butler, also acknowledges prudence, which with benevolence and conscience it describes as principles, as well as what Butler called particular passions. This set of distinctions makes the useful point that prudence and benevolence are of a second-order character and presuppose other desires — my own in the case of prudence, those of others in the case of benevolence — to supply them with content, since they are aimed at maximizing the satisfaction of those two classes of desire.

But Butler makes no explicit provision for the kind of action to which Kant's rules of skill would lead us. At least that is correct if the most straightforward interpretation is put on the phrase "particular passions." It suggests a sudden, emotionally intense state of mind, demanding immediate expression in action. Much the same is true of the words "desire" and "appetite." One desires an attractive person as a sexual partner; one has an appetite for food. But it would be absurd to speak of an appetite for good health (served by dieting, exercise, and giving up cigarettes), and it would at least be very artificial to describe good health as something one desired.

Now these facts about idiomatic correctness are trivial in themselves. But they bring to notice some questionable implications of the unidiomatic uses. In the first place it suggests that the purposes of human action are generally of a primordial, bodily kind, calling for little or no intellectual effort from those who entertain them. Second, their bodily character attracts a measure of moral stigma to the nonmoral springs of human action in general. It serves to obscure the fact that most human desires are not what puritanical moralists call animal desires. (For that matter, many of the desires of animals are not animal desires in that sense either.)

It might be thought that these historical considerations are not relevant to current thinking about morality. But that is far from true. In the English-speaking world, at any rate, moral philosophers have been obsessed with the cognitive problem of whether and how it is possible to establish the truth of moral beliefs. Their role in guiding action has either been ignored altogether or it has been explained by interpreting moral utterance as a kind of imperative, without pausing to consider the question of the circumstances in which it is reasonable for someone who issues an order to expect that it might be obeyed. Where the motives of action have been considered in any detail it is either in the course of discussing moral responsibility and the freedom of the will or as a problem in the philosophy of mind.

One striking example of the contemporary vigor of the dualism of morality and desire is the fact that in the copious index to the eight volumes of the best and most recent large-scale encyclopedia of philosophy in English, neither prudence nor efficiency is mentioned. I shall mention other examples when I come to discuss the bad effects on moral philosophy that I take the neglect of nonmoral values to have had. So far, I admit, I have been concerned with the variety of nonmoral springs of action or motives, rather than of nonmoral values. But the two things are directly connected. To want something, to have a preference for it, to have a favorable attitude toward it, to strive to get it or bring it about, to desire it — all this is to ascribe some sort of value to it. The ascription may be mistaken. In that case the rational agent modifies his wants, attitudes, preferences, or desires and hopes to do better next time.

III

The practice of treating nonmoral values as an undifferentiated mass (conceived sometimes as the objects of desire in general, sometimes as rationally calculated, systematic self-interest), although widespread, is not universal. One large, although little remembered, exception is that of R. B. Perry, biographer of William James. His last major work, *Realms of Value* (1954) investigates a long list of different values. In building it up he follows the clue that, just as kinds of knowledge can be distinguished by looking at different intellectual or knowledge-seeking institutions, so kinds of value correspond to different institutions offering practical guidance for conduct. The main values he comes up with are moral, political, legal, economic, customary, scientific or intellectual, and aesthetic.

There is an evident bias in Perry's list in favor of the public and cooperative kinds of value. Unless these categories of the economic and the aesthetic are stretched in such a way as to detach them altogether from the institutions in relation to which they were introduced, there is no provision in his list for the greater part of the objects of human striving and for the values realized by it to the extent that it is successful. In nearly five hundred pages he has nothing, or next to nothing, to say about health, food and drink, sexuality, friendship, or the family.

His bias is to a great extent corrected in the other main treatise that sets out to expound the plurality of values. In G. H. von Wright's *The Varieties of Goodness* (1963) the crucial clue is, in accordance with the spirit of its epoch in English-speaking philosophy, rather minutely linguistic. It starts from the modest consideration of the different prepositions that can be attached to the word *good*: a thing or person can be good *at* or good *for* or good *as* something or other.

The kinds of goodness he enumerates are instrumental (as of knives), technical (as of carpenters), medical (as of eyesight), beneficial or utilitarian (as of advice), hedonic (as of a dinner or the weather), eudaemonic (as of the circumstances of life), and moral (as of the characters and acts of human agents). He admits that his list is not exhaustive. It strikes one as also perhaps insufficiently exclusive, but I shall not pursue that point here. He distinguishes, persuasively, happiness from welfare, taking the latter to be the good of man, which it is the task of moral action to preserve and promote. Happiness, he says, in a suggestive but, as he admits, obscure and metaphorical way, is the consummation of welfare. He has nothing to say of aesthetic and intellectual value.

A third exception to the rule of neglect of the plurality of nonmoral values is C. I. Lewis, particularly in his *The Ground and Nature of the Right* (1955). He correctly points out that far from being simply moral words, "good," "right," and "ought" and their opposites apply to intellectual activities of believing and reasoning as literally and straightforwardly as they do to action. Second, they are far from confined to the domain of morality when they are applied to action. "The field of judgement of right and wrong," he says, "extends to whatever is subject to human deliberation and calls for decision." [2]

In listing the kinds of value he starts from a Kantian list of varieties of right conduct: the technical, the prudential, the moral. The end of technique is the minimally costly realization of some particular good. Prudence aims at maximizing the good of the individual in his life as a whole. Morality is directed toward maximizing the good of all. I believe that to define morality in such terms as these is a mistake, particularly when it is combined with the assumption that morality ought to prevail over prudence where the requirements conflict. For the fact is that they nearly always will. In every situation where we can choose what to do there is always something we *could* do which would augment the good of others at the expense of our own unless we are in the most dejected circumstances of anyone, so the assumption that morality should always override prudence implies that we should always sacrifice our own well-being for the sake of others. But I defer consideration of this topic for the moment.

In Lewis's conception, technique finds means for ends that are inherently valuable, means that are on that account instrumentally

[2] C. I. Lewis, *The Ground and Nature of the Right* (New York: Columbia University Press, 1955), p. 9.

valuable. These elements of value contribute to, or where negative presumably detract from, well-being, the systematized good of a life as a whole, and such individual well-beings add up to the good of all.

Inspired, but not dominated, by these three conceptions of the plurality of value, I propose the following list, not as a final account of the matter, but using each to compensate for the limitations of the others. There is the hedonic value of simple pleasure or enjoyment; the technical value of efficiency in the pursuit of any valuable end; the economic value of material benefit or advantage; the aesthetic value of what satisfies disinterested contemplation (a well-born cousin, perhaps, of hedonic value); the medical or hygienic value of health, physical and mental; the intellectual value of knowledge.

These valued things are occasionally but not necessarily or usually the objects of passions in any sense we could give the term, although any persistent desire is likely to become emotionally intense from time to time. Unless there were elemental or primary values there would be nothing for prudence or for morality to apply to. Hedonic and aesthetic value, as well as medical disvalue — pain and inability to function — are the most elemental values. Technically right action enables them, and, of course, other, secondary values, to be realized. Economically right action is, from one point of view, a form of technically right action, but of a more systematic and comprehensive kind. From another point of view it provides a simple means of getting valuable things without making them. The intellectual value of knowledge is valued for its own sake, as the object of a desire to know which is inadequately described either as curiosity or by Aristotle's term, "wonder." Knowledge is also, and more fundamentally, valuable as a means, supplying the causal information needed for technical skill.

It does not matter that the list I have proposed makes no claim to completeness, so long as it is at least representative of the main kinds of value in a way that the earlier lists I have mentioned are not. It is clear what steps need to be taken to improve on it. There is a large body of literature concerned with the rational conduct of life to be consulted in which that inquiry is not only not confined to morality but may be concerned with it only to a small extent. The genre begins with the wisdom components of the scriptures of China, India, and the Jews. It is largely disentangled from religion in the post-Aristotelian philosophers of classical Greece. It reappears in the long sequence of essayists and aphorists from Erasmus, Montaigne, and Bacon, by way of French *moralistes* and Voltaire down to Schopenhauer.

IV

For a number of reasons it is a mistake to describe these particular values as all being kinds of pleasure, even if books with such titles as *The Major Pleasures of Life* are sources it is sensible to consult in seeking inventories and accounts of them. The first is that pleasure suggests, even if it does not strictly imply, passive enjoyment. Human beings find their most intense and persisting satisfactions in activity; if they are fortunate, indeed, in their work. But work and pleasure are conventionally opposed, as when an immigration official inquires into the purpose of a traveler's visit to a foreign country.

Second, there is also an informal association of the same kind between pleasure and bodily enjoyment. That is not to say that the phrase "pleasures of the flesh" is a pleonasm, but only that it is to these that the mind turns first when pleasure is mentioned. That is no doubt a distortion brought about by religious asceticism. It is a distinction of the same sort as that which leads to the identification of morality with sexual abstinence in unreflective thought and colloquial speech.

Third, and still as a matter of rhetoric more than semantics, the ordinary conception of pleasure is of an enjoyment or satisfaction that is atomic or instantaneous. But most satisfactions or realizations of value are much more systematic than that. Listen-

ing to a symphony or eating a good dinner is not ordinarily a
sequence of momentary delights whose total value is the sum of
the value of its parts.

Nevertheless, something which could, with suitable precau-
tions, be described as pleasure, but which is better described as
enjoyment or satisfaction, is the ultimate basis of all value. It is
what is crucially present in what I have called the more elemental
cases of value: the hedonic, the aesthetic, and the medical. Derivative values — the technical, much of the economic, much of the
intellectual — depend on their service as a means to these ends.
The "principles" of prudence and morality, to the extent that they
are seen as the harmonious maximization, respectively, of individual and general good, are directed to the realization of no
proprietary value of their own but are applied, as devices of
rational selection, to potential values of the elemental type or to
values instrumental to them.

Besides morality, then, in human choice and direction of conduct are prudence, like it a procedure for the maximization of
prior values, and a great range of specific values and disvalues,
varying greatly among themselves as immediate or instrumental,
as atomic or systematic, as passive or active, as bodily or mental,
as momentary or enduring and so on. This conception corrects
two erroneous pictures of the objects of human wants and efforts.
The worse of the two simply identifies all the nonmoral values as
mere inclinations or desires, aimed at pleasure conceived in the
narrowest, most colloquial sense. The second opposes morality
to self-interest, taking all particular desires to be self-interested.
Neither view is usually affirmed explicitly. But Kant, although
he knew better, usually writes as if the first mistaken picture were
correct.

V

Bishop Butler's term for the nonmoral, self-related maximizing
principle of conduct, "self-love," is unfortunate. It suggests self-

admiration rather than a concern with the interests of the self. Two other terms for what he has had in mind are "self-interest" and "prudence." Neither of them is altogether saitisfactory.

The defect of self-interest as a term for the disposition to guide one's choices so as to have the best life possible is that it is connected too closely to the pursuit of competitive satisfactions or values. There are many objects of human desire which are competitive in that their realization or enjoyment by one person inevitably excludes their enjoyment by another. The most obvious examples are material possessions and money. But there is also status, since ruling political elites, Olympic teams, titles of nobility, and so forth are inevitably limited in number. Power, to some extent associated with status, is scarce as a matter of logical necessity. It is an asymmetrical relation: if A has power over B in some respect, then B does not have power in that respect over A. Furthermore power does not amount to much unless it is power over a number of people.

We call someone self-interested if he is predominantly concerned to maximize his competitive satisfactions. But many of the values which people want to realize are noncompetitive. Many more are countercompetitive in that the satisfaction of people other than the agent is an essential part of them. The desire for knowledge that leads someone to make new discoveries yields something that he wants and would not have been available to be advantageous or otherwise satisfying to other people unless he had discovered it. There are three qualifications to this thesis, but they are all contingent. The first is that what is discovered may be something that other people do not want to know, not merely in the sense that it does not interest them, but that they wish that it was not known. A prime instance is scandalous information about some public figure. Perhaps in most such cases more people will want to know than will desire that the fact should not be known, although the desire of the interested majority is likely to be less intense.

A second qualification is that some discoveries confer a competitive advantage on their discoverers: money, reputation, Nobel Prizes. A third is that the effort the discoverer puts into his inquiries might have been put into some form of activity even more beneficial to other people. This possibility of subtraction from benevolence is not a very serious one. The discoverer is more likely to have selected as an alternative course of action either some other line of research or else something even more remote from benevolence, although no more hostile to it, like working in his garden or sailing a small boat. But then there is also the chance that he might have chosen to do something malevolent. Work can keep people out of mischief as well as preventing them from doing straightforward public good.

It would be quite inappropriate to describe someone who labors at an engrossing intellectual or artistically creative task as self-interested on that account alone. Further conditions must be satisfied; for example, that he has taken it on only as a means to the acquisition of competitive goods — "money, fame, power and the love of women" in Freud's phrase — or that in carrying it out he has neglected some specific obligations, to his family, perhaps, or his creditors.

It is not merely inappropriate but absolutely mistaken to describe as self-interested the action of someone whose purpose in doing it is the satisfaction of someone else. Although universal benevolence, altruism in the fullest sense, is rare, and perhaps nonexistent, everyone but a small minority of psychological monsters has a direct interest in the well-being of some people other than himself. As Hume rightly observed, our generosity is somewhat confined. The theory of kin selection, by supplying the evolutionary explanation of our concern for those who share our genes, puts this limited instinctive modicum of altruism on a scientific basis. But beyond this there is in most people a measure of what Hume called sympathy. By that he meant that a desire, on the whole, and other things being equal, that other people, whoever they may be, should not suffer. There is also acquired or learned altruism, which takes the form of a direct concern for the well-being of people to whom one is not related.

Concern for the welfare of others, or moral action generally, may of course be prompted by self-interest as a means to the agent's individual advantage. Most often, perhaps, that takes the negative form of acting so as not to incur their hostility and the unpleasant consequences to which it may lead. In that case the concern for others is self-interested. But even if that motive were operative in all of an agent's altruistic conduct to some extent, it would not follow that he was entirely self-interested. Our motives are often mixed.

I am inclined to think that there is an intermediate region between calculating, self-interested altruism and an immediate desire for the well-being of others. This is where an agent forgoes an advantage he would get at their expense because of what taking it would do to his self-respect or, again, where he is driven to act in such a way by feelings of guilt. But, although these sorts of cases show concern with the self rather than others, they are not directed toward a competitive advantage and could not reasonably be called instances of self-interested conduct.

VI

"Prudence" is a better word than "self-interest" for the disposition to pursue the greatest good for oneself in one's life as a whole or, as one might put it, to pursue a good life by rational means. Its fault is a certain negative, defeatist quality. It implies a strategy of minimizing losses rather than of maximizing gains, of caution and wariness rather than adventure and enterprise. The rationality it enjoys is limited in the way that economic rationality is limited. A man may feel that his life is less good than it might have been if he had given more of his attention to listening to serious music. In criticizing his current conception of a good life for himself he is not accusing himself of imprudence. Prudence, as we ordinarily understand it, is a resolute avoidance of harm. It is also opposed to spontaneity, presumably on the ground that more surprises are unpleasant than agreeable.

Nevertheless prudence is well-established, and much less misleading than self-interest as a name for the rational pursuit of a good life by an individual, and it does apply well enough to the style of consideration an agent would give, if rational, to the major decisions of life, those on which his long-run happiness or well-being depend: of what career to follow, of whom to marry, of where to live. So I shall continue to use it and the adjective "prudential," with the added warning that these words are not to be interpreted in a purely negative sense.

The intellectual aspect of that concern with rational pursuit of a good life whose motivational aspect is prudence is wisdom, the common subject matter of the books which I suggested earlier as a source for a fuller list of the varieties of value than I had provided. More precisely it is worldly wisdom, or *Lebensweisheit*. That, of course, is what most unsophisticated people mean by the word "philosophy." The adverb "worldly," often put in front of "wisdom," tends to invest the wisdom referred to with a morally questionable or disreputable air, as if it were inevitably cynical. However, it was probably put there in the first place to distinguish it from the sort of wisdom that is concerned with what, if anything, happens to us after death.

VII

So far I have been arguing that the nonmoral ends of action cannot be treated as the objects of an undifferentiated mass of desires nor, collectively, as the objects of self-interest. Desires for specific things differ in many ways. Some of them are for competitive goods, but others are not. Desires for competitive goods are, no doubt, self-interested, but self-interest as a disposition is not simply having and acting on such desires. Every time I eat something I am taking out of circulation something someone else hungrier than I might have eaten. Self-interestedness, as a trait of character, is a relative notion, like tallness. To be self-interested is to be more than usually indifferent to the claims of others to the objects of one's competitive desires.

Other desires are for noncompetitive objects; others again, for countercompetitive ones. Among these last are those desires for the well-being of others which are among our motives for moral conduct. As such, along with other elemental incentives, like hunger, sexual appetite, curiosity, taste for the beauty of nature, and so on, they help to constitute the raw material on which prudence or practical wisdom operates to arrive at the largest possible system of harmonious satisfactions.

What this appears to imply is that prudence is ultimately sovereign over morality, since part of the rational conduct of life is a matter of deciding what part morality shall play in it, to what extent the various desires which impel us to moral action should be indulged. (Prudence is in addition *epistemically prior* to morality, to the extent that morality is a matter of protecting and promoting the well-being of others, since to pursue the well-being of others we have to know in what it consists, what, as the sometimes insincere saying goes, their best interests are. But that is another matter.)

In accepting the implication of the sovereignty of prudence or wisdom over morality it seems that I am in direct collision with the widespread conviction that moral reasons for conduct override all other claims, or, more extremely, that its overridingness is what makes a reason for action moral. There are obvious difficulties with the theory of overridingness. What *in fact* overrides other reasons for action in cases of conflict is quite commonly not supposed, by either the agent or anyone else, to be the moral element in the conflict. But if the overridingness of the moral is its being *right that it should* override then the question is: what sort of "should" is this? If it is a moral "should" the thesis is empty. It must be, then, a prudential "should" and, to the extent that the

thesis is defensible, it is. The question Why should I be moral?
is a question as to the place of morality in the good life rationally
pursued. Self-interest and morality are calculated to come into
conflict. But since prudence and self-interest are far from the
same thing, prudence can enjoin abstention from self-interest, and
it does.

But does it enjoin complete abstention? Many theories of
morality, intentionally or not, imply what could be called moral
imperialism or moral totalitarianism. By that I mean the view
that in every situation of choice there is something the agent
morally ought to do, from which it follows that every other choice
in that situation would be morally wrong. Ordinary utilitarianism,
and any unguarded consequentialist theory, has this implication
when it proclaims that one ought always to do that which contributes most to the general happiness or to the good of all.

On the reasonable assumption that the most comprehensive
account of the goal of moral action is the increase of the general
good and the reduction of its opposite, it becomes necessary, if
this excessive moralism is to be contained, to recognize distinctions
within morality. I suggest that, first of all, there is the field of
moral obligation proper, which requires us not to act so as to harm
or cause suffering to others. Here are to be found the almost
universally recognized rules which forbid killing and injuring
others, stealing from them, deceiving and defaming them. It also
includes the keeping of promises. The expectations and plans of
others depend on our honoring our undertakings to them. If we
do not, harm will generally ensue to them.

Second, there is the field of charity, in which the aim is to
reduce or prevent by our action harm to others that has not been
caused by us but by natural causes or the actions of yet other
human beings. Here, as in the first field, the aim is negative, the
elimination of harm or suffering. But the requirements of charity
are open-ended. As far as a single human agent is concerned there
is no limit to the opportunities he is presented with of charitable

action. It is probably correct that no one has ever seized all the opportunities for charitable conduct that it was practically possible for him to take, themselves only a small part of those it was conceivable for him to respond to. Of course people are charitable to markedly different extents. The more charitable are more morally admirable than the less. But the noncharitable are not wicked or, at any rate, not in the way or to the extent that those who fail in their duty are.

Third, there is action directed toward the positive increase of the general good, of well-being or happiness. This is morally admirable so far as it is motivated by a direct concern for human welfare. When it is, it is neither a matter of obligation nor a form of charity; it should be called, rather, generosity or, perhaps, benevolence. The opportunities for the exercise of generosity are as boundless as those of charity. If it, as well, is included in the scope of duty or obligation, as it is by most consequentialist theories of morals, even if inadvertently, a quite unacceptable concept of morality is implied. As Popper has commonsensically observed we surely do not feel that there is any moral claim on us to augment the happiness of those who are already reasonably content. It is more important to concentrate our concern for others on cases where we can reduce suffering.

Most positive contributions to the general well-being are probably motivated not by a general concern for the greater well-being of mankind but by impulses of personal affection for family and friends, at the smaller end of the scale, and by such factors as ambition, the love of knowledge, or the desire for artistic expression at the larger end.

I am proposing as rational a conception of morality which is both finite and negative, at least in its primary part, the domain of obligation. It is negative, but not finite, in its secondary part, the domain of charity. It is rational because it takes account of the differences both of importance and of practicability of the two kinds of requirements of conduct. An indication of the higher

importance of obligation is that the legal systems of all politically
organized societies include the enforcement of the rules of duty
as their primary constituent.

It is a mistake to run obligation and charity together, since it
is to ask too much. By treating what it is reasonable to insist on
with what it is reasonable only to encourage, it tends to weaken
the more important claims of obligation. By setting an unrea-
sonably high standard of conduct it is calculated to bring about
inadequate performance over the whole range of morally desirable
conduct.

The need for some sort of distinction along these lines has
long been evident to those engaged in practical moral thinking
of a reflective kind. Catholic moral theology, from an early stage
of its history, accepted the idea of supererogation, the doing of
morally good deeds beyond the call of duty. That admission
recognized that most human beings would not adopt morality as
a vocation. To absorb the full claims of charity into the domain
of the obligations one recognizes is to aspire to sainthood. The
first Christians, convinced that the destruction of the world was
imminent, did have this aspiration. So, from time to time, have
various Protestant groups. Moral utopianism, however, is hard to
sustain when the millennium obstinately fails to arrive.

But a distinction between the morally essential and the morally
optional is seldom to be found in philosophical treatments of
morality. Views which imply that there is no distinction are
embraced without awareness of what they entail.

On the other hand, the inclusive, nonfinite view is ultimately
a necessary consequence of the conception of human nature embodied in supernaturalist religion. If human beings are really
immortal rational souls in temporary association with desiring
bodies, it is the welfare of the soul that must determine the character of a good life, and it will be one in which moral claims of
obligation and charity prevail over all others. The acceptance of
supererogation by the church is a makeshift or compromise, a

reluctant accommodation to human moral weakness. It is altogether more at home in a secular ethics.

In claiming that only the primary, strictly obligatory part of morals — not harming others and keeping one's promises to them — is essential and compulsory it may seem that I have run into inconsistency. For did I not say that morality is subject to prudence, rather than the other way round? But primary morality is that part of morality as a whole, I should contend, that prudence endorses as overriding other ends of conduct and motives directed toward those ends. To follow it is to satisfy elemental impulses of our nature. It is also desired as enabling us to be the kind of person we want to be. Furthermore it is prudent, in the narrowest, calculating sense, in two ways. It preserves us from the hostility of others and it contributes to the maintenance of social peace and of practices that are indispensable for effective human cooperation.

We should not think of morality as somehow uniquely imposing obligations *ab extra* on unregenerate human nature. Exactly analogous conflicts between what we unreflectively want to do and what we realize would, on rational consideration, be best for us to do crop up in other domains of conduct. There is nothing particularly moral about our struggles to resist the temptation provided by delicious but fattening food; by the greater easiness of not bothering to fix the leaky tap; by the pleasure of spending money it would be more prudent to save.

VIII

I have been arguing that morality is not the same thing as the good life, even if its primary part is an essential constituent of the good life and its secondary, charitable, part is a desirable constituent of such a life, to be fostered by moral education but not to the extent of obliterating all other human purposes. I have represented our impulses to dutiful and charitable action as part of ordinary, earthly human nature and not tied up with some quite distinct, and, indeed, opposed, supernatural ingredient in our constitution. I have claimed, too, that most positive good is secured by action in which moral motivation plays little or no part. I have assumed that there must be nonmoral goods to give morality, as a second-order mode of determining action, a content, namely, the desired ends of others which it is the task of morality to promote, in its negative way.

I began from the fact that, apart from aesthetics, morality is the only major field of practical thinking which has received serious and systematic attention from philosophers. I shall finish by discussing two bad consequences which follow from this narrowness of view. It should, perhaps, be added that these are, in themselves, intellectually bad, although like other intellectual mistakes, they may indirectly have morally bad consequences as well, may lead to avoidable harm to people other than the mistaken theorists.

The first of these bad results is that a number of areas of first-order reflection about practice are insufficiently investigated. The most important of them are the technical, the economic, and the medical. There are large bodies of doctrine about the way in which to pursue efficiency, economic advantage, and health. But the general assumption prevails that there is nothing problematic about these ends themselves. The usual assumption is that efficiency, economic benefit, health, and other nonmoral values are entirely uncontroversial and objective. It is assumed that we all agree in our criteria of these values and that we can unquestionably set about the discovery of rules which order actions as better or worse means of realizing them. That assumption is mistaken.

Consider the case of health. It is an interesting and somewhat suspect fact that textbooks of pathology tend to define disease or illness, the lack of health, in statistical terms. They identify it as a condition of body or mind that deviates from the average to a pronounced degree. As it turns out, they do not adhere to this principle. Pathologists do not regard being two meters tall or having red hair, both properties of a small minority of the human race, as forms of illness. More fundamentally, they do not answer the question Why should the medical profession strive to bring everyone into much the same bodily and mental condition as everyone else? To the extent that they are right to do so is precisely to the extent to which being in the average condition is one that people generally want to be in or enjoy being in or that leads to persisting states of that kind.

But people's wants and satisfactions vary. One person's health could be another person's illness. There is, plainly, room for dispute. So is there in matters of efficiency and economic benefit. A precise and conclusive procedure can be imposed to settle questions about them. But, like the criterion of statistical normality in the case of health and sickness, this smothers the contestable nature of the value in question rather than eliminates it.

To make this point about health, efficiency, and so on is not to take a skeptical attitude toward medical and technical judgments. There is possibility of dispute here, but it is comparatively marginal. The range of relevant factors is sharply limited: to pain, dysfunction, and death in the medical case, to time and cost in the technical case. That consideration leads into the second bad consequence of the obsession with morality at the expense of other fields of practice.

In emphasizing the distinction between morality and the undifferentiated remainder of forms of practice and particularly by detaching moral motivation from ordinary human nature, from desires and emotions, ethical theorists have exaggerated beyond reason the difference between them as matters of knowledge or justified belief. For the past half-century ethical theory in the English-speaking world has been dominated by the noncognitivist account of moral convictions and utterances which takes them, not, as they seem to be, as statements, true or false, reasonable or unreasonable, but as interjections or imperatives.

That point of view draws strength from the association of moral judgment with the elevated kind of aesthetic judgment that is regarded as the only kind of valuation seriously comparable with it. If the object of comparison had been the humbler aesthetics of food and clothing, of furniture and scenery, the outcome could well have been different. For there, there is much less disagreement than there is about art, particularly about art that has been recently created and to which people have not had time to become accustomed. Apparently unresolvable disagreement about art is, in fact, much greater than it is about moral issues. The comparison, then, exaggerates the variety of moral opinions, in one way, as, from the other end, does the mistaken assumption that in the domain of technical, economic, and medical value disagreement can, in principle, be conclusively resolved. The obsession of theorists with morality, to the exclusion of other forms of practice, deprives the latter of the philosophical attention they deserve and encourages radical misunderstanding about morality itself.

The Study of Human Nature and the
Subjectivity of Value

BARRY STROUD

THE TANNER LECTURES ON HUMAN VALUES

Delivered at
The University of Buenos Aires

June 7, 1988

BARRY STROUD is Professor of Philosophy at the University of California, Berkeley. He was born in Toronto, Canada, and attended East York Collegiate, the University of Toronto, and Harvard University. He has spent research leaves in Oxford and in Venice and has held visiting academic appointments in Great Britain, Canada, Norway, Mexico, Australia, and the United States. In 1986–87 he was John Locke Lecturer at the University of Oxford and Visiting Fellow of New College and of All Souls College. He is the author of *Hume* (1977) and *The Significance of Philosophical Scepticism* (1984) as well as numerous essays on a variety of philosophical topics. He is a fellow of the American Academy of Arts and Sciences.

I believe that the philosophical study of moral and other values is filled with difficulty. Our best attempts to understand evaluative thought of all kinds — all questions of good and bad, better and worse — seem to me to distort or threaten to obliterate the very phenomenon we want to understand. But if we refrain from pressing for a philosophical exposé of values we appear to ourselves to be simply acquiescing in a way of thinking and acting without understanding it. And that leaves us dissatisfied. So we persist, and end up misrepresenting and so still not understanding the phenomenon of value.

I would like to present at least the outlines of the dilemma I see. Having it clearly before us is a necessary step toward finding some way out of it. In these two lectures I can explain it only sketchily and at a regrettably high level of generality.

I stress that it is a philosophical way of thinking about values in general that I am interested in, not any particular morality or political arrangement or set of values in itself. It is a very powerful conception of what is really going on when human beings deliberate, evaluate courses of action, and make choices, or assess the choices and actions of others. If some such conception really is at work in our understanding of ourselves, it can be expected to affect the way people think concretely about what they are doing, and why. And it can come in that way to affect what people actually do. There are perhaps good reasons in general to doubt that such an abstract, purely philosophical theory could ever have such palpable effects. But on the other hand it seems hard to deny that many of the ways we think and speak about our current social arrangements, and the justification typically offered for them, do rest on some such conception of value in general. I will not have time to go into the question of the extent to which that is really so.

I will first try to describe the main outlines of the conception of evaluative thought that I have in mind and then identify the kind of distortion or denial I think it leads to. Then, in the second lecture, I will turn to the question of how and why we are so inevitably driven toward that dead end. I think it comes from nothing more than our desire to understand ourselves in a certain way.

I

Any attempt in philosophy to understand morality or evaluative thought generally leads almost inevitably to what I shall call "subjectivism." It is not always easy to notice this tendency, let alone to lament it, since the kind of view one is led to appears to have gained the status of orthodoxy. There seems to be no other way to think about values. And so, we think, nothing true is being distorted or denied at all.

The idea, in a word, is that values are "subjective," that questions of value are not questions with "objective" answers, that the goodness or badness of a thing or a course of action is not something that belongs to the world as it is in itself, independently of us. There are many different versions of this single thought. I will not be concerned with each one of them. It is what they all have in common that leads to the difficulties I see.

What they all have in common is the thought that there are no evaluative facts. In general, when we say or believe something, if things are the way we think they are, if the world is in fact the way we say it is, then what we say or believe is true. When what we say is false, things are not that way, the world is not in fact as we say it is. In science and all other forms of inquiry we seek the truth. By that I mean nothing lofty, abstract, or metaphysical. I mean only that in this or that particular way we want to find out what is so, how things are, what the world is like in one or another respect. The question can be quite particular and trivial (e.g., Where is that book I was reading yesterday?) or extremely general and profound (e.g., What, if any, are the fundamental ele-

ments of the universe?). It is always a question of what is so —
what are the facts. Whether or not something is so, whether there
is anything there to be discovered or not, is in general something
that holds quite independently of whatever we might happen to
think about it, however we might feel about it, or even whether
we are at all interested in it or not.

On the "subjectivist" view, matters of value — of the goodness
or badness, the beauty or worth, of a thing or action — are not in
this way anything to be found among the facts of the world at all.
They are therefore not part of anything that scientific or any other
kind of cognitive investigation could study and try to make progress on. There is in that sense no possibility of moral or aesthetic
or, in general, evaluative knowledge. Not because our faculties
are too weak to discern the true value of things, and not even
because evaluative matters are so complex that we can never expect
universal or even widespread agreement about them. It is, rather,
that in the realm of values there is simply no "objective" truth to
be known. The world in itself is just what it is; it is simply there.
It is the totality of facts, and it is value free.

Of course, human beings do take an interest in certain facts.
They care about certain things and not about others, they want
certain things, they try to bring about certain states of affairs and
to prevent others. Those are undeniably facts of the world. Human
beings are part of the world, and they do think and feel and act
in those ways. In short, human beings value some things or states
of affairs more highly than others. That is a fact of the world, but
it is not an evaluative fact. It is not a matter of one thing's being
better than another. It is simply a matter of human beings' regarding one thing as better than another. For the "subjectivist," there
are "objective" facts of what humans do, but not of the value of
what they do, or of the value of anything else.

What "subjectivism" denies, then, is not that human beings do
place value on certain things, but only that there is such a thing as
being correct or incorrect in those valuings, as we can be correct or

incorrect in our beliefs about the facts. When we say or think that something is good or worthwhile, or evil or ugly, our thinking or saying it is certainly something that is so, but either there is nothing at all that makes what we think true or false, or if in some way there is, it is only something about us, something "subjective." And it is nothing evaluative.

Hume put the view this way:

> Take any action allow'd to be vicious: Wilful murder, for instance. Examine it in all its lights, and see if you can find that matter of fact, or real existence, which you call *vice*. In which-ever way you take it, you find only certain passions, motives, volitions and thoughts. There is no other matter of fact in the case. The vice entirely escapes you, as long as you consider the object. You never can find it, till you turn your reflexion into your own breast, and find a sentiment of disapprobation, which arises in you, towards this action. . . . So that when you pronounce any action or character to be vicious, you mean nothing, but that from the constitution of your nature you have a feeling or sentiment of blame from the contemplation of it. Vice and virtue, therefore, may be compar'd to sounds, colours, heat and cold, which, according to modern philosophy, are not qualities in objects, but perceptions in the mind.[1]

Hume thought this "discovery" about the nature of morality was a great advance in the study of human nature. It was the "discovery" (although Hume, of course, was not the first to make it) or what I am calling the "subjectivity" of value.

Hume thought that not only values and colors are "subjective," but also, most famously, causality itself. Given the way human minds work, we will inevitably come to believe in necessary causal connections between some of the things we experience. But nothing in the world corresponds to that belief. "Necessity is

---

[1] David Hume, *A Treatise of Human Nature*, ed. L. A. Selby-Bigge (Oxford: Clarendon Press, 1958), pp. 468–69.

something, that exists in the mind, not in objects," he said.[2] We
think causal necessity is something "objective," but it is really
nothing but a "subjective" "determination of the mind." [3] This
famous treatment of the idea of causality can still serve today as
our best model of "subjectivism." Other more recent varieties can
all be measured against it.

There are many different positive versions of the "subjectivist"
idea. For Hume, in speaking of necessity there is really nothing
to speak of except what is in your own mind. And, as he says,
when you "pronounce" upon the value of something "you mean
nothing, but that . . . you have [a certain] feeling or sentiment"
toward it. Taken literally, that implies that value judgments are
really just statements of feeling. That particular idea is not essential to "subjectivism." Another version says that if you say that
something is vicious you are not stating that you have got a certain
feeling but rather are simply expressing or giving vent to a feeling
or attitude you have toward the thing. Your remark is like a cheer
or a sigh and is therefore neither true nor false.[4] Or you might be
both stating facts about the action and expressing a feeling toward
it. Another version says that you are reporting or expressing a
feeling and also encouraging others to have that same feeling or
attitude.[5] For some "subjectivists" feelings are not involved at all;
in "pronouncing" upon the value of something you are recommending or prescribing it, not saying anything that is true or false
of it.[6] A quite different kind of theory holds that when you say
that something is vicious you are saying only that the thing is such
as to produce certain feelings or experiences or desires in human

[2] Ibid., p. 165.

[3] Ibid.

[4] See, e.g., A. J. Ayer, *Language, Truth, and Logic* (New York: Dover Publications, 1946), chap. 6.

[5] See, e.g., C. L. Stevenson, *Ethics and Language* (New Haven: Yale University
Press, 1958), chaps. 2, 4, 9.

[6] See, e.g., R. M. Hare, *The Language of Morals* (Oxford: Clarendon Press,
1952), chaps. 1, 12.

beings of such-and-such kinds. Whether the thing does or would
have such effects is a straightforward matter of fact. But for the
"subjectivist" there is nothing evaluative in the facts such judgments state. There couldn't be. They speak only of nonevaluative
effects to be brought about in human beings by certain "objective,"
nonevaluative states of affairs.

"Subjectivism" carries with it a certain view of moral discussion or disagreement. It cannot see it as a dispute as to how things
are, or what is so. Those who dispute about whether it is better
to do X or to do Y when it is not possible to do both do not dispute about any matter of fact. Of course, they might disagree
about certain facts as well, but the purely evaluative dispute is not
factual. The disputants' valuings or attitudes or feelings are
opposed to each other, so that at most only one of them can prevail, but the one who does prevail cannot be said to be getting
things right while the other is getting them wrong. The one who
prevails gets, or gets more of, what he values. But their dispute,
if it is evaluative, is not a dispute about whether the world is such
that X is better than Y or that Y is better than X.

The theory obviously has great appeal. It is extremely widely
believed, in one form or another. In fact, it can seem to be the
only kind of account there could be, largely because it alone among
all theories avoids what would otherwise be an apparently in-
soluble problem. If values were part of the "objective" world,
what sort of thing could a value be? How could there be such a
thing as an evaluative fact or state of affairs? We know that
where a thing is, what shape it is, how much it weighs, even what
color it is or how much it costs, even whether human beings want
it or get pleasure from it — are all matters of "objective" fact. But
how could there be an additional fact to the effect that the thing
is good or bad, or better than something else? The unintelligibility
or "queerness" of what values would apparently have to be if they
were "objective" has been one of the strongest arguments for "sub-

jectivism." As befits a metaphysical theory, it is defended on what are really metaphysical grounds.

The theory also has its moral or political appeal. It seems to express something to which we attach positive value — the idea that nothing or nobody can push me around in matters of evaluation. There is no position from which one person's values can be criticized as incorrect or misguided. Nor is a person's choice of what to do or the best way to live constrained by some "objective" standard against which it can be measured. The thought that the world cannot force us to accept one set of values rather than another can be liberating. It does not necessarily make life easy. There are great differences and conflicts among people's valuings, and social and political life is a matter of resolving those conflicts and reconciling opposed interests. But what calls for solution is the question of which is to prevail. Each opposing interest must somehow be accommodated. All are there to be dealt with, and there are none that can be dismissed on the grounds that they are mistaken.

I have called what is common to all forms of "subjectivism" a metaphysical theory. It involves a conception of what the world is really like — a specific, determinate idea of the nature of "objective" reality. It is a world that lacks some of the things that most people appear to believe it contains. It is in that sense a more restricted world than what we seem to accept in everyday life. For Hume it contained no necessary causal connections between events, and no colors or sounds. No causal sentences or color sentences were true of the world. For the "subjectivist" about values no evaluative sentences are true of the world, even though we appear to say and think that some things are good, or are better than others. Evaluative thoughts or beliefs or attitudes are part of the world, but there is nothing in the world that makes those thoughts true or false. All such evaluative facts have been eliminated from the subjectivist conception of what the world is like.

Eliminating something from our conception of the world is in ordinary circumstances a familiar procedure. We could be said to be doing it whenever we find out that something we used to believe is not so. This happens every day in small matters and, over longer periods of time, cosmically. Great scientific breakthroughs are sometimes needed to bring about an altered conception of the world. Other, smaller changes take less. But in every case those old ways of thinking are then abandoned.

With the metaphysical theory of "subjectivism" things are different. Human beings — even "subjectivists" — continue to talk about and appear to believe in those very things that the theory claims are not really part of the world. There is a sense in which they are not abandoned. We cannot help getting experiences of color and believing on that basis that objects around us are colored. We do inevitably come to value certain things more than others. The "subjectivist" philosopher of human nature says that those things we inevitably perceive and come to believe in are not in fact to be found in the "objective" world. But any such theorist, being human, will inevitably get those very perceptions and beliefs that the theory says are only fictions and cannot be true. The "subjectivist" will inevitably believe that grass is green, for example, while also holding that no object in the world has any color. And he or she will regard a particular murder as vicious or bad while also insisting that no value statements are true, that the viciousness or badness of something is nothing in the world.

This seems to require of "subjectivism" both detachment from and engagement with the very same experiences, ideas, and beliefs. We must stand apart from our color beliefs and our evaluations while also holding onto them. Given the force with which the world inevitably operates on us, this would seem to make reflection on the austere, restricted reality of "subjectivism" at best unstable — a momentary grasp of what you take to be the way things really are, from which your humanity immediately rescues you, plunging you back into a rich world of colors and vice and virtue which reflection had apparently revealed to be nothing but illusions generated only by your own constitution. No one has given more poignant expression to this plight, while remaining in the grip of both sides of it, than Hume.[7]

But it is not just a matter of psychological instability, or oscillation. It is a question of whether that restricted view of the fully "objective" world can even be reached. That is the question I want to ask. Can we coherently think of a world in which all our valuings are exposed as only "subjective"? Could we then continue to understand ourselves to be making any evaluations at all? I think neither defenders nor opponents of "subjectivism" have taken this question seriously enough.

We say how we think the world is by saying what we believe to be so. But as long as we simply specify how things are, or how we take them to be, we will never arrive at the view that I am calling "subjectivism." In fact, if we tried to specify all the things we believe, and we took that list to express our conception of what the world is like, what we believed would be incompatible with "subjectivism." One thing I believe is that grass is green; another is that some acts are vicious murders, that the deliberate killing of a human being is a very bad thing. If I take these beliefs to express part of my conception of the world, I will have to conclude that it is a fact, or part of the way the world is, that grass is green, that some acts are vicious murders, and that the deliberate killing of a human being is a very bad thing. My conception of the world will not then be "subjectivistic" about colors or values. So at the very least the "subjectivist" account of the world must not include the contents of any of those beliefs. In saying how things really are it must not mention the colors of things or their value.

But merely leaving such things out of one's conception of the world is not enough in itself to express the "subjectivist" concep-

---

[7] See especially *Treatise*, book 1, part 4, section vii.

tion. To leave certain features out of my conception of the world is not necessarily to conceive of a world which lacks those features. I might concentrate for some reason on only certain aspects of things. For example, I might think only about the size of the objects in my house, without mentioning their location, where I got them, or how much they cost. But that does not mean that I think that only their size is real, that they do not really have any location, any origin, or any cost. Similarly, I might specify a huge number of physical facts about the movements of particles, the presence of certain forces in the world, and so on, without mentioning the colors of anything. But I do not thereby imply that I think things have no color. I simply say nothing about their color one way or the other. And if I say only that certain physical movements occurred and the effect was the death of a human being, I say nothing about the value of what went on, but I do not imply that it was not in fact a vicious murder, or that I believe it was not. So merely stating some of one's beliefs about the world without mentioning the colors of things, or their value, does not automatically make one a "subjectivist" about colors or about values. Leaving something out is not the same as saying that there is no such thing.

"Subjectivism" clearly needs the thought, then, that colors, or values, or whatever is said to be purely "subjective," are *not* part of the world. Rather than merely conceiving of a world without conceiving of colors or values, it must conceive of a world which lacks colors and values. It involves a claim of exclusiveness. The negative claim about what the world does *not* contain is as essential to "subjectivism" as the positive claim about what the world is really like.

But "subjectivism" also requires the thought that people nevertheless do have beliefs about, or experiences of, those very features which it holds are not part of reality. The point of calling the source of those beliefs or experiences merely "subjective" is that we only *think* things are that way, or we have experiences which we wrongly *take* to represent the way things are. Without that, there would be nothing to be a "subjectivist" about. The theory is a theory about human thoughts or beliefs or experiences. So it cannot deny that we have such thoughts and beliefs and experiences.

If all this is what "subjectivism" requires, how is it to be shown that "subjectivism" is true in a particular domain? How is it to be shown, for example, that there is nothing in the world corresponding to our beliefs about colors or about values — nothing to make them true or false? With a theory like Hume's it can look easy. He thought that all that was available to us in perception of the world were momentary, independent atoms of sensory information. Anything we ever think about must somehow be constructible out of such meager data. The task of his science of man was to explain how we develop our elaborate conception of the world with so little information to go on. Given only such restricted data, various features of our own minds will obviously have to play a large role. To the extent that our own mental operations alone can explain the origin of ways of thinking that go beyond what is available in the minimal data, those ways of thinking will be seen to have a wholly "subjective" source. The world would not have to contain anything corresponding to those ways of thinking in order for them to arise quite naturally in us as they do.

This is a strategy that many "subjectivist" philosophers since Hume have made use of, and continue to make use of today. If you can explain how people come to think or experience something without having to suppose that those thoughts or experiences represent anything that is so in the world that gives rise to them, you will have exposed the thoughts or experiences as "fictions" with a wholly or partly "subjective" source. "Objective" reality would therefore include no more than what is found to be essential for explaining everything that happens, including human beings' getting the thoughts and beliefs and experiences we know they get. So to say that colors are not part of the world, or that nothing in the world as it is in itself has any value, would be to say that nothing like "Grass is green" or "That was a vicious murder" has to be taken to be true in order to explain why people come to think that grass is green or that an act was a vicious murder. No colors would need to be ascribed to anything in the world in order to explain people's color perceptions and beliefs. And no values would need to be ascribed to anything in the world in order to explain why human beings value things as they do.

I call such explanations, if they are successful, "unmasking" explanations. They unmask or expose some of our beliefs or experiences as illusory in the sense of not actually representing the way things are in the world, even though it is perfectly understandable why we inevitably get such beliefs or experiences, given what we are like and the way the world works on us. Whatever we cannot help regarding as true in order to explain our thinking and experiencing what we do must be reckoned as part of the way the world is. Those indispensable beliefs about the world will not then have been exposed or unmasked by an explanation of their origins. On the contrary, they will have been vindicated. They will have been shown to represent things as they really are. But for all the rest, the world is not really the way they represent it as being.

This might be called an explanatory test or criterion of reality. The world as it is in itself amounts to all, but only all, those truths that are sufficient to explain what is so. Anything that is not needed for that explanatory purpose is not to be reckoned as part of the way things are.

I have said that this is one possible route to "subjectivism" about values, or about colors. It seems to rely on a certain faith in the simplicity of the universe. It sees the world as highly efficient and economical, as no richer than it needs to be for the explanatory purposes of science. I do not want to speculate about the origins of such a faith. Nor will I go into the details of any particular attempts to establish "subjectivism" by an appeal to unmasking explanations. I can only say that it seems to me extremely implausible to think that they alone could do the job. They seem to work best, as in Hume's case, when you have already arrived at a restricted conception of what the world really contains. But establishing "subjectivism" in a particular area is a matter of arriving at that appropriately restricted conception of the world in the first place.

I want to turn away from all questions about how "subjectivism" about values might be established and look instead at what must be an essential ingredient in any form of the view, however it is arrived at. There must be some way of understanding the presence of what those unmasking explanations, if they were appealed to, would be supposed to explain or unmask. The "subjectivist" view of the world, for all its zeal in eliminating certain features we unreflectively seem to think are there, still must acknowledge as part of the world all those perceptions, beliefs, and attitudes of human beings which it claims have only a "subjective" source. And there is a question of how the presence of those perceptions, beliefs, and attitudes is to be understood.

The question arises as much for colors as it does for values, and it will be helpful to look at that case first. To entertain the view that colors do not belong to the "objective" world, but are at best projected onto, or falsely believed or perceived to be present in, a world that does not really contain them, we must ourselves attribute no color to anything (since we say there is none in the world) while nevertheless believing that there are many perceptions of and beliefs about the colors of things. The question is whether we can do that. It obviously depends on what perceiving colors or believing that things are colored amounts to, and on what it takes for us to understand that such psychological phenomena occur. If we are "subjectivists," it cannot depend on our supposing that any of the contents of such perceptions or beliefs are actually true of the world they are about. Can we make sense of the perceptions or beliefs if we no longer make that assumption?

We can, of course, understand people to have many beliefs about, and perhaps even perceptions of, things which we ourselves know do not exist. I understand that people believe in, and sometimes describe themselves as seeing, for example, ghosts or angels. People also think about centaurs and golden mountains. There is no doubt that such psychological phenomena occur. The explanation traditionally offered for our understanding of such facts relied on a simple compositional theory of thought. The concept of a ghost or a centaur was said to be a complex idea. It represents nothing that exists in the world, but it is a compound made up of simple elements, some of which do indeed find counterparts in the world. Our attributing thoughts or beliefs about nonexistent things to others therefore does not require that we ourselves believe the world to be populated with the things those complex ideas represent. We can see how people come to think that way without our agreeing that the thoughts they have are true.

Even this theory does not completely sever our understanding of the thoughts of others from all our own beliefs about the way things are. The presence in our common world of objects like horses' bodies or the heads of men (or other even simpler things) is what enables us to think about such things and to attribute thoughts with those contents to the minds of our fellow humans. But even if that theory is perfectly satisfactory for thoughts about centaurs or golden mountains — which I do not believe it is — it would be of little help in explaining how the "subjectivist" can understand the presence of thoughts and perceptions of color. Surely our idea of color cannot be built up out of simpler elements that are not themselves colors at all. Perhaps some particular colors or shades can be understood as mixtures or combinations of other colors or shades, but there are no "elements" which are not colors but which somehow could be combined in thought or experience to give us the idea of color in the first place.

Particular shades of color have traditionally been thought to be so simple that we can all understand what it is to have a perception of them simply by having such perceptions. It has been suggested that we each understand in our own case what it is to have a perception of green, say, simply by perceiving green; we know what that is like. If we could each understand it in that way, we could perhaps then say that what others have when they have a perception of green is just the same as what we have. We know in that way what green is, so we know that the feature that others perceive when they perceive green is that same feature. And that is what we all ascribe to objects when we believe that they are green. This seems to involve no ascription of green to anything in the world and yet to acknowledge the presence of perceptions of green and beliefs about green things on the part of human beings constituted more or less as we are.

I do not find this traditional theory plausible, for reasons I will only state and not develop. I believe we could never come to understand in that first-person way what it is to have a perception of green. The theory says that having a perception of green, or perhaps several of them, is enough to teach us what having a perception of green is. But simply having perceptions of green could never be enough. There is no way of being directly acquainted with something, or simply gazing at or experiencing a particular item, and from the mere occurrence or presence of the thing somehow coming to understand it as a thing of a certain sort rather than of some other sort. That is what we must do if we are to understand something as a perception of green rather than, say, as a remarkable event, which it might also be. Nor is there any possibility, on the sole basis of "having" it, of understanding that we have got the same sort of thing this time as we have had before. Every two things are the same in some respect or other, and also different in countless respects, so whether we have got the same kind of thing on a second occasion depends on which respects are relevant and which not. And that cannot be fixed by an original item about which we understand nothing but which we merely "have."

Some surroundings are needed to make a thought into the thought of a certain kind of thing, so some surroundings are needed to make a thought about a psychological occurrence into a thought about a perception of green, say, and not something else. But if in trying to supply the surroundings needed to ascribe perceptions of particular colors to perceivers we find that we ourselves must also ascribe colors to some of the things we take them to be perceiving, we will have abandoned the "subjectivist" conception of reality. We will be conceiving of the world as containing colored things. The "subjectivist" thought must leave room in the world for perceptions of and beliefs about color, but the price of our understanding such things to be part of the world would be our also taking the world to contain colored things. Color perceptions and beliefs could not then be unmasked as illusory or as having no counterparts in the way things are. So "subjectivism" could not be established.

It might seem that that is not so, since there is at least one version of "subjectivism" on which it remains true that objects are colored. It says that what is ascribed to objects when we apply color words to them is a disposition to produce perceptions of color in appropriately placed perceivers in certain specified conditions. Objects really do (or do not) have such dispositions. So on that view our beliefs about the colors of things would indeed describe things as they are in the world. We would not be precluded from truly ascribing colors to objects.

But that dispositional theory does not really avoid the difficulty. It explains what it is for an object to be colored in terms of perceptions of color, but it says nothing about what a perception of color is, or what it takes for us to understand that there are such things as perceptions of color. Nor does it explain what a perception of green in particular is a perception of. The greenness involved in perceptions of green — what makes them perceptions of green — cannot itself be equated with a disposition to produce perceptions of green, even if the greenness of objects can be explained that way.

That dispositional account of the greenness of an object makes essential use of an idea of green that cannot in turn be explained in that same dispositional way. So it must hold that there are perceptions of green even though no objects in the world possess that feature that they are perceptions of. And that is the same problem that faced other versions of "subjectivism" about colors. It must explain how we can understand particular perceptions to be perceptions of, say, green and not something else, while at the same time we hold that no objects in the world possess that feature that they are perceptions of.

When we think about what actually happens in everyday life, it seems that we constantly do rely on the public accessibility of such states of affairs as the greenness of grass in ascribing perceptions of greenness to our fellow human beings. We attribute color to objects in the world as a condition of attributing particular contents to perceptions. If that is so, and inescapably so, we will not be able to think of the world in the way "subjectivism" requires.

We can now see, I hope, a parallel difficulty for the "subjectivity" of values. This is where the threat of distortion or denial comes in. Those who think that a particular act was an act of murder and was vicious or wrong seem to have a certain thought about that act: they think it was wrong. Perhaps they think in general that the deliberate killing of a human being is a very bad thing. We can speak of such persons as having certain moral views or beliefs or opinions (in this case not very controversial). "Subjectivism" cannot deny that people have such views. It must insist on the fact. The question is how it can acknowledge and understand that fact while also holding that no such thoughts are ever true or false of the world.

I have said that there are many different positive theories of evaluative judgment which are all compatible with the negative "subjectivist" thesis that values are not part of the "objective" world. One view is that the assertion of "That act was wrong" reports the presence of a certain feeling that the speaker has toward that act (for Hume, a "sentiment of disapprobation"). Another view holds that what is being said is that the act is such that all human beings of certain kinds would get a certain feeling toward it if they knew of it. Both these views see the so-called evaluative judgment as a factual assertion about actual or hypothetical feelings on the part of certain human beings. In that respect they are like the dispositional analysis of an object's color.

One merit of all theories of this sort is that they preserve one striking feature of our evaluative thought. They allow that our reactions to the world do involve genuine beliefs about the goodness or badness of things. They see us as asserting what we take to be truths about the world. And there is very good reason for insisting that we think of our moral judgments as either true or false. Not only do we seem to believe them and assert them and try to support them by reasoning. Moral sentences can also be embedded in other sentences in what certainly looks like a purely truth-functional way.

For example, from the sentence "That act was wrong" and the sentence "If that act was wrong then whoever did it deserves to be punished" it follows logically that whoever did that act deserves to be punished. Any view which says that moral or other evaluative judgments are not assertions or are not, strictly speaking, true or false has great difficulty in accounting for that logical implication. Take the extreme emotivist view which says that in uttering "That was wrong" I am not asserting anything but only expressing my own distaste or my disapprobation of the act in question. That view can really give no account of the validity of the inference at all. In saying "If that act was wrong then ——" my "If" does not signify that I am somehow hypothetically or conditionally expressing a feeling. There is no such thing as hypothetically expressing a feeling. Of course, I can say "If I feel such-and-such then ——" and then reflect on what follows from my having a certain feeling, or what would be true if I had one. I can also draw conclusions from the supposition not that I have a certain feeling but that a certain feeling has been expressed. But the antecedent in all those reasonings would be a straightforward factual proposition about feelings or the expression of feelings. They would not be mere expressions of feeling which are neither true nor false.

Other kinds of nonpropositional theory are more complicated, but they all face similar difficulties. Some hold that to make a moral judgment is not to say anything true or false but to prescribe a certain course of action in the way that imperatives order or demand certain courses of action. But still there is a difficulty about how one can hypothetically prescribe or recommend something. One can certainly prescribe or order something that is hypothetical or conditional — "If you go out, shut the door after you." But that is an order to do something if certain conditions are fulfilled. The imperative does not appear as the antecedent of a conditional proposition. Moral judgments like "That was wrong," it appear, do occur as the antecedents of conditional propositions, and inferences are validly drawn from them. But if they are prescriptions, it would seem that in such positions they serve to issue prescriptions only conditionally. And what could that be? It would not be entertaining the hypothesis that a certain prescription has been made or that a certain course of action has been recommended. Those are both straightforward factual propositions which are either true or false. They can easily be embedded in other sentences. But how could a prescription itself be embedded in a conditional sentence? It seems that it would have to be something like a hypothetical issuing of a prescription. But there is no such thing.

Another type of view, perhaps closest to what Hume says about causal necessity, is that in making moral judgments we do take ourselves to be expressing beliefs which are either true or false, but we are deeply confused and mistaken. What we are really doing is projecting something we feel when perceiving or thinking about an action onto that action itself and mistakenly supposing that it "objectively" resides there. "The mind," Hume says, "has a great propensity to spread itself on external objects, and to conjoin with them any internal impressions, which they occasion, and which always make their appearance at the same time that these objects discover themselves to the senses." [8] In making moral judgments we think we are ascribing moral characteristics to the acts we observe; we treat our moral views as if they were, so to speak, propositional, but in fact they are mere projections. We "gild" or "stain" the facts with our feelings, but all that is strictly true in what we say is the purely factual, nonevaluative content to which something in the value-free world could correspond.

This kind of view seems to me to serve the interests of "subjectivism" best. But so far it gives no account of what our making a moral judgment really amounts to. It does not explain what we are saying when we say or believe that a particular act was wrong. We are said to take something we feel and project it onto the world, believing it to be a property belonging to things that exist there. But how do we do that? We do not think that objects and events in the world actually have the very feelings that give rise to our own "pronouncements." The most that could be said is that we ascribe to things in the world, not the feeling itself, but what the feeling is a feeling of — that very feature that we are aware of "in our own breast." In the case of causality Hume thinks we get what he calls an impression of necessity, and it is that very feature — necessity — that we ascribe to the connections between some of the events we observe. In the case of color it is, say, greenness that we perceive and then project. What is the corresponding feeling or impression in the moral case? What we think or judge is that the act was bad, or vicious, or wrong, so it would

[8] *Treatise*, p. 167.

seem that it must be a feeling of badness, or vice, or wrongness. But what *is* such a feeling? The question for "subjectivism" is whether and how we can understand those particular feelings that it says either generate or are referred to in our moral judgments or opinions.

Hume calls the feelings in question sentiments of approbation or disapprobation. But what makes a feeling a feeling of disapprobation or disapproval? Not just any bad or negative feeling will count. To disapprove of something is to think it bad, to make an unfavorable evaluation of it. So a particular feeling will be a feeling of disapproval only if it is generated by or suffused with the thought that the thing in question is bad. But that is precisely the evaluative thought that the theory is trying to account for. It must explain how we can think something is bad or wrong without itself attributing badness or wrongness or any other evaluative feature to anything.

This same difficulty faces other versions of "subjectivism" in which feelings are said to play an essential role in moral judgments. If my moral judgment is a report that I have a certain feeling, or that all human beings would get a certain kind of feeling under certain conditions, the kind of feeling in question must be identified before we can know what is being said. Not just any feeling will do. Hume says that the feeling arising from virtue is "agreeable," and the feeling of vice is "uneasy" or unpleasant, but in saying that an act is wrong, even if I am indeed saying something about how people do or would feel, I am not saying only that they would get unpleasant or disagreeable feelings from the act. They might get unpleasant feelings from something they eat, but that would not make what they eat bad, or vicious, or wrong. So we still need some explanation of what it is to think that something is bad, or vicious, and some account of how we can intelligibly attribute such thoughts or attitudes to people.

I do not mean to suggest that, as things actually are, there is any special difficulty about our doing that. We often agree in our moral assessments of particular acts and in many of our more general evaluative opinions. We come to share values, when we do, by growing up and living in a culture in which they are endorsed and acted on. We recognize the badness of certain acts, and we recognize that other people have beliefs or reactions that are appropriate to the badness of the acts we all observe. Their responses count as disapproval because they involve the thought that the acts are bad — a thought which we know to apply truly to just such acts as these. Our ascriptions of evaluative attitudes or feelings to human beings go hand in hand with our ascriptions of value to things and actions in the world.

I need not share all those moral assessments that I can correctly attribute to others. I can recognize that others think that a certain sort of thing is bad even if I do not think the thing is bad, because I too can have that same thought about other things. I do not have to agree in each particular case, any more than I must agree with someone else's judgment about the color of something in order to attribute a belief about or a perception of color to that person. Knowing that a blue light is shining on a white wall, I will know that a person looking at it sees blue and, if he doesn't know about the light, that he also believes that the wall is blue. I know the belief is false, but I can attribute that belief to him. I can do that because of my own general competence in the language of color and my knowledge of what colors things are in the environment. Similarly, if I do not agree with a person's evaluative judgment, I can still correctly attribute it to him and understand what it is for him to hold that view, because of my own general competence in the language of evaluation and my knowledge of the evaluative features of the environment — what things are good or bad, better or worse than others.

The traditional theory of simple and complex ideas was a way of accounting for the possibility of false belief or of a lack of correspondence between people's ideas and the world. But that theory seems no more plausible here as a way of understanding the possibility of evaluative thought in general than it seemed in the case of color. Perhaps some particular evaluative concepts can be defined in terms of others, but surely we cannot expect all evaluative notions to be reduced to terms that are not evaluative at all. There are no simple nonevaluative "elements" which could somehow be combined in thought or experience to give us the idea of value, and hence the possibility of evaluation, in the first place. This irreducibility is one of the few things on which most modern moral philosophers would seem to agree.

There is no question that we do make moral judgments or evaluate things or states of affairs, and that we do attribute such judgments, or reactions involving such judgments, to others. The question is not whether we all do it in real life. The question is whether someone who consistently holds to the "subjectivity" of all values could do it. Could someone make sense of the idea of there being feelings or attitudes of disapproval, say, if that person did not also hold the view that certain kinds of acts are bad, or wrong, or worthy of disapproval? What made it seem possible in the case of color was the thought that perceptions could somehow be directly recognized as intrinsically of a certain specific kind — that we can simply read off from our perceptions themselves what features they are perceptions of — whatever we take the world to be like, whether we think it contains any colored things or not. I think there is a tendency to rely on a similar thought in the case of values. We are thought to be able to recognize what we feel simply by feeling it, by being aware of some felt feature in our experience, whatever we take the world to be like, whether we attribute any negative or positive value to anything in the world or not.

I have already suggested why I think that sort of view could not be right even about perceptions of color. I do not think its prospects are any better in the case of values. Even supposing that we could isolate in our experience some feeling or attitude or response which plays an essential role in moral or evaluative judgment, there would still be the problem of what that feeling could be said to be like. It would have to be identified and classified only in terms that are somehow immediately available to consciousness, not in terms of any evaluative judgments that define or accompany it. It would have to be the kind of feeling or response that a person could have without having any moral or evaluative opinions at all.

This would have the consequence that the only materials available to us for understanding what appears to be evaluative thought and for seeing how it figures in human action and human social arrangements would be simple, isolated feelings with no evaluative content. They might be such things as pleasant or unpleasant sensations, feelings of satisfaction or dissatisfaction, or simple likes or dislikes. Or, moving away from feelings, they might be such things as basic unmotivated desires or wants or preferences, or even more indiscriminately, those all-purpose motivators called "pro-attitude" and "con-attitude."

Even such apparently scaled-down materials are not necessarily on the nonevaluative ground floor. One can feel pleased that justice has been done, for example, and if that is a feeling of pleasure it is still not independent of its evaluative content. Someone who did not think that justice had been done could not have such a feeling. And liking something or somebody can be a matter of thinking well of the thing or person, and that again has an essential evaluative component. Even wanting, or preferring, or simply being for or against a certain thing can also be an evaluative attitude or state. Preferring that virtue be rewarded, for example, or being for a just solution, or being against the unjust acts of one's government — these are moral attitudes and not simple motivating feelings or wants that might rise up in a nonevaluating agent. It is not clear to what extent there could even be such a thing as a nonevaluating agent — at least, a human agent.

I have suggested that it is the thought that values and evaluation would not otherwise be intelligible that can lead to the idea that they must ultimately be explained only in terms of likes and dislikes, pleasures and pains, or basic human desires. Perhaps something like that is what finds expression in the popular half-thought that morality is after all just a matter of what people want, or what they like or don't like. Or worse still, the thought that it is just a matter of whose likes and dislikes are going to prevail. And now there is the view, in the United States at least, that morality is itself just one among a great many "special interests" that have to be accommodated in society. People are thought to be just pushing their own personal interests or seeking their own "gratifications" in one way or another, and the "morality lobby" is encouraged to fight it out with the military, the corporations, the doctors, the judges, and so on.

Whether such views are really derived from the position I am calling "subjectivism" I don't know. But it does seem to me that to hope that the feelings or attitudes essential to evaluative judgment can be identified and understood neutrally, on the basis of some intrinsically felt quality alone, would be disastrous for making sense of what is, after all, a fundamental aspect of human life. If it is only our very engagement in a set of values that makes it possible for us even to recognize the phenomenon of evaluation, the demand of evaluative neutrality would have the effect of denying or obliterating the very phenomenon we want to understand. If engagement or participation is essential, we can never get ourselves into a position to discover that all values are "subjective," that the goodness or badness of something is not part of the way things are.

II

I have been trying to identify some of the difficulties in "subjectivism" and to draw attention to what looks like a serious obstacle to our ever even arriving at that conception of the world. If we tried to adhere strictly to what "subjectivism" requires of us, it seems that we could not consistently or coherently come to think that it is true of our evaluative thought. But even if that is so it might not seem like much of a threat. Why can't we simply abandon "subjectivism" and look elsewhere for a more satisfactory understanding of evaluative thought and its role in our lives? I now want to suggest why I think that will not be easy.

"Subjectivism" in one form or another appears to be the inevitable result of our trying to understand ourselves in a certain way, and the goal of understanding ourselves that way is not easily abandoned. It seems impossible to conceive of a better way of understanding how human beings work. The model goes back to one of the greatest achievements of the Enlightenment — the idea of a "science of human nature." It was to be a thorough, systematic investigation of the principles of human nature that would eventually explain every aspect of the personal, social, cultural, and political life of human beings. That the proper aims of individual human beings and the best social and political arrangements among them should somehow be determined in the light of truths about their nature and the world they live in was not in itself a new idea. What was unique to the Enlightenment was an open-ended curiosity about what that human nature is really like and, most important, an empirical, secular idea of how it is to be known.

If human beings were endowed by a supernatural power with certain capacities and goals and were placed in a specially ordained position in the world, that would obviously limit both the content and the justification they could find for the beliefs they arrived at and the goals they aspired to. The source of any knowledge they acquired or any values they pursued would then lie in something other than those human beings themselves and the familiar world they could know they inhabit. Their behavior in pursuit of that knowledge and those values would therefore not be fully understandable to them by human intellectual means alone. There could be no properly scientific understanding of human behavior or human life.

The impressive growth in understanding the inanimate physical world, culminating in the work of Isaac Newton, was the decisive step toward the downfall of that traditional picture. The mathematical science of nature was seen to rest on no supernatural hypotheses and to proceed carefully no further than experience, and solid reasoning based on that experience, could take it. It does not matter now whether that really was a correct perception of the revolution in physical science or not. In any case it served as the source of the Enlightenment ideal of understanding what we might call the human world through the application of just such a broadly scientific enterprise to the study of human nature and human life. It put human beings at the center, and it insisted that the way things should be in any human world must be based only on what human beings can reliably find out about themselves and the natural observable world they live in.

One of the earliest and still one of the best statements of this goal is Hume's *A Treatise of Human Nature*. It was written in the belief that "all the sciences have a relation, greater or less, to human nature. . . . Even *Mathematics, Natural Philosophy, and Natural Religion*, are in some measure dependent on the science of MAN; since they lie under the cognizance of men, and are judg'd of by their powers and faculties." [9] The aim of the book was to lay the foundations of a genuine science of man that was to be like nothing that had gone before.

Hume had found that the "moral Philosophy transmitted to us by Antiquity," like ancient "Natural Philosophy," was "entirely Hypothetical, & depend[ed] more upon Invention than Experience. Every one consulted his Fancy in erecting Schemes of Virtue & of Happiness, without regarding human Nature, upon which every moral Conclusion must depend." [10] His plan was to appeal to nothing but experience—to "introduce the experimental method

[9] Ibid., p. xix.

[10] *The Letters of David Hume*, vol. 1, ed. J. Y. T. Grieg (Oxford: Clarendon Press, 1969), p. 16.

of reasoning into moral subjects." He would take human beings as they are, he would observe them "in the common course of the world, . . . in company, in affairs, and in their pleasures," [11] and he would try eventually to explain all the overt and hidden richness of their behavior, thought, and feeling. That would require the discovery of general principles of human nature, but the only possible access to such principles and explanations would be judicious generalization from whatever we can find out by "the cautious observation of human life." [12] Where our best experience remains still silent on some question of human nature or human destiny we must willingly confess our ignorance and perhaps try harder to discover how we work and what the world holds in store for us. But we must not let the natural human desire for some answer or other lead us to invent comforting stories for which we can honestly find no support in experience, or impose such conjectures or hypotheses on the world and then base our beliefs and behavior on such creatures of the imagination.

The positive project of a naturalistic study of human beings is familiar to us today in what we call the social sciences. They are such a pervasive and powerful feature of the modern world that it is sometimes difficult to remember that they have not always been with us. Ideally, they promise a dispassionate, scientific understanding of thought, feeling, and behavior in every area of human life. The information they would provide is to be the basis of all personal, social, and political organization and improvement, just as the physical sciences provide the facts and theories that engineering and technology then make such spectacular use of in the purely inanimate domain. By now we are used to a division of the study of human behavior into different, highly specialized fields such as economics, psychology, and sociology. Hume probably never envisaged the technical professionalism of today. But

[11] *Treatise*, p. xxiii.
[12] Ibid., p. xxiii.

the idea that human beings can be studied and understood in this
way is an Enlightenment idea. It is just what he had in mind.

Hume's enthusiasm for the idea went beyond the social benefits to what he saw as the directly cognitive or intellectual payoff
of a science of man. Since all sciences — even mathematics and
physics — fall under the cognizance of men, he thought it was
"impossible to tell what changes and improvements we might
make in these sciences were we thoroughly acquainted with the
extent and force of human understanding, and cou'd explain the
nature of the ideas we employ, and of the operations we perform
in our reasonings." [13] These hopes have scarcely been vindicated.
It is difficult to point to concrete advances in the sciences that have
been generated by Hume's own epistemological theory of our ideas
and reasonings, and presumably few today would think of looking
to psychology, say, or sociology, as a possible source of breakthroughs in mathematics or physics. But even without the hope
of such direct scientific consequences, the Enlightenment idea of
the study of human nature still serves to determine our culture's
conception of understanding ourselves. It remains difficult to
imagine any other way of getting the kind of understanding of
ourselves that we seek.

The goal is an understanding of human nature. The method
is to study human beings in interaction with the world and thereby
to explain how they come to think, feel, and act as they do. But
not just any story — even any true story — about the relation
between human beings and the world will give us what we want.
For instance, we are interested in how people come to believe
and know what they do about the world around them, but we
would not be satisfied with the obvious truth that they learn to
think and speak and they come to know things about the world
by seeing and touching things and in other ways perceiving what
is true of the things around them. That is all true, but it does not

13 Ibid., p. xix.

explain what we want to understand. Similarly, we are interested in how people come to value things and why they endorse the particular values that they do, but we would not be satisfied with the obvious truth that they grow up and are socialized into a particular culture and come to accept many of the value beliefs current in that culture. That again is certainly true. But such general truths about human beings and human life do not explain what we want the philosophical study of human nature to explain.

It is not just a question of detail. Even a full, detailed story of how a particular person or a particular group comes to know or to value a certain sort of thing would not satisfy us. We want to understand certain pervasive or fundamental aspects of human life *in general*.

Morality, for example, is a quite general phenomenon which seems distinctive of the human species. No other creatures seem moved by considerations of good and bad, right and wrong. To understand that aspect of human life, then, would be to understand how there comes to be such a thing as morality at all, how it works, and what makes it possible. Our possession of an elaborate conception of the world we live in and its history, how it works, and how it affects us, is also something a science of human nature should be able to explain. We want to know how there comes to be any such thing at all. The same is true of our beliefs about the colors of things in particular, or all our beliefs to the effect that certain things are causally connected with other things. The question in each case is how we come to have any thoughts or beliefs or responses of that general kind at all.

There is implicit in this kind of question a certain idea of how best to answer it. It seems to be the only way in which it could be answered. Obviously, if human beings come to act or think or feel a certain way only after interaction with the world around them, there must be something about human beings — something about what we are like — and something about what the world is like which combine to produce in human beings the way of acting or thinking or feeling in question. Even if facts of the world affected us directly by simply impressing themselves on our minds whenever we opened our eyes or ears, there would still be something true of us that was partly responsible for our getting all the beliefs we get. It would be because we are capable of passively receiving information about the world in that way. So it seems that any explanation of distinctive, pervasive features of human life would have to be a two-part explanation. It would involve an "objective" factor — what the world is like, or how things are independent of us — and a "subjective" factor — what we are like, or how things are with us.

If both factors are always present, if human beings themselves always play some role in acquiring their conception of how things are, then the study of human nature will naturally take the form of asking how much, and what, the human subject does contribute. That would be to isolate and identify those elements of human nature that are responsible for our conceiving of and responding to the world in the ways we do. How much of what we think or feel about the world is due to us, to the way we are, to the "subjective" factor, and how much is due to the way things are independently of us, to the "objective" factor? The intellectual goal expressed in terms of this bipartite conception serves as our model for understanding ourselves, for seeing how we work, for identifying what is distinctively human.

Hume's Enlightenment project of a "science of human nature" embodied just this conception of how to understand ourselves. It was the search for, among other things, "principles of human nature" — those features of human minds and sensibilities that are responsible for our thinking, feeling, and acting as we do. Hume sought those "principles" which he called "permanent, irresistable, and universal." They are the "foundation" of all our thoughts, feelings, and actions in the sense that, as he put it, "upon their removal human nature must immediately perish and go to ruin." [14] They will be those "principles" that are at work in anything recognizable as human life as we know it — ways of thinking and acting without which nothing would think or act as humans do. They are to be identified by asking what must be true of human beings as we know them in order for them to think and feel and act in the ways we know they do.

This Enlightenment project of isolating and identifying the "subjective" factor in human thought and experience is by no means only a thing of the past. We find it in any philosopher who would distinguish in general between the "given" and the "interpretation," between the "data" we receive and the construction we put upon them, or between the "flux of experience" and the "conceptual scheme" we impose upon it to make sense of our experience and to learn from it. In our own day, for example, W. V. Quine in his *Word and Object* has put his task almost mathematically as follows: "we can investigate the world, and man as a part of it, and thus find out what cues he could have of what goes on around him. Subtracting his cues from his world view, we get man's net contribution as the difference. This difference marks the extent of man's conceptual sovereignty." [15]

It is not just a matter of how the world affects us. We know that something outside us acts on us; our cognitive and affective responses are caused by something in the world. So in that sense we know that there is something or other in the world which, in conjunction with facts about us, makes us think and feel as we do. But it is not merely a question of causation. We are interested in a more complex relation between our beliefs and responses and the world. We want to know the nature of whatever causes there are. Is there anything in the world that not only causes but somehow matches up with, or corresponds to, or is adequately repre-

[14] Ibid., p. 225.

[15] W. V. Quine, *Word and Object* (Cambridge, Mass.: Technology Press of MIT and John Wiley & Sons, 1960), p. 5.

sented by, those things that we think and feel? Is the world, or does the world have to be, anything like the way we think it is, in order for it to have given us the thoughts and feelings about it that we have? What is there, if anything, that renders those thoughts or responses true? Or are they merely "subjective" responses with nothing corresponding to them in the "objective" world? And with these questions we have arrived at the inquiry that I have already suggested seems so easily to lead to "subjectivism" with respect to many of the things we believe.

It leads easily to skepticism about the world too. Descartes's evil demon represented the threat that the way things are independently of me might be extremely different from the way I take them to be. If the demon exists, he alone exists beyond me, and his clever machinations make me think that I live in a world of earth and water, trees and buildings, and other people with human bodies like the one I think I've got. He gives me such thoughts and beliefs, so they are produced by something "objective" and independent of me, but there would be almost nothing in that world corresponding to any of those thoughts. They would almost all be false. The challenge of skepticism is to show how I know that I do not live in such a world. Once we see human knowledge as a combination of an "objective" and a "subjective" factor in this way, and we acknowledge the possibility of a largely or even entirely "subjective" source for most of our beliefs, it seems impossible to explain how those beliefs could ever amount to knowledge or reasonable belief.

But our concern here is not the epistemological question of knowledge or the reasonableness of our beliefs. The "subjectivism" I have been describing results from a metaphysical project which relies on some unquestioned knowledge of the world. It subtracts from some of our beliefs, not the causes that produce them, and not necessarily our warrant for accepting them, but rather their correspondence with anything that holds in the way things are independently of us. Whatever support we might have for them therefore cannot be "objective." It cannot be based in anything that is to be found in the way things are. The same bipartite conception of the ultimate source of all our beliefs and responses is at work in this project. Everything is to be assigned either to an "objective" or to a "subjective" source.

It is because we want to understand human values or human valuing in general in terms of this bipartite picture that I think we are inevitably driven toward "subjectivism." To understand the general phenomenon of human evaluation we want to understand the content of such evaluative thoughts — what exactly is being said or thought when someone says, "That was a vicious act" or "It is better to comfort someone than to kill him." To ask what is involved in such a thought is to ask what, if anything, could make it true, or false. If we answer, simply, that it is the goodness or badness of things that makes such remarks true or false, we feel we are not really explaining the content of those evaluative "pronouncements." In saying that it is true that an act is vicious if and only if the act is indeed vicious we are making use of the idea of viciousness, but we are not explaining it. We feel we will understand evaluation only when we know, as it is often put in philosophy, *what it is* to be vicious, or bad, or wrong.

When Hume investigated that fundamental feature of human life which he called our "reasoning from causes to effects," our getting beliefs about the necessarily causal connections between things, he did not restrict himself simply to identifying the circumstances in which we get such beliefs. If he had, he could have said that a belief that two things are causally connected arises in us whenever we are presented with instances in which one thing causes another. Even if that were true, it would not help us understand human thought about causality in general because it does not explain what it is for one thing to cause another. It was because Hume wanted to explain not just the origin but also the contents of our causal beliefs that he was able to find nothing in the world corresponding to their special claim of necessity. Necessity, then, could be only something "subjective," or nothing at all. It was the very desire for a completely general account that would explain how any thought about necessity is possible at all that led to "subjectivism" about necessity.

If the contents of our evaluative beliefs are going to be explained in terms of what is or could be the case in the world, it does seem that we will have explained evaluative thought in general in that way only if whatever we find in the "objective" world to explain it is something nonevaluative. Otherwise, there will still be some evaluative content that will not have been explained. And since the nonevaluative always falls short of exhausting the special, apparently evaluative, content of our thought, the source of that special evaluative element will inevitably have to be located in us, not in things as they are independently of us. It will be assigned to the "subjective" and not the "objective" factor. All our value beliefs, then, insofar as they are really evaluative, will be "subjective" and will not assert anything that is or even could be true of the way things are.

In the first lecture I tried to cast doubt on our ability to carry out this metaphysical project of conceiving of a world in which we have genuinely evaluative beliefs or attitudes while holding that none of them is true of the world. It requires detachment from, or nonendorsement of, the contents of all our evaluations. And it requires an acknowledgment of the fact that we nevertheless do make such evaluations. But the fulfillment of either one of those two requirements threatens the possibility of fulfilling the other. Without ascribing value to things in the world, and hence holding evaluative beliefs of our own that we take to be true, it is difficult to see how we could interpret and hence understand other people, as well as ourselves, as holding any evaluative beliefs at all. We would not have what it takes to see the world as containing genuine evaluations — any thoughts to the effect that something is good or bad, or better or worse than something else. If we do find thoughts in the world which we understand to be genuinely evaluative, then it seems that we must already hold certain evaluative beliefs or opinions of our own. But then our disengagement from all values would have been abandoned. We would be taking certain value sentences as true.

I did not try to prove any of that. I said what I could to make it plausible. Without offering further argument for it here, I want to examine some of its consequences. Suppose, as I have been suggesting, that there is simply no understanding of evaluation in completely nonevaluative terms. It has long been accepted that there is no hope of strictly *defining* evaluative notions somehow in purely nonevaluative terms. That is, perhaps, the real lesson of G. E. Moore's misnamed "naturalistic fallacy," which preoccupied moral philosophers for so long.[16] I am suggesting, not an obstacle to definition of the contents of our evaluations, but rather an obstacle to our even understanding or acknowledging the phenomenon of human evaluation at all. Evaluation is a fact of human life — something that human beings do — which it seems we cannot acknowledge without our also engaging in the practice ourselves. And that means that we cannot even understand that it is going on without our being prepared to take certain evaluative beliefs or "pronouncements" to be true.

Just suppose for a moment that that is right. Now if it is also right (as I think it is) that accepting "subjectivism" about values would have to involve our disengaging from all values while still making sense of evaluative thought, then we would not really be able to accept a "subjectivist" picture of human values. We could not coherently get ourselves into the position of discovering that none of the evaluative beliefs or attitudes of human beings corresponds to anything that is so in the way things are. But then, if "subjectivism" is the inevitable outcome of trying to understand human values in terms of that traditional bipartite conception of human beings and their relation to the world, it would follow that

---

[16] G. E. Moore, *Principia Ethica* (Cambridge: Cambridge University Press, 1956), chap. 1.

we cannot really carry out the Enlightenment project of determining the "objectivity" or "subjectivity" of values in general. The detachment or disengagement we would need would rule out the very understanding that we seek. That would be disturbing, and dissatisfying, given the natural appeal of that picture. It seems like a perfectly comprehensible intellectual goal — in fact, the very model of what it would be to understand general aspects of human nature in the right way. But it would be unattainable. We could never fully understand ourselves in that way.

This is not to say that we could not study the phenomenon of human evaluation, and indeed human values themselves, and learn much more than we now do. There is a great deal that we do not know and should be trying to find out, not only about what things are good and bad, and why, but also about how people acquire the values they do. How does it happen that an infant who comes into the world with needs and impulses and a native set of behavior patterns comes by the time it is an adult to possess a complex set of evaluative beliefs and responses? How do adults with firmly held evaluative opinions about certain matters come over the course of time to change them? And how can we arrange things in society so that people on the whole make such changes in the direction of more informed, more considerate — in a word, better — evaluative attitudes? There is no answering such questions in the abstract. It obviously depends on the particular people and the particular culture and on countless other factors in ways we still do not understand very well. But such questions, however complex, can be answered — or at least progress can be made.

Any study of human socialization or human development along these lines would be a study of how a human being or a group of human beings gets absorbed into a culture whose members already have some values or other, or how the possession of one set of values gets transformed into possession of another. It would explain at most the transmission of values, perhaps even the transmission of the very idea of value, from those who have it to those who do not. But to explain how something is transmitted or changed is not necessarily to explain what it is that is transmitted or changed. It is not necessarily to explain what those attitudes are, or what it is to hold them. What is it to think that deliberate killing of a human being is a very bad thing, or to think anything evaluative about anything? This is a philosophical question about human valuing as such.

If that is what we want to understand about ourselves or about human nature in general, then the metaphysical project I have been describing seems inevitably to come into play. This is what leads us to "subjectivism." We want to understand the nature of any evaluative thoughts or attitudes. We ask what their special content is, what is really being thought. And that first takes the form of asking what would be so if they were true. In trying to answer that question, either we merely repeat the thought — "Killing a human being is bad" is true if and only if killing a human being is bad — and so we do not feel we are explaining it, or we try to express its content in other terms that reveal in some illuminating way what is really being said. If those further terms are still evaluative, we will not feel that we have explained what it is for any evaluative thought or attitude to be true; we will simply have exchanged one such thought for another.

So if we are going to make any progress in explaining the evaluative as such, we will either say that having what we call an evaluative attitude or opinion is not really a matter of thinking something to be true — but instead is expressing a feeling or issuing a prescription or making a recommendation or some such thing — or we will say that it is a matter of our thinking true something that is really nonevaluative and so could hold in the "objective" world — perhaps something about nonevaluative feelings that we and others do or would feel under certain conditions. Each of these alternatives is a version of what I am calling "subjectivism": there are no "objective" evaluative facts or states of affairs. And each of these alternatives appears to deny or obliterate the very phenomenon we set out to understand. That looks like the inevitable outcome of our trying to understand human evaluation in general.

It is this very desire to explain human evaluation in general that seems to preclude us from invoking unexplained evaluative truths or states of affairs in any account of the special contents of human evaluations. Thus do we inevitably banish genuinely evaluative facts from any world in which we can make sense of what seems to be evaluation. But in trying consistently to adhere to nothing more than that shrunken conception of what is really so we would fail to make sense of the idea that human beings have such things as evaluative thoughts, attitudes, or responses. We would lose those very attitudes that "subjectivism" about values claims have nothing corresponding to them in reality but are nothing more than our "subjective" responses to an "objectively" value-free world.

I would draw here on the parallel I see with the case of colors. If we did not make categorical ascriptions of colors to things around us we could not acknowledge the existence of such things as perceptions of colors or beliefs about the colors of things on the part of human beings. We could not conceive of the world as containing those very perceptions and beliefs that "subjectivism" about colors claims have nothing corresponding to them in reality and are nothing more than our "subjective" responses to an "objectively" colorless world.

I want to say more about what this idea amounts to and exactly what it implies about our understanding of values and colors, and what it does not. It says in its strongest form that we cannot think of a world in which people perceive particular colors or believe that things are colored without ourselves being prepared to ascribe color categorically to things in the world. We cannot understand human beings to have evaluative opinions or attitudes to the effect that such-and-such is good or bad without ourselves sometimes recognizing the goodness or badness of certain things. And in making those ascriptions of color, or of value, we are taking certain things to be true. We take it to be part of the way things are, for example, that grass is green, or that the deliberate killing of a human being is a very bad thing. Our engagement with, or endorsement of, aspects of the world of those general types is required for our ascribing to human beings beliefs or attitudes with those types of contents. What we take to be facts of the world are implicated in our making sense of thoughts of the world. The two cannot be pried apart completely.

I am here endorsing particular instances, having to do with colors and with evaluation, of what appears to be a quite general fact about our understanding one another in the ways we do. There are conditions of the successful ascription to human beings of beliefs, attitudes, perceptions, or feelings with specific contents. This is something that I believe lies at the heart of Wittgenstein's later work. Donald Davidson has stressed its importance in what he calls "radical interpretation." [17]

If we are to interpret someone as believing or perceiving or feeling some particular thing or as having a certain specific attitude, we must somehow connect those specific psychological states we are attributing to that person with facts or events or states of affairs in the world that we take them to be about. If we ourselves had no opinions about what is so and what other people are most likely to be attending to in the environment, we would be in no position to attribute any beliefs or perceptions or attitudes to them at all. We interpreters and ascribers of beliefs and other psychological states must therefore be engaged in the world and take certain things to be true of it if we are ever going to attribute psychological states to anyone. And we have no choice but to ascribe to others, at least in general, beliefs in and perceptions of and attitudes toward some of the very things we ourselves take to be true of the world. We cannot make sense of other people

---

[17] See, e.g., Donald Davidson, *Inquiries into Truth and Interpretation* (Oxford: Clarendon Press, 1984), essays 9–12.

as believing something we know to be obviously false unless we
have some explanation in the particular case of how they come
to get it wrong. And that explanation will work only if we understand them to share in common with us other beliefs and attitudes
in the midst of which their particular, localized error (as we see it)
can be made intelligible.

This still leaves considerable room for difference or disagreement. Whole areas of belief or perception might be found to
diverge if there remains enough overlap to serve as the shared
base of what the interpreter could then see as the others' deviance.
But it seems to me, as I have been suggesting, that the deviance
could not go as far as the interpreter's finding that others had perceptions of color and beliefs about the colors of things which he
held did not agree with anything at all that he took to be true in
the world. Nor could he find that they had evaluative beliefs or
attitudes about the goodness or badness of things none of which
he shared because he had no evaluative beliefs or attitudes at all.

Davidson has sometimes drawn from his main claim about
interpretation the conclusion that most of our beliefs must therefore be true.[18] They must be, if we can even understand the fact
that we and other people have any beliefs at all. And this seems
to imply that the truth of the majority of our beliefs is a necessary
condition of our having them — that if we have any beliefs or
atttiudes at all, the list of sentences which state the contents of
those beliefs or attitudes will contain mostly truths. That would
connect our beliefs necessarily with the way the world is. If I am
right to apply this thesis about interpretation to color beliefs in
particular, that would imply that most of our color beliefs are true.
It would mean that we are getting the colors of things, on the
whole, right. We can't help it. And applied to our evaluations it
would mean that, in general, our beliefs about what is good and
bad, better and worse, are true. On the whole, the things that we

18 Donald Davidson, "A Coherence Theory of Truth and Knowledge," in *Kant
oder Hegel*, ed. D. Henrich (Stuttgart: Klett-Cotta, 1983).

think are good, or bad, really are good, or bad. Of course, in the case of values there appears to be much less widespread agreement, so it is not easy to speak without further qualification of what "we" believe, what "our" evaluative beliefs are. But despite that apparent lack of agreement, there must still be enough common ground somewhere among all those who hold evaluative beliefs to make possible the ascription of such beliefs to them. That common core, or at least the major part of it, is then said, on Davidson's view, to be true.

This is not a conclusion I wish to draw — at least not if it is taken as a defense of the "objectivity" of colors or values as opposed to their alleged "subjectivity." If we knew, by this kind of transcendental argument, that most of our beliefs had to be true, and in particular that most of our color beliefs are true, and that most of our evaluations are true, we could easily be led to ask, in the spirit of the traditional metaphysical project, how that could possibly be so. How could it be that our believing what we do requires that the world should be a certain way? This will make us look once again at the contents of those beliefs. What exactly are we believing when we believe that, say, grass is green, or that the deliberate killing of a human being is a bad thing? And what is it to believe such things? We want to understand such beliefs in general. Just as that quest drove us toward "subjectivism" earlier, so it would drive us toward "subjectivism" again. There seems to be no other way to account for the necessary connection that would have been proven to hold between the body of our beliefs as a whole and their truth.

This is just the position of Kant's *Critique of Pure Reason*, perhaps the greatest attempt there has ever been to prove that the truth about the way the world is cannot come apart in general from our thinking and perceiving in the ways we do. Kant thought there were necessary conditions of the possibility of all thought and experience, and that not all those necessary conditions are themselves just further thoughts or beliefs. They include as well many nonpsychological truths, so not only must we think a certain way, but the world independent of us must be a certain way, in general, if we are even able to think of or perceive anything at all.

Kant saw that some philosophical theory was needed to explain this necessary link between thought and experience and the world, and his explanation was the theory of transcendental idealism. It was the only explanation he thought there could be. We can know that the world in general must conform to our thinking and perceiving in certain ways because our being able to think and perceive what we do actually "constitutes" the world that we perceive and believe in. The price of showing that our thoughts and perceptions and the truth of their contents cannot come apart in general was that the truth of what we believe about the world somehow consists in our having the kinds of thoughts and perceptions that we do. The world turns out to be dependent on our thoughts and perceptions in some way after all. That is a form of idealism, which is one variety of what I am calling "subjectivism."

If we ask in a similar vein how our color beliefs, or our evaluative beliefs, could not fail to be true, a more particular version of that same idealism or "subjectivism" will seem like the only possible answer. What it is for color judgments to be true, for there to be a world of colored objects, it would say, is just for human beings to agree for the most part in their ascription of colors to things. There might be considerable disagreement in particular cases, but on the whole there would be nothing more to things' being colored than human perceivers agreeing in general in the perceptions they have and the judgments they make about the colors of things. Similarly, for things to have value, and to have the particular values they have, would simply be for human beings to agree in general in their ascriptions of value to things. Again, there is room for wide disagreement and uncertainty, but on the whole the truth of value judgments would amount to nothing more than agreement, or the possibility of agreement, in human beings' evaluative beliefs.

This is clearly just "subjectivism" approached from a different direction. In terms of the traditional dichotomy, it locates the source of the truth of color judgments and of value judgments on the "subjective" side. Or rather, like all forms of idealism, it in effect collapses what was originally thought of as the "objective" into the "subjective." The facts of the "objective" world that make our color judgments or our value judgments true would be facts only about us, about what we say and do, and not about an independent world that we say those things about. The only form of so-called "objectivity" granted to those judgments would be intersubjective agreement. And understood in terms of the traditional dichotomy that is not really "objectivity" at all.

This is precisely the kind of view of the world that I have been suggesting we can never reach. Describing it this way perhaps brings out why. We cannot make sense of the idea that the truth of judgments of a certain kind amounts to nothing more than human agreement with respect to the contents of those very judgments. If human beings agree in certain judgments, there must be something they agree about. We must be able to make independent sense of their making such judgments in the first place if we are to find anything for them to be in agreement about. That is the point of Davidson's requirements on interpretation. The content of the judgment must be identifiable independently of the fact that the judgment is made. And that is why our taking certain things to be true of the world must be involved in interpretation from the beginning.

Davidson himself would make no appeal to idealism or any form of "subjectivism" to explain why he thinks most of our beliefs must be true. It comes from the conditions of interpretation alone. But making sense of what people are saying and doing, and ascribing various psychological states to them, is something that we human beings do. The conditions of interpretation or understanding are conditions of our doing something, or our succeeding in doing it, not simply conditions of something's being so independently of our efforts to understand. If our taking certain things to be true is a condition of ascribing to people beliefs and perceptions and attitudes with specific contents, then there will necessarily be considerable agreement among us. But that does not strictly imply that what we largely agree about must be true. The truth of something does not in general follow from the fact that some or many or even all human beings agree about it. Nothing about the conditions of interpretation can obliterate that fact.

Of course, if we all agree about many things then we will *regard* them all as true. We will hold, of those things that we all agree about, that they are all true. But it still does not follow from our acknowledged agreement that they are all true, even if we insist that agreement is indeed necessary for interpretation and mutual understanding. So even if we must all share certain evaluative (or color) judgments if we are to see ourselves as having any evaluative (or color) opinions at all, I do not see that the truth of any evaluative (or color) statements themselves, as opposed to our believing them to be true, would follow from that. Since we do believe them, we will assert them to be true. But no fact of the world would have been shown to be a necessary condition of our believing things about the world. This is still compatible with our insisting that we must take certain things to be true of the world in order to see ourselves as believing or having any opinions or attitudes about anything.

The fact about interpretation and the ascription of belief is the important point. I think it is enough in itself to prevent us from ever arriving at the "subjectivist" picture of the world. By that I mean only that we could never consistently arrive at the "subjectivist" conception of values or color, not that that conception is false, or necessarily false, or a contradiction, as it would have to be on the stronger conclusion that sees a necessary connection between the body of our beliefs as a whole and their truth. That stronger conclusion would say that there could not possibly be such things as evaluative beliefs, or color beliefs, unless they were on the whole in fact true. And that is the kind of necessary connection that only idealism or some form of "subjectivism" would seem able to explain.

To think that we are forced to that strong conclusion by what I am calling the fact about interpretation would be to take the kind of step Bishop Berkeley took to his form of idealism. Because he thought that we cannot conceive of an object without perceiving it, he thought that we cannot conceive of an object that remains unperceived. He concluded that an object could not possibly exist unperceived — it is inconceivable. But that is to start with the fact that we cannot do something, that we cannot perform a certain feat, and to conclude that a certain thing could not possibly be so. If we distinguish, as we must, between what we cannot do and what cannot be so, between what we cannot consistently think and what is in itself inconsistent, the fact about the conditions of interpretation will not support the idea that our color beliefs or our evaluative beliefs are simply such that most of them must be true. That conclusion anyway would once again encourage idealism or "subjectivism." But the fact about interpretation would mean that that is no threat. We would be in no position to deny or refute "subjectivism" on the grounds that it is inconsistent, but we would never be able consistently to reach the thought of the truth of "subjectivism" either. Denying "subjectivism" is not the only way of avoiding it.

So although I strongly resist the "subjectivity" of value, I do not wish to be understood as defending the idea that on the contrary values are "objective." The tendency to draw that conclusion directly from the unacceptability of "subjectivism" is good evidence, if more were needed, of the power of that traditional metaphysical dichotomy. It still represents the structure in terms of which we want to understand things. We feel that colors, or values, or whatever it might be, must be either "subjective" or "objective." We think that either there is something corresponding to our thoughts about them in the fully "objective" world or there is not. So if we cannot really understand values to be "subjective," we think they must be "objective" after all.

I believe that we cannot get a satisfactory understanding of ourselves in that way. That leaves us dissatisfied. It seems as if it couldn't be simply impossible. So we persist. And once again we apply the traditional dichotomy. This tendency, I believe, is the place to look for the real source of "subjectivism" about values. It would help explain why we can expect that some form of the view will always be with us.

THE TANNER LECTURERS

1976–77

OXFORD — Bernard Williams, Cambridge University

MICHIGAN — Joel Feinberg, University of Arizona
"Voluntary Euthanasia and the Inalienable Right to Life"

STANFORD — Joel Feinberg, University of Arizona
"Voluntary Euthanasia and the Inalienable Right to Life"

1977–78

OXFORD — John Rawls, Harvard University

MICHIGAN — Sir Karl Popper, University of London
"Three Worlds"

STANFORD — Thomas Nagel, Princeton University

1978–79

OXFORD — Thomas Nagel, Princeton University
"The Limits of Objectivity"

CAMBRIDGE — C. C. O'Brien, London

MICHIGAN — Edward O. Wilson, Harvard University
"Comparative Social Theory"

STANFORD — Amartya Sen, Oxford University
"Equality of What?"

UTAH — Lord Ashby, Cambridge University
"The Search for an Environmental Ethic"

UTAH STATE — R. M. Hare, Oxford University
"Moral Conflicts"

1979–80

OXFORD — Jonathan Bennett, Univ. of British Columbia
"Morality and Consequences"

CAMBRIDGE — Raymond Aron, Collège de France
"Arms Control and Peace Research"

HARVARD — George Stigler, University of Chicago
"Economics or Ethics?"

[261]

MICHIGAN   Robert Coles, Harvard University
                "Children as Moral Observers"

STANFORD   Michel Foucault, Collège de France
                *"Omnes et Singulatim: Towards a Criticism
                of 'Political Reason' "*

UTAH   Wallace Stegner, Los Altos Hills, California
                *"The Twilight of Self-Reliance: Frontier Values
                and Contemporary America"*

1980–81

OXFORD   Saul Bellow, University of Chicago
                "A Writer from Chicago"

CAMBRIDGE   John A. Passmore, Australian National University
                "The Representative Arts as a Source of Truth"

HARVARD   Brian M. Barry, University of Chicago
                *"Do Countries Have Moral Obligations? The Case
                of World Poverty"*

MICHIGAN   John Rawls, Harvard University
                "The Basic Liberties and Their Priority"

STANFORD   Charles Fried, Harvard University
                "Is Liberty Possible?"

UTAH   Joan Robinson, Cambridge University
                "The Arms Race"

HEBREW UNIV.   Solomon H. Snyder, Johns Hopkins University
                "Drugs and the Brain and Society"

1981–82

OXFORD   Freeman Dyson, Princeton University
                "Bombs and Poetry"

CAMBRIDGE   Kingman Brewster, President Emeritus, Yale University
                "The Voluntary Society"

HARVARD   Murray Gell-Mann, California Institute of Technology
                "The Head and the Heart in Policy Studies"

MICHIGAN   Thomas C. Schelling, Harvard University
                "Ethics, Law, and the Exercise of Self-Command"

STANFORD   Alan A. Stone, Harvard University
                "Psychiatry and Morality"

UTAH R. C. Lewontin, Harvard University
  "Biological Determinism"

AUSTRALIAN
NATL. UNIV. Leszek Kolakowski, Oxford University
  "The Death of Utopia Reconsidered"

1982–83

OXFORD Kenneth J. Arrow, Stanford University
  "The Welfare-Relevant Boundaries of the Individual"

CAMBRIDGE H. C. Robbins Landon, University College, Cardiff
  *"Haydn and Eighteenth-Century Patronage
  in Austria and Hungary"*

HARVARD Bernard Williams, Cambridge University
  "Morality and Social Justice"

STANFORD David Gauthier, University of Pittsburgh
  "The Incompleat Egoist"

UTAH Carlos Fuentes, Princeton University
  "A Writer from Mexico"

JAWAHARLAL
NEHRU UNIV. Ilya Prigogine, University of Brussels
  "Only an Illusion"

1983–84

OXFORD Donald D. Brown, Carnegie Institution of Washington,
  Baltimore
  "The Impact of Modern Genetics"

CAMBRIDGE Stephen J. Gould, Harvard University
  "Evolutionary Hopes and Realities"

MICHIGAN Herbert A. Simon, Carnegie-Mellon University
  *"Scientific Literacy as a Goal in a High-Technology
  Society"*

STANFORD Leonard B. Meyer, University of Pennsylvania
  "Ideology and Music in the Nineteenth Century"

UTAH Helmut Schmidt, former Chancellor, West Germany
  "The Future of the Atlantic Alliance"

HELSINKI Georg Henrik von Wright, Helsinki
  "Of Human Freedom"

1984–85

OXFORD   Barrington Moore, Jr., Harvard University
              *"Authority and Inequality under Capitalism
              and Socialism"*

CAMBRIDGE   Amartya K. Sen, Oxford University
              "The Standard of Living"

HARVARD   Quentin Skinner, Cambridge University
              "The Paradoxes of Political Liberty"
              Kenneth J. Arrow, Stanford University
              "The Unknown Other"

MICHIGAN   Nadine Gordimer, South Africa
              "The Essential Gesture: Writers and Responsibility"

STANFORD   Michael Slote, University of Maryland
              "Moderation, Rationality, and Virtue"

1985–86

OXFORD   Thomas M. Scanlon, Harvard University
              "The Significance of Choice"

CAMBRIDGE   Aldo Van Eyck, The Netherlands
              "Architecture and Human Values"

HARVARD   Michael Walzer, Institute for Advanced Study
              "Interpretation and Social Criticism"

MICHIGAN   Clifford Geertz, Institute for Advanced Study
              "The Uses of Diversity"

STANFORD   Stanley Cavell, Harvard University
              "The Uncanniness of the Ordinary"

UTAH   Arnold S. Relman, Editor, *New England Journal
              of Medicine*
              "Medicine as a Profession and a Business"

1986–87

OXFORD   Jon Elster, Oslo University and the University of Chicago
              *"Taming Chance: Randomization in Individual and
              Social Decisions"*

CAMBRIDGE   Roger Bulger, University of Texas Health Sciences Center, Houston
"On Hippocrates, Thomas Jefferson and Max Weber: the Bureaucratic, Technologic Imperatives and the Future of the Healing Tradition in a Voluntary Society"

HARVARD   Jürgen Habermas, University of Frankfurt
"Law and Morality"

MICHIGAN   Daniel Dennett, Tufts University
"The Moral First Aid Manual"

STANFORD   Gisela Striker, Columbia University
"Greek Ethics and Moral Theory"

UTAH   Laurence H. Tribe, Harvard University
"On Reading the Constitution"

1987–88

OXFORD   F. Van Zyl Slabbert, South Africa
"The Dynamics of Reform and Revolt in Current South Africa"

CALIFORNIA   Wm. Theodore de Bary, Columbia University
"The Trouble with Confucianism"

CAMBRIDGE   Louis Blom-Cooper, Q.C., London
"The Penalty of Imprisonment"

HARVARD   Robert A. Dahl, Yale University
"The Pseudodemocratization of the American Presidency"

MICHIGAN   Albert O. Hirschman, Institute for Advanced Study
"Two Hundred Years of Reactionary Rhetoric: The Case of the Perverse Effect"

STANFORD   Ronald Dworkin, New York University and University College, Oxford
"Foundations of Liberal Equality"

UTAH   Joseph Brodsky, Russian poet
"A Place as Good as Any"

BUENOS AIRES   Barry Stroud, University of California, Berkeley
"The Study of Human Nature and the Subjectivity of Value"

MADRID   Javier Muguerza, Institute of Philosophy of the Superior
                 Council of Scientific Investigations, Madrid
                 "The Alternative of Dissent"

WARSAW   Anthony Quinton, London
                 "The Varieties of Value"

1988–89

OXFORD   Michael Walzer, Institute for Advanced Study

CALIFORNIA   S. N. Eisenstadt, The Hebrew University of Jerusalem

CAMBRIDGE   Albert Hourani, Oxford University
                 *"Islam in European Thought — the Nineteenth Century
                 and After"*

MICHIGAN   Toni Morrison, Princeton University
                 *"Unspeakable Things Unspoken: the Afro-American
                 Presence in American Literature"*

STANFORD   Stephen Jay Gould, Harvard University

UTAH   Judith N. Shklar, Harvard University

YALE   John G. A. Pocock, Johns Hopkins University
                 *"Edward Gibbon in History: Aspects of the Text
                 in* The Decline and Fall of the Roman Empire*"*

CHINESE
UNIVERSITY OF
HONG KONG   Fei Xia-tong, Peking University
                 *"Unity and Plurality: Reflections on Ethnic Relations
                 in China"*

1989–90

MICHIGAN   Carol Gilligan, Harvard University

UTAH   Octavio Paz, Mexico City, Mexico

YALE   Edward Nicolae Luttwak, Georgetown University

INDEX TO VOLUME X, 1989

THE TANNER LECTURES ON HUMAN VALUES

Le Bon, Gustave. Work: *Psychologie des foules*, 19–21
Lee Kuan-yew, 134
Legalists (Chinese philosophical school), 139–40, 149, 151
Legality, vs. morality, 80, 81–89, 99–110
Legal realism, 89–91
The Leopard (Baron of Lampedusa), 9
Levitin, Theresa, 49
Lewis, C. I. Work: *The Ground and Nature of the Right*, 195–96
Liang Ch'i-ch'ao, 169, 175, 176. Work: *Intellectual Trends in the Ch'ing Period*, 164–65
Liberalism, protest against Chinese autocracy, 159–70
The Liberal Tradition in China (de Bary), 158, 159
Liberty, as fundamental human right, 108–9, 110, 123, 128
Lijphart, Arend, 66n.21
"The Limits of Social Policy" (Glazer), 26
Lincoln, Abraham, 40
Li Ssu, 151, 172; on seditiousness of Confucians, 149–50
Lorenzen, Paul, 106
Losing Ground (Murray), 23–24, 25
Lowell, A. Lawrence, 45
Lowi, Theodore, 66–67
Lu Hsun, 133
Lü Liu-liang, 168, 170, 171, 176, 177; anti-Manchu radicalism of, 162–64
Lu Lung-ch'i, 163, 164

McGovern-Fraser Commission, 66
MacIntyre, Alasdair, 123n
McKinley, William, 64
Madison, James, 38n, 39, 56, 61. Work: *The Federalist Papers*, 55
Maine, Sir Henry, 45
Maistre, Joseph de, 26, 28, 82n.18. Work: *Considérations sur la France*, 16
Malem, Jorge. Work: *Concept and Justification of Civil Disobedience*, 127

Malthus, Thomas Robert, 22, 24
Manchu dynasty, 161; liberal protest against, 162–64
Mandates, dynastic, and public trust, 142–43
Mandates, Presidential: exploitation of, 67–68; history of, 35–43; theory of, 43–45; validity of, 45–51
Mandeville, Bernard, 14, 23, 27
The Man versus the State (Spencer), 21
Maoism, 178
Mao Tse-tung, 133, 140; mobilization of populace by, 181
Maritain, Jacques, 75, 95–96
Marshall, T. H., 3–4, 5, 11
Marx, Karl, 81, 121
Masses, political participation of, 17–21
Mass media: and mass education, 182; and political processes, 69
Means and ends, morality of, 113–17, 122–23
Meiji dynasty, 176
Mencius, 135, 150, 151, 155, 172, 175, 181; critique of the powerful, 147; on mission of noble man, 147–49; on nature of public service, 178
Mephisto (Goethe's character), 14
Metzger, Thomas, 157
Mexican Constitution (1917), 111
Miller, Warren E., 49
Ming dynasty, 162, 168, 180; despotism of, 156, 158–59, 160; position of Confucianism in, 154–57
Minimum-wage laws, 22
Mohists (Chinese philosophical school), 139–40
Monopolies, state, in Han dynasty, 151
Monroe, James, 39
Montaigne, 197
Moore, Barrington, 126–27. Work: *Injustice: The Social Basis of Obedience and Revolt*, 126
Moore, G. E., 248
Morality: basis in human nature, 242; conflict with prudence, 195, 203–4; of consensus, 96–100; of ends and

278   *The Tanner Lectures on Human Values*

"Wie ist Legitimität durch Legalität möglich?" (Habermas), 100

Wilson, James, 38n

Wilson, Woodrow, 64, 67; claim to mandate, 37, 40–42. Works: *Congressional Government*, 41–42; *Constitutional Government in the United States*, 42

Wisdom: in pursuit of good life, 202; of sacred texts, 197

Wittgenstein, Ludwig Josef Johann, 252

Women, exclusion from franchise, 57

Word and Object (Quine), 244

Workhouses, 24

Wright brothers, 51, 56

Wu, Emperor, 150, 151

Yao, Emperor, 137–38

Yi dynasty, 155, 157

Yüan dynasty, 154

Yung-cheng, 163–64

For EU product safety concerns, contact us at Calle de José Abascal, 56–1°, 28003 Madrid, Spain or eugpsr@cambridge.org.